English & Grammar
START

왕초보에게 꼭 필요한
영문법 8코스

박연우 지음

English& 북스

English&
Grammar
START

초판 1쇄 발행 2023년 9월 15일
초판 2쇄 발행 2023년 12월 15일

지은이 박연우
펴낸이 박성호
펴낸곳 잉글리쉬앤(주)

편　집 장서원
영업마케팅 여주형, 김성윤, 방성출, 박훈효, 조민형, 이달님, 강정구, 이진희, 조병운,
변중구, 정노을, 조예선, 조광민, 이현정, 김정민, 최희성, 최인태, 윤종철,
엄주아, 윤지원, 우민지, 이가은

주　소 서울 특별시 관악구 쑥고개로 67-1
대표전화 (02) 878-1945
출판등록 2002년 3월 3일 제 320-2002-00045호

ISBN 978-89-6715-167-6　13740

저작권자 2023 잉글리쉬앤(주)
이 책은 잉글리쉬앤(주)에 의해 출간되었으므로
저자와 출판사의 서면에 의한 허락 없이 글과 그림의 인용, 복제, 발췌를 금합니다.

* 가격은 뒤표지에 있습니다. 파본은 바꾸어 드립니다.
www.english.co.kr

서문

영어의 중요성은 아무리 강조해도 지나치지 않습니다. 취업, 진학, 승진 등 모든 분야에서 활용되고 있고 개인의 능력을 평가하는 잣대가 되기도 하니 한국이 영어에 열중하는 것은 어찌 보면 당연한 일일 수도 있습니다.

저에게 "어떻게 하면 영어를 잘 할 수 있겠냐"라고 묻는 사람들이 많습니다. 저는 그때마다 '최고의 비결은 꾸준함'이라고 답합니다. 여러분이 어린 시절을 회상해 보면, 모국어도 한순간에 여러분에게 체득된 게 아닙니다. 옹알이를 할 때부터 십 수 년을 꾸준히 연습한 결과 한국어를 구사할 수 있게 된 거죠. 어찌 보면 여러분들은 아직도 한국어를 연습하고 있는 중입니다.

영어도 마찬가지입니다. 꾸준하게 연습하고 익혀야 합니다. 강의 현장에서 지켜보면 영어에 대한 기초 문법이 부족하여 많은 학생들이 영어 공부를 힘들어하고, 심지어 포기하는 경우가 적지 않습니다. 너무 안타까운 일입니다.

'잉글리쉬앤 그래머 START'는 영어의 문법 공부를 시작하는 수험생들이 흥미를 잃지 않고 익힐 수 있도록 영문법의 기초를 다지는 데 초점을 맞췄습니다. GRAMMAR POINT에서 학습한 이론을 GRAMMAR PRACTICE로 문제를 풀며 확인하고, GRAMMAR IN SENTENCE를 통해 독해력도 향상시킬 수 있도록 구성했습니다. '잉글리쉬앤 그래머 START'를 통해 영어에 대한 자신감을 갖고 승승장구 할 수 있기를 바랍니다.

마지막으로 '잉글리쉬앤그래머 START'를 집필할 수 있도록 해주신 박성호 대표님, 여주형 이사님, 변중구 과장님 그리고 장서원 편집자님께 진심으로 감사드립니다.

저자 **박연우**

차 례

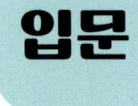

서문 · 8
이 책의 구성과 특징 · 10

입문

1코스
Unit 1 | 명사 · 12
Unit 2 | 대명사 · 18
Unit 3 | 동사 · 24
Actual Test 1 · 30

2코스
Unit 4 | 형용사 · 34
Unit 5 | 부사 · 40
Unit 6 | 전치사 · 46
Actual Test 2 · 52
Mini Test 1 · 54

3코스
Unit 7 | 문장의 성분, 1형식 · 58
Unit 8 | 2형식, 3형식 · 64
Unit 9 | 4형식, 5형식 · 70
Actual Test 3 · 76

4코스
Unit 10 | 구 · 80
Unit 11 | 절 · 86
Unit 12 | 문장의 종류 · 92
Actual Test 4 · 98
Mini Test 2 · 100
입문 Final Test · 102

기본

5코스
Unit 13 | 명사와 대명사 ········· 106
Unit 14 | 형용사와 부사 ········· 112
Unit 15 | 동사와 전치사 ········· 120
Actual Test 5 ·············· 126

6코스
Unit 16 | 시제 ················ 130
Unit 17 | 수일치 ·············· 136
Unit 18 | 태 ················· 142
Actual Test 6 ·············· 148
Mini Test 3 ················ 150

7코스
Unit 19 | 부정사 ·············· 156
Unit 20 | 동명사 ·············· 162
Unit 21 | 분사 ················ 168
Actual Test 7 ·············· 174

8코스
Unit 22 | 접속사 I ············ 178
Unit 23 | 접속사 II ··········· 184
Unit 24 | 관계사 ·············· 190
Actual Test 8 ·············· 196
Mini Test 4 ················ 198
입문 Final Test ············· 202

정답 및 해설 ················· 210

문법 개념 학습과 문제 풀이 적용을 한번에!

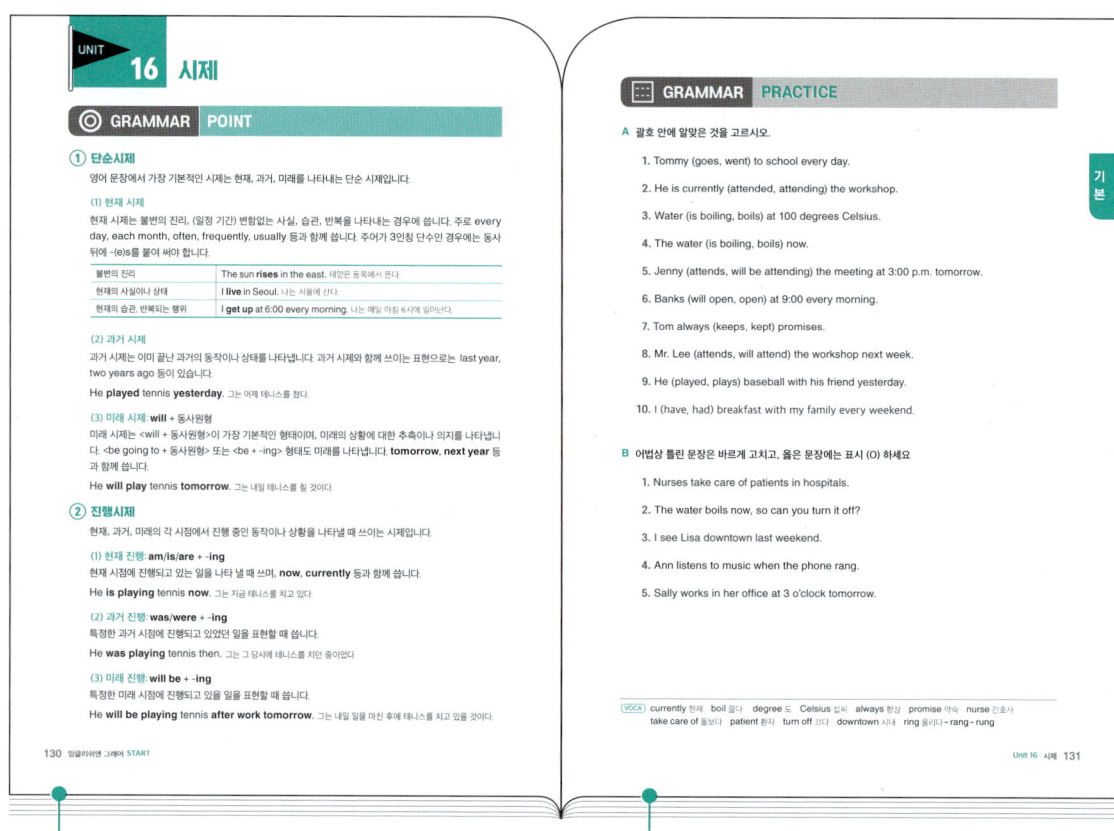

쉽고 상세한 문법 설명
천천히 읽고 개념에 익숙해지세요.

방대한 문법 체계 안에서 무엇부터 공부해야 할지부터 막막하지 않았나요?
가장 암기하기 쉬운 개념부터 심화 개념까지 효율적인 순서대로 학습합니다.

방금 배운 알게 된 문법 개념을
오픈북 방식으로 문제를 풀어보세요.

처음부터 외우려고 부담 갖지 마세요!
처음에는 문법 개념에 익숙해지고 이해하고 정리된 내용을 보고 문제에 적용하는 연습을 해봅니다.

문장 안에서 학습한 문법 개념을 독해까지 적용하기

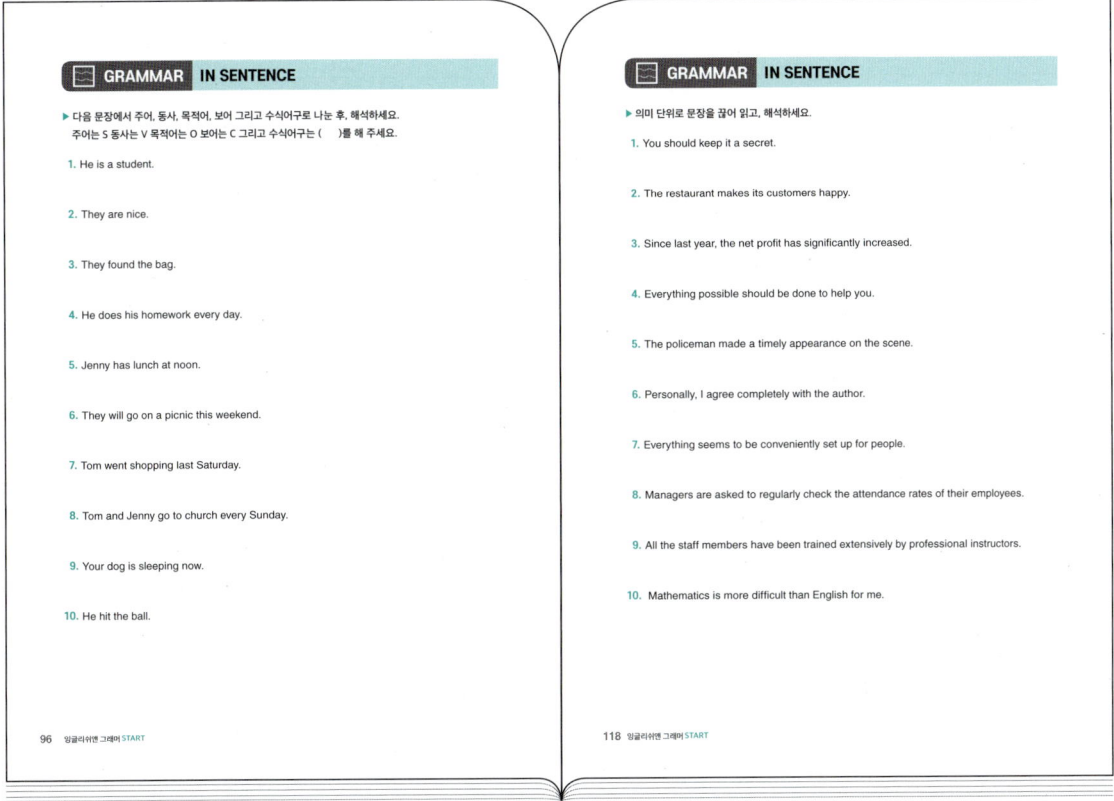

유닛별로 문장 안에 문법 개념을 적용해서 해석해보세요.

문법 개념을 배울 때는 이해가 됐는데 막상 문장이나 지문을 봤을 때 해석이 막혀서 답답한 적 없었나요? 문법을 문장 안에서 다시 적용해보고 나면, 학습한 문법 개념이 독해에 적용되어 어느새 끊어 읽기를 자연스럽게 하고 있는 자신을 발견하게 됩니다.

Unit과 Unit 사이 핵심 개념 요약으로 다시 또 정리!

요약된 중요 개념 포인트를 보며 단번에 전체 내용을 정리해볼 수 있습니다.

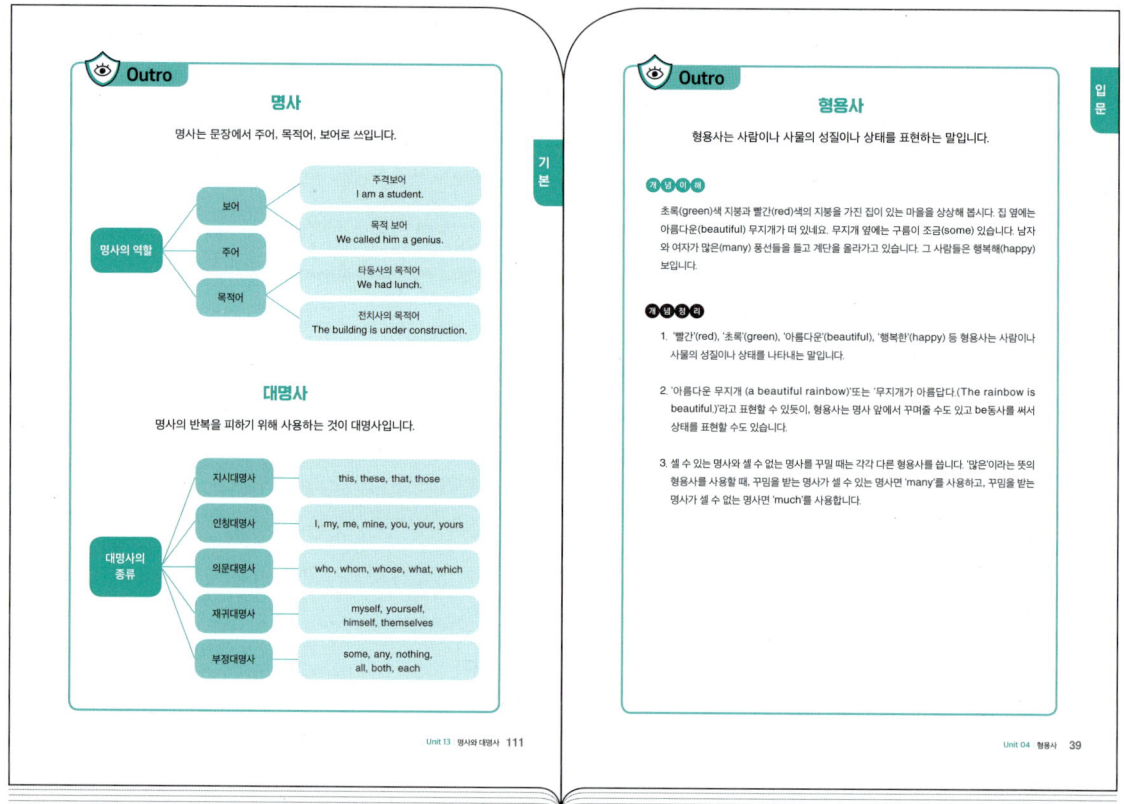

새로운 문법 개념을 공부하기 전, 바로 직전에 배웠던 문법 개념을 짧게 훑어보세요.

문법은 서로 서로 개념이 연결되어 있어 중요한 포인트를 암기하고 있지 않으면 다른 개념 학습에도 어려움이 있습니다.
그 많은 양을 언제 다 복습하지? 머리가 아파오는 순간, 그때 이 Outro 한 페이지를 활용해보세요.

* OUTRO 요약본 PDF 무료 제공!

코스와 코스 사이 TEST로 마무리!

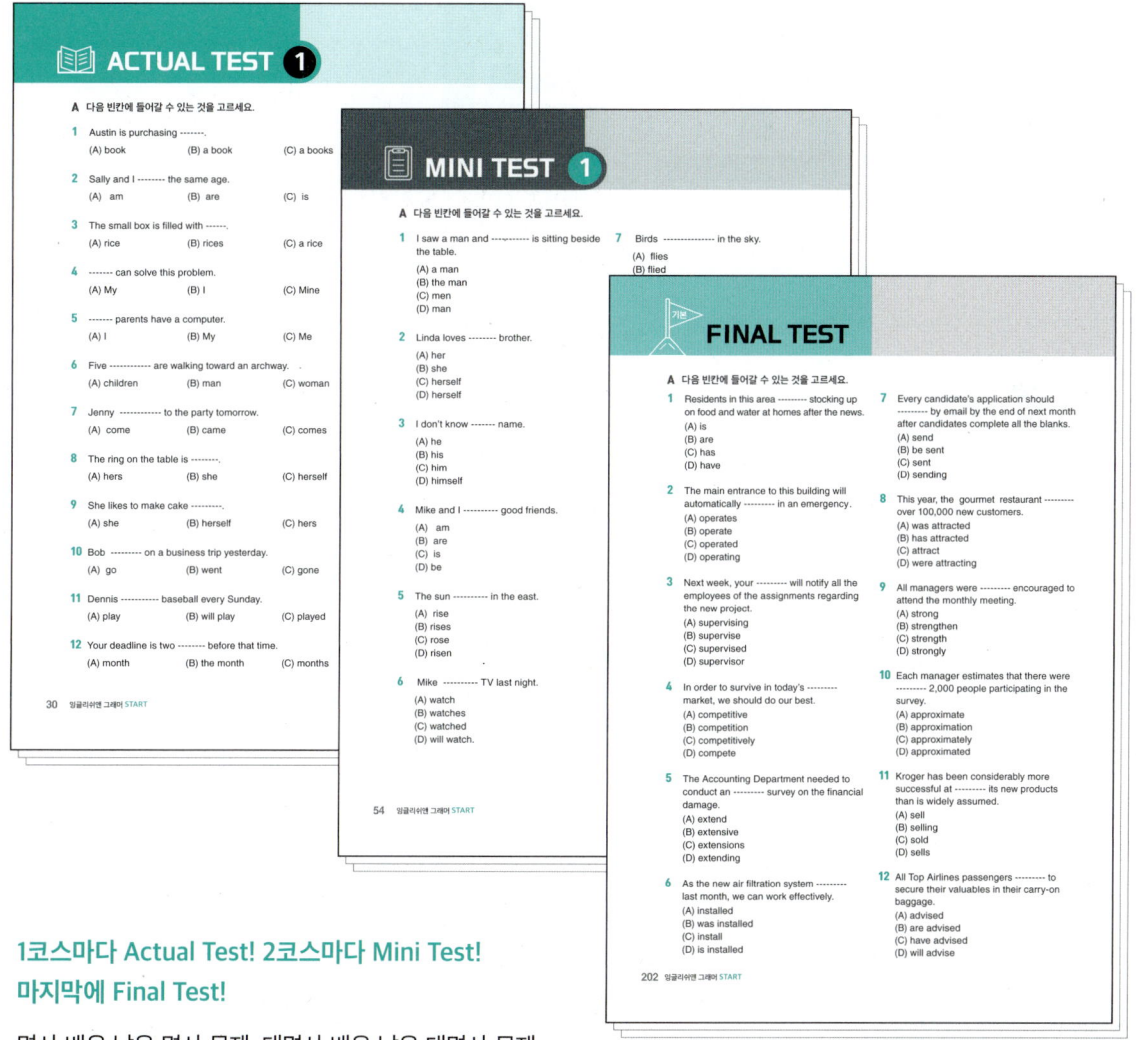

1코스마다 Actual Test! 2코스마다 Mini Test!
마지막에 Final Test!

명사 배운 날은 명사 문제, 대명사 배운 날은 대명사 문제. 문법서에서 문제는 잘 풀렸는데 막상 시험장에서 문제는 안 풀리지 않았나요? 학습 범위가 누적될수록 Test에도 진도가 넓어집니다. 전체 범위에서 학습한 문법 개념을 적용하여 시험까지 준비할 수 있어요.

잉글리쉬앤 그래머 START

입문편

 코스

Unit 1 명사
Unit 2 대명사
Unit 3 동사

1코스
2코스
3코스
4코스
5코스

UNIT 01 명사

◎ GRAMMAR POINT

고양이(cat), 책상(desk), 우유(milk), 제니(Jenny)등 어떤 사람이나 사물은 그 이름들이 있습니다. 이렇게 어떤 대상에 붙여진 이름을 '명사'라고 합니다. 하지만 사랑(love), 분위기 (atmosphere), 대화 (conversation)와 같은 것들은 그게 어떤 것인지는 알지만 우리 눈에는 보이지 않습니다. 하지만 이들도 모두 이름을 가지고 있으므로 명사에 포함됩니다.

① 명사의 정의와 종류

(1) 명사의 정의

눈에 보이는 사물, 동물의 이름	가게(store), 과일(fruit), 여자(woman), 손(hand), 고양이(cat), 남자(man)
사람의 이름	Tom, Jennifer
눈에 보이지 않는 추상적인 것의 이름	사랑(love), 분위기(atmosphere), 대화(conversation), happiness (행복)
눈에 보이지만 셀 수 없는 것의 이름	소금(salt), 설탕(sugar), 우유(milk)

(2) 명사의 종류

셀 수 있는 명사	뜻	하나, 둘, 셋 등으로 셀 수 있다.
	예시	bird 새, desk 책상, chair 의자, letter 편지
셀 수 없는 명사	뜻	셀 수 없이 수가 많거나, 어떤 형태가 존재하지 않는다.
	예시	coffee 커피, milk 우유, rice 쌀, advice 충고

② 명사의 수

(1) 셀 수 있는 명사 - 셀 수 없는 명사

셀 수 있는 명사	하나	개수가 1개이면 명사 앞에 a(n)를 쓴다. ex) a book, a desk, a pen, a chair, a machine
	둘 이상	개수가 2개 이상이면, 대개 명사 끝에 -s를 붙인다. ex) books, desks, pens, chairs, machines
셀 수 없는 명사		셀 수 없으므로 앞에 a(n)를 쓸 수도 없고, 명사 끝에 -s를 붙일 수 없다. ex) milk, beer, rice, advice, news 등

(2) 셀 수 없는 명사의 수량 표현

셀 수 없는 명사는 복수형이 없으므로, 그 앞에 단위를 나타내는 명사를 붙여서 셀 수 있다.

a glass of water (milk) 물(우유) 한 잔	two glasses of water (milk) 물 (우유) 두 잔
a sheet of paper 종이 한장	five sheets of paper 종이 다섯 장

GRAMMAR PRACTICE

A 다음 중 명사인 것을 고르세요.

(A) salt (B) small (C) bread (D) listen
(E) good (F) restaurant (G) fast (H) soccer
(I) baseball (J) run (K) pizza (L) she
(M) sugar (N) air (O) go (P) they
(Q) big (R) you (S) water (T) fresh

B 다음 중, 명사의 성격이 나머지와 다른 하나를 고르세요.

1. (A) book (B) pen (C) rice (D) desk
2. (A) beer (B) sugar (C) salt (D) letter
3. (A) Jennifer (B) chair (C) Tom (D) Ford
4. (A) air (B) child (C) crisis (D) person
5. (A) breakfast (B) lunch (C) meal (D) dinner
6. (A) sugar (B) salt (C) milk (D) egg
7. (A) banana (B) tomato (C) flour (D) cookie
8. (A) butter (B) water (C) coffee (D) apple
9. (A) advice (B) book (C) news (D) money
10. (A) insect (B) coin (C) information (D) newspaper

C 다음 중, 바르게 표현한 명사를 고르세요.

1. (A) a boy (B) two book (C) three milk (D) four milk
2. (A) a beer (B) three desk (C) five books (D) ten advice
3. (A) an advice (B) six students (C) twenty pen (D) a pens
4. (A) a water (B) two bird (C) three sheet (D) a machine
5. (A) a cup of coffee (B) two waters (C) five news (D) five beer

GRAMMAR POINT

(3) 여러 개의 명사 표현하기

1) 두 개 이상의 명사

원래 모양	두 개 이상 일 때	예
일반적인 경우	단어 뒤에 -s를 붙임	book**s**, car**s**
어미가 s, x, ch, sh	단어 뒤에 -es를 붙임	bus**es**, fox**es**, bench**es**, dish**es**
어미가 자음 + o	단어 뒤에 -es를 붙임	potato**es**
어미가 자음 + y	y를 i로 바꾸고 es를 붙임	city → cit**ies** , lady → lad**ies**
어미가 f, fe	f를 v로 바꾸고 es를 붙임	shelf → shel**ves** , knife → kni**ves**

> **Tip** chiefs 의장 cliffs 절벽 roofs 지붕 safes 금고 등은 예외이다

2) 복수 명사의 불규칙한 형태

하나	둘 이상	하나	둘 이상
man	men	child	children
woman	women	foot	feet
person	people	crisis	crises
tooth	teeth	mouse	mice

3) 형태가 같은 경우

하나	둘 이상	하나	둘 이상
fish	fish	sheep	sheep

③ a / an 과 the 의 쓰임

(1) a, an

셀 수 있는 명사 앞에 하나를 셀 때만 a 또는 an을 쓸 수 있다. 명사의 시작이 자음 발음이거나 'y'발음으로 시작될 때는 a를 사용하며, [a, e, i, o, u]등의 모음 발음으로 시작되거나 h가 묵음일 때는 an 을 사용한다.

명사의 발음이 자음으로 시작되면 a를 사용	명사의 발음이 모음으로 시작되면 an을 사용
a dog, a book , a movie	an idea, an apple, an hour

(2) the

모든 명사 앞에 모두 쓰며, 특정한 셀 수 없는 명사 앞에도 씁니다.

전에 말했던 그 사람 (것)	I know a boy. **The boy** is nine years old. 나는 한 소년을 안다. 그 소년은 아홉 살이다.
모두 아는 그 사람 (것)	Can you open **the window**? 그 창문을 열어 주시겠어요?
특정한 그 사람 (것)	I like **the music**. 나는 그 음악을 좋아한다.
유일한 사람 (것)	**The sun** rises in the east. 태양은 동쪽에서 뜬다.
악기 이름 앞에	Can you play **the piano**? 피아노 칠 수 있어요?

> **Tip** 식사 이름 앞(breakfast, lunch, dinner), 스포츠 이름(baseball, soccer), by + 교통, 통신, 결제 수단(by cash, by bus) 등에는 a(an), the를 붙이지 않습니다.

GRAMMAR PRACTICE

A 다음 단어들이 여러 개 있을 때의 형태로 고치세요.

1. book →
2. fox →
3. bus →
4. bench →
5. child →
6. man →
7. foot →
8. shelf →
9. frog →
10. house →
11. tree →
12. potato →
13. roof →
14. city →
15. crisis →
16. fish →
17. woman →
18. person →
19. tooth →
20. mouse →

B 빈칸에 **a** 또는 **an** 을 넣으세요.

1. _____ insect
2. _____ window
3. _____ apple
4. _____ nose
5. _____ orange
6. _____ red apple
7. _____ book
8. _____ hour
9. _____ umbrella
10. _____ old man
11. _____ young boy
12. _____ elephant

C 다음 중, 필요한 곳에는 **a(n)** 또는 **the**를 쓰고, 필요 없는 곳에는 **X**를 하세요.

1. I have _____ breakfast every morning.
2. I play _____ flute in my free time.
3. We played _____ soccer yesterday.
4. Look at _____ moon!
5. Let's save _____ earth!
6. What's for _____ lunch today?
7. Let's play _____ tennis this afternoon!
8. _____ sun is shining in _____ sky.
9. Jenny wants to talk with you by _____ phone.
10. I know a girl. _____ girl is beautiful.

GRAMMAR IN SENTENCE

▶ 다음 문장에서 명사를 찾고 해석하세요.

1. I have breakfast every morning.

2. I play the piano in my free time.

3. We played baseball yesterday.

4. Look at the moon!

5. Let's save the earth!

6. What's for dinner today?

7. Let's play tennis this afternoon!

8. The sun is shining in the sky.

9. Jenny wants to talk with you by phone.

10. I know a girl. The girl is beautiful.

 **Outro**

명사

명사는 어떤 대상의 이름을 가리키는 말입니다.

식료품점에서 쇼핑을 하는 가족(a family)을 상상해 봅시다. 신선한 과일(fruits)과 야채(vegetables)도 있고, Jenny 라는 이름의 한 여자아이(a girl)는 사과(an apple)를 바라보고, Tom 이라는 이름을 가진 남자아이(a boy)는 야채를 들고 있습니다. 요리를 맛있게 하려면, 소금(salt)과 설탕(sugar)도 사야 합니다. 서로 사랑(love)하는 한 가족이 대화(a conversation)를 하며 쇼핑하는 분위기(an atmosphere)가 무척 좋아 보일 것 같습니다.

개념정리

1. 과일(fruit), 야채(vegetable), 사과(apple) 등은 우리 눈에 보이는 사물이며, 어떤 물건이나 사물을 지칭하는 이름입니다. 이러한 이름들을 '명사'라고 합니다. 사람의 이름, 즉 Tom 이나 Jenny 등도 명사입니다.

2. 소금(salt), 설탕(sugar) 등은 우리 눈에는 보이지만 셀 수는 없습니다. 이런 단어들도 모두 명사입니다.

3. 위에 언급된 단어 중에서 사랑(love), 분위기(atmosphere), 대화(conversation) 등은 우리 눈에 직접적으로 보이지 않지만 모두 명사에 속합니다.

UNIT 02 대명사

GRAMMAR POINT

사람이나 사물, 동물 등의 이름을 대신해서 부르는 말을 대명사라고 합니다.

① 대명사의 역할과 형태

대명사는 문장 내에서 다양한 역할을 나타내며, 역할이 변할 때마다 그 형태도 바뀝니다.

역할	뜻	형태						
		단수(한 명, 하나)				복수(두 명, 둘 이상)		
주격	~은, ~는(~이, ~가)	I 나는	you 너는	he 그는	she 그녀는	it 그것은	we 우리는	you 너희는	they 그들은
소유격	~의	my 나의	your 너의	his 그의	her 그녀의	its 그것의	our 우리의	your 너희의	their 그들의
목적격	~을, ~를	me 나를	you 너를	him 그를	her 그녀를	it 그것을	us 우리를	you 너희를	them 그들을

② 대명사의 종류

(1) 인칭대명사

인칭대명사란 사람을 가리키는 대명사를 말합니다.

나(I)는 1인칭, 너(you)는 2인칭, 나와 너를 뺀 제3자들(he, she, they 등)은 모두 3인칭이라고 일컫습니다.

인칭	단수	복수
1인칭	I 나는	we 우리는
2인칭	you 너는	you 너희들은
3인칭	he 그는	they 그들은
	she 그녀는	
	it 그것은	

(2) 소유대명사

소유대명사는 우리말의 '~의 것'이라는 뜻에 해당합니다. 따라서 대명사 소유격과 명사를 합쳐 놓은 한 단어라고 생각하면 됩니다. [소유를 나타내는 대명사 = 소유대명사]

소유격 + 명사 = 소유대명사	
my car = mine 나의 것	our car = ours 우리의 것
your car = yours 너의 것	your car = yours 너희들의 것
his car = his 그의 것	their car = theirs 그들의 것
her car = hers 그녀의 것	

GRAMMAR PRACTICE

A 다음 중 대명사인 것을 고르세요.

(A) he	(B) birthday	(C) they	(D) Tom	(E) she
(F) family	(G) happy	(H) we	(I) she	(J) are
(K) his	(L) gift	(M) visit	(N) yours	(O) is
(P) her	(Q) its	(R) advice	(S) rice	(T) them
(U) nice	(V) hers	(W) Jenny	(X) my	(Y) I

B 주어진 우리말에 해당하는 대명사를 ( ) 안에서 고르세요.

1. 나는 (I, my, me)
2. 그녀의 (she, her, his)
3. 그의 (he, her, his)
4. 우리는 (I, we, they)
5. 그들의 (they, their, them)
6. 너희들을 (us, them, you)
7. 너의 (your, you, their)
8. 우리를 (me, them, us)
9. 그녀를 (her, him, she)
10. 그것을 (it, its, they)

C 다음 문장과 일치하도록 대명사를 사용하여 빈칸을 완성하세요.

[보기] An elephant has a long nose. = Its nose is long.

1. He has a blue hat. = _____ is blue.
2. She has a red bag. = _____ is red.
3. You have a nice car. = _____ is nice.
4. They have a yellow ball. = _____ is yellow.

D 다음을 동일한 표현의 대명사로 바꾸세요.

1. my chair = _____
2. your ring = _____
3. his money = _____
4. her bag = _____
5. our house = _____
6. their shoes = _____
7. her books = _____
8. my computers = _____
9. his dog = _____
10. Their car = _____

VOCA advice 충고　visit 방문하다

◎ GRAMMAR POINT

(3) 지시대명사
대명사에는 '이것, 저것'처럼 손가락으로 지시하듯이 가리킬 때 사용하는 지시대명사가 있습니다.

	하나(한명)를 가리킬 때	두 개(두 명) 이상을 가리킬 때
가까이 있는 것(사람)	**this** 이것, 이분	**these** 이것들, 이분들
	This is a book. 이것은 책입니다.	**These** are books. 이것들은 책들입니다.
멀리 있는 것(사람)	**that** 저것, 저분	**those** 저것들, 저분들
	That is a car. 저것은 자동차입니다.	**Those** are cars. 저것들은 자동차들입니다.

(4) 재귀대명사
재귀대명사는 문장에서 목적어가 주어 자신일 때, 혹은 주어나 목적어를 강조할 때 쓰입니다.
어미에 -self/-selves를 붙여서 표현합니다.

수	주격(~은, ~는)	재귀대명사(주어 자신)
한 명 / 하나	**I** 나는	**myself** 나 자신
	you 너는	**yourself** 너 자신
	he 그는	**himself** 그 자신
	she 그녀는	**herself** 그녀 자신
	it 그는	**itself** 그것 자체
두 명 / 둘 이상	**we** 우리는	**ourselves** 우리 자신
	you 너희들은	**yourselves** 너희들 자신
	they 그(것)들은	**themselves** 그들 자신

① 주어 = 목적어
주어와 목적어가 같을 때, 즉, 주어가 자기 자신의 주어에게 행위를 할 때 목적어로 재귀대명사를 씁니다.
이 때 생략할 수 없고, 반드시 재귀 대명사를 써야 합니다.

I looked at **myself** in the mirror. 나는 내 자신을 거울로 봤다. * I = 목적어 myself

② 강조
재귀대명사는 '자신이 직접'이라는 의미로 주어나 목적어를 강조할 때 쓰기도 합니다.
문장에서 강조하는 역할을 하므로 생략해도 됩니다.

I made dinner. = I made **myself** dinner. = I **myself** made dinner. = I made dinner **myself**.
내가 저녁을 만들었다.

GRAMMAR PRACTICE

A 빈칸에 **this** 또는 **these**를 알맞게 넣으세요.

1. _____ is a puppy.
2. _____ are pink.
3. _____ books are for me.

B 빈칸에 **that** 또는 **those**를 알맞게 넣으세요.

1. _____ men are my friends.
2. _____ is her ring.
3. What is _____ sound?

C 밑줄 친 부분에 주의하여 다음 문장을 해석하세요.

1. Mike : Hello, **This** is Mike. Is **this** Ann?
2. Ann : Yes, **this** is she. What's up, Mike?
3. Mike : Did you hear the news? We will go on a picnic **this** weekend.
4. Ann : Oh, I didn't know **that**.

D 다음을 재귀대명사의 형태로 바꾸세요.

1. 내 자신 → _____
2. 너 자신 → _____
3. 그 자신 → _____
4. 그녀 자신 → _____
5. 우리 자신 → _____
6. 그들 자신 → _____
7. 그것 자체 → _____
8. 너희들 자신 → _____

E 괄호 안에 알맞은 말을 고르세요.

1. May I introduce (me, myself) right now?
2. They enjoyed (them, themselves).
3. Tom gave (her, herself) a ring.
4. We finished the project (us, ourselves).
5. I (my, myself) made lunch.

VOCA sound 소리 go on a picnic 소풍가다 introduce 소개하다 enjoy 즐기다
gave give의 과거형(give - gave - given) finish 마치다 project 프로젝트

GRAMMAR IN SENTENCE

▶ 다음 문장에서 대명사를 찾고, 해석하세요.

1. You have a nice car.

2. They have a yellow ball.

3. These books are for me.

4. Did you hear the news?

5. We will go on a picnic this weekend.

6. May I introduce myself right now?

7. They enjoyed themselves yesterday.

8. Tom gave her a ring.

9. We finished the project ourselves.

10. I myself made lunch.

 **Outro**

대명사

대명사는 명사를 대신하여 사용하는 말입니다.

개념이해

오늘은 Tom의 생일이라고 상상해 봅시다. Tom은 자신을 소개할 때, Tom이라는 이름 대신 '나(I)'라고 소개할 것입니다. Tom이 친구에게 말할 때도, 친구의 이름 대신 '너(you)'라고 하겠죠. Tom은 자신과 친구들을 '우리(we)'라고 말할 것입니다.
이제 여러분의 입장에서 생각해 봅시다. Tom은 남자이므로 '그(he)'라고 지칭할 수 있고, Tom의 친구가 여자이면, '그녀(she)'라고 지칭할 것입니다. Tom과 친구들을 함께 '그들(they)'이라고 지칭할 수 있습니다.

테이블 위에 선물들이 있습니다. 친구들이 Tom에게 '이것은 너의 선물이야.(This is your present.)'또는 '이 선물은 너의 것이야. (This present is yours.)'라고 말할 수 있습니다.

개념정리

1. 사람이나 사물을 가리킬 때 그 사람이나 사물의 고유한 이름을 대신해서 사용하는 말을 '대명사'라고 합니다. 대명사에는 나(I), 너(You), 그(he), 그녀 (she), 그들(they), 우리(we) 등이 있습니다.

3. 나(I), 나의 (my), 나를(me), 나의 것(mine), 너(you), 너의(your), 너를(you), 너의 것(yours), 그(he), 그의(his), 그를(him), 그의 것(his), 그녀(she), 그녀의(her), 그녀를(her), 그녀의 것 (hers)등과 같이 대명사도 다양하게 사용합니다.

UNIT 03 동사

◎ GRAMMAR POINT

'타다(ride)', '붙잡다(hold)', '입다(wear)', '서다(stand)'와 같이 사람이나 사물의 동작이나 상태를 나타내는 말을 '동사'라고 합니다.

① 동사의 종류와 형태

동사는 크게 be 동사와 일반 동사로 나뉩니다.

(1) be 동사의 형태

be 동사는 '~이다'의 뜻으로, 어떤 대상이 '~한 상태에 놓여있다'는 의미를 나타냅니다.

수	인칭	주어	be 동사			수	인칭	주어	be 동사		
			현재	과거	미래				현재	과거	미래
한명, 하나	1인칭	I	am	was	will be	두 명, 둘 이상	1인칭	we	are	were	will be
	2인칭	you	are	were			2인칭	you			
	3인칭	he / she / it	is	was			3인칭	they			

(2) 일반 동사의 형태

일반 동사는 현재 '~하다(한다)'의 뜻으로 사람이나 사물의 동작이나 상태를 나타냅니다.

원래 모양	주어가 3인칭 단수(he, she, it 등) 일 때	예
일반적인 경우	동사 뒤에 -s를 붙임	wants, reads
어미가 o, s, x, ch, sh로 끝날 때	동사 뒤에 -es를 붙임	goes, teaches, fixes, misses
어미가 자음 + y로 끝날 때	y를 i로 바꾸고 -es를 붙임	study → studies, cry → cries

Tip 이 외에 동사의 형태가 완전히 바뀌는 경우도 있다. 이런 동사들은 따로 그 형태를 외워야 합니다.

② 시제 (tense)

주어의 동작이나 상태를 시간과 연관 지어 나타내는 말을 시제라고 합니다.
기본 시제로는 현재, 과거, 미래가 있습니다.

현재시제	과거부터 지금까지 그리고 미래에도 계속 반복될 일을 나타낼 때 씁니다.
	Mike **gets** up 7 o'clock **every day**. (습관) Mike 매일 7시에 일어난다.
과거시제	이미 지나간 일이나 과거에 끝난 일을 말할 때 씁니다. 동사의 원래 모양에 -ed를 붙입니다. 불규칙 동사는 따로 암기해야 합니다.
	Mike **got** up 10 o'clock **yesterday**. Mike 어제 10시에 일어났다.
미래시제	미래에 대한 의지(~하겠다), 예측(~할 것이다), 계획(~할 예정이다)을 나타냅니다. 주로 will, be going to 동사원형 등과 함께 씁니다.
	Mike **will get** up at 6 o'clock **tomorrow**. Mike는 내일 6시에 일어날 것이다.

* get - got - got (gotten)

동사의 불규칙 변화는 p.262의 동사 변화표를 보면서 확인하기 바랍니다.

GRAMMAR PRACTICE

A 다음 중 동사인 것을 고르세요.

(A) go   (B) children   (C) sit   (D) bench   (E) ride
(F) he   (G) they   (H) come   (I) stand   (J) is
(K) are   (L) young   (M) walk   (N) tree   (O) learn
(P) news   (Q) study   (R) was   (S) chair   (T) call
(U) eat   (V) have   (W) nice   (X) were   (Y) people

B ( ) 안에 알맞은 be 동사를 고르세요.

1. I (am, is, are) a student.
2. She (am, is, are) a teacher.
3. They (am, is, are) happy.
4. This (am, is, are) a book.
5. It (am, is, are) big.
6. We (am, is, are) students.
7. He (am, is, are) young.
8. You (am, is, are) nice.
9. They (was, were) happy.
10. She (was, were) a doctor.

C 다음을 주어가 he, she, it 일 때, 현재시제의 형태와 과거, 과거분사 형태를 쓰세요.

1. do →
2. pass →
3. watch →
4. mix →
5. play →
6. fly →
7. enjoy →
8. cry →
9. buy →
10. dream →
11. teach →
12. miss →
13. fix →
14. go →
15. live →

D 괄호 안에 알맞은 동사를 고르세요.

1. Ann (go, goes, went, will go) to church every Sunday.
2. I (play, plays, played, will play) baseball last weekend.
3. He (go, goes, went, will go) to school next year.
4. They (get, gets, got, will get) up at 6 o'clock tomorrow.
5. David (drink, drinks, drank, will drink) a glass of milk every day.

VOCA learn 배우다   call 부르다   pass 통과하다   teach 가르치다   miss 그리워하다, 놓치다   fix 고치다   live 살다

◎ GRAMMAR POINT

② 조동사

말 그대로 동사를 도와주는 동사입니다. 미래, 가능, 추측, 허가, 의무 등의 의미를 추가하는 동사입니다. 조동사 뒤에는 반드시 본동사의 원래 형태가 와야 합니다.

(1) 조동사의 위치

조동사 뒤에는 반드시 본동사의 원래 형태가 와야 하며, 항상 동사원형 앞에 옵니다.

I **can go** there tomorrow. (O) 나는 내일 거기에 갈 수 있다.
  조동사 본동사

(2) 조동사의 종류와 의미

① will (= be going to) ~을 할 것이다

미래의 일을 예측하거나 앞으로의 일정, 계획 등을 나타낼 때 쓸 수 있습니다.

I **will study** English tomorrow.
= I **am going to study** English tomorrow. 나는 내일 영어 공부를 할 것이다.

② can (= be able to) ~할 수 있다, ~ 해도 좋다

능력을 나타낼 때 쓸 수 있습니다.

I **can play** the piano.
= I **am able to play** the piano. (능력) 나는 피아노를 칠 수 있습니다.

You can go now. 이제 가도 좋다.

③ should (= ought to) ~해야 한다

사회적 관습이나 도덕적인 양심에 비추어 당연히 해야 하는 일을 표현 할 때 씁니다.

You **should tell** the truth.
= You **ought to tell** the truth. 당신은 진실을 말해야 합니다.

④ may (= can) 아마 ~일 것이다, ~해도 좋다

추측이나 허가를 나타낼 때 씁니다. '~해도 좋다'라는 의미를 가지고 있으며, Can 허락의 의미로 쓰이는 경우도 있습니다.

May I **open** the window?
= **Can** I **open** the window? 창문을 열어도 될까요?

⑤ must (= have to) 반드시~해야 한다

반드시 해야 할 의무를 나타낼 때나 강한 추측을 나타낼 때 씁니다.

You **must keep** the secret.
You **have to keep** the secret. 당신은 비밀을 지켜야 합니다.

GRAMMAR PRACTICE

A 다음 중, 조동사인 것을 고르고 뜻을 적으세요.

(A) can   (B) went   (C) sat   (D) desk   (E) did
(F) the   (G) will   (H) came   (I) run   (J) have
(K) sheet   (L) old   (M) work   (N) jog   (O) may
(P) advice   (Q) sleep   (R) make   (S) should   (T) been
(U) must   (V) going   (W) book   (X) had   (Y) change

B 다음의 조동사를 넣어서 문장을 다시 적으세요.

1. It is perfect. (may) → _____

2. He swims. (can) → _____

3. It rains tomorrow. (will) → _____

4. You meet Jenny. (should) → _____

5. You keep your word. (must) → _____

C 같은 의미가 되도록 빈칸을 채워 넣으세요.

1. I will go shopping next weekend.
= I _____ go shopping next weekend.

2. Tom can drive a car.
= Tom _____ drive a car.

3. Linda must call the police.
= Linda _____ call the police.

4. I ought to go to bed now.
= I _____ go to bed now.

5. May I speak to John, please?
= _____ I speak to John, please?

VOCA perfect 완벽한   keep one's word 약속을 지키다

GRAMMAR IN SENTENCE

▶ 다음 문장에서 동사 (조동사와 본동사) 를 찾고 해석하세요.

1. Ann goes to church every Sunday.

2. I played baseball last weekend.

3. He will go to school next year.

4. They will get up at 6 o'clock tomorrow.

5. David drinks a glass of milk every day.

6. I will go shopping next weekend.

7. Tom can drive a car.

8. Linda must call the police.

9. I should go to bed now.

10. May I speak to John, please?

 **Outro**

동사

동사는 움직이는 동작이나 상태를 나타내는 말입니다.

개념이해

한가로운 공원의 풍경을 상상해 봅시다. 한 소년이 자전거를 타고(ride) 있습니다. 뒤에는 소년의 아버지가 자전거를 잡아주고(hold) 있습니다. 옆에는 소년의 어머니로 보이는 스커트를 입은 (wear) 한 여자가 가 서서(stand) 사진을 찍고 있네요. 이렇게 한가로운 공원에는 사람들이 다양한 동작을 하고 있습니다.

개념정리

1. '타다(ride)', '붙잡다(hold)', '입다(wear)', '서다(stand)'와 같이 사람이나 사물의 동작이나 상태를 나타내는 말을 '동사'라고 합니다.

2. '이다'는 사람이나 사물의 동작이 아닌 상태나 성질을 나타내는 말에 붙습니다. 이렇게 사람이나 사물의 상태나 성질을 나타내는 말에 붙는 동사를 'be동사'라고 합니다.

3. 미래를 나타낼 때는 'will ride'와 같이 동사 ride앞에 will이라는 동사를 보조해 주는 동사가 붙습니다. 이렇게 동사를 보조해 주는 동사를 '조동사'라고 합니다. 동사 '타다(ride)'는 시간이 흐름에 따라 과거 현재 미래의 동작을 나타낼 수 있습니다. 현재 '타고 있습니다.'는 ride로 표현하고, 과거에 '탔어요.'는 rode로, 미래에 '타겠군요.'는 will ride로 표현합니다.

ACTUAL TEST 1

A 다음 빈칸에 들어갈 수 있는 것을 고르세요.

1 Austin is purchasing -------.
(A) book   (B) a book   (C) a books   (D) two book

2 Sally and I -------- the same age.
(A) am   (B) are   (C) is   (D) be

3 The small box is filled with ------.
(A) rice   (B) rices   (C) a rice   (D) two rices

4 ------- can solve this problem.
(A) My   (B) I   (C) Mine   (D) Me

5 ------- parents have a computer.
(A) I   (B) My   (C) Me   (D) Mine

6 Five ------------ are walking toward an archway.
(A) children   (B) man   (C) woman   (D) boy

7 Jenny ------------ to the party tomorrow.
(A) come   (B) came   (C) comes   (D) will come

8 The ring on the table is --------.
(A) hers   (B) she   (C) herself   (D) her

9 She likes to make cake ---------.
(A) she   (B) herself   (C) hers   (D) her

10 Bob --------- on a business trip yesterday.
(A) go   (B) went   (C) gone   (D) goes

11 Dennis ----------- baseball every Sunday.
(A) play   (B) will play   (C) played   (D) plays

12 Your deadline is two -------- before that time.
(A) month   (B) the month   (C) months   (D) a month

B 다음 문장에서 틀린 부분을 찾아 바르게 고치세요.

1 I put my books on the shelfs.   ( ) → ( )

2 Asher has a idea for the project.   ( ) → ( )

3 Bradley had two bowls of rices.   ( ) → ( )

4 Parents take care of its children.   ( ) → ( )

5 Mr. Cooper stays at him grandparents' house.   ( ) → ( )

6 This coffee taste very good.   ( ) → ( )

7 You wasn't old at that time.   ( ) → ( )

8 You eyes are very beautiful.   ( ) → ( )

9 Jenny will passes the exam next month. ( ) → ( )

10 My grandmother read the newspaper in the morning.   ( ) → ( )

C 다음 밑줄 친 부분 중 어법상 틀린 것을 두 개 고르세요.

From : Elizabeth Linn
Received : October 10, 3:31 P.M.
To : David Manning

Good morning, Mr. Manning. (1) <u>These</u> is Elizabeth from Star Graphic Design. We (2) <u>discussed</u> the (3) <u>designs</u> in your office last Tuesday. The (4) <u>design</u> are ready. I (5) <u>was</u> hoping to schedule a meeting to review which ones you'd like to use in (6) <u>your</u> new catalog. Thank you.

잉글리쉬앤 그래머 START

입문편

- Unit 4 형용사
- Unit 5 부사
- Unit 6 전치사

6코스
7코스
8코스

UNIT 04 형용사

◎ GRAMMAR POINT

형용사는 사람이나 사물의 성질이나 상태를 표현하는 말입니다.

① 형용사의 역할

형용사는 명사를 앞, 뒤에서 꾸며주는 역할을 합니다.

(1) 명사를 꾸며주는 형용사

형용사 + 명사	■ 대부분의 형용사가 명사 앞에서 꾸며줍니다. I bought **a new** car. 나는 새 자동차를 샀다.
명사 + 형용사	■ -thing 이나 -body(-one)이 끝나는 대명사 뒤에서 꾸며줍니다. I want **something new**. 나는 새로운 무언가를 원한다.

(2) 명사를 설명하는 형용사

주어 설명	■ be 동사 뒤에 와서 주어의 상태를 설명합니다. **Tom** is **happy**. Tom은 행복하다.
목적어 설명	■ 목적어 뒤에 와서 목적어의 상태를 설명합니다. Tom made **me happy**. Tom이 나를 행복하게 해 주었다.

② 감정동사의 형용사

excite (흥분시키다), interest(흥미를 갖게 하다), bore(지루하게 하다), exhaust (지치다) 등 감정을 나타내는 감정동사는 동사 뒤에 -ing를 붙이거나 -ed를 붙여서 형용사의 역할을 합니다.

감정을 유발하는 -ing	감정을 느끼는 v-ed.
The **game** is **exciting**. 그 경기는 흥미진진하다.	**Spectators** are **excited**. 관중들이 흥분했다.
This is an **exciting game**. 이것은 흥미진진한 경기이다.	I saw an **excited spectators**. 나는 흥분한 관중들을 보았다.
The **class** is **boring**. 수업이 지루합니다.	**Students** are **bored**. 학생들이 지루합니다.
It is a **boring class**. 그것은 지루한 수업입니다.	**Bored students** are talking to each other. 지루해 진 학생들이 서로 이야기를 합니다.

GRAMMAR PRACTICE

A 다음 중 형용사인 것을 고르세요.

(A) green (B) full (C) flower (D) news
(E) wife (F) pretty (G) drive (H) nice
(I) happy (J) roof (K) big (L) is
(M) small (N) red (O) boring (P) listen
(Q) large (R) possible (S) beauty (T) fresh

B 주어진 형용사를 이용하여 <보기>처럼 문장을 완성하세요.

> 보기 He is a student, (smart) → He is a **smart student**. = The **student** is **smart**.

1. This is a car (small) → _____. = _____.
2. He is a teacher. (new) → _____. = _____.
3. It is tea. (hot) → _____. = _____.
4. That is a rainbow. (beautiful) → _____. = _____.
5. It is a roof. (red) → _____. = _____.

C 괄호 안에 알맞은 형용사를 고르세요.

1. I watched an (interesting, interested) movie.
2. People were (disappointing, disappointed) with the result.
3. The students are (surprising, surprised) by the news.
4. I read a (boring, bored) book.
5. I saw (exciting, excited) people.

D 다음 빈칸에 알맞은 말을 보기에서 찾아 쓰세요.

> 보기 shocking, shocked / boring, bored / interesting, interested

1. It was _____ news. 그것은 충격적인 소식이었다.
2. The students are _____. 학생들은 지루해 하고 있다.
3. This book is _____. 이 책은 재미있다.

VOCA large 큰 possible 가능한 fresh 신선한

◎ GRAMMAR POINT

② 수와 양을 나타내는 형용사

(1) 셀 수 있는 명사와 함께 쓰이는 형용사

수를 나타내는 형용사인 many, a few, few, several 등은 두 개 이상의 셀 수 있는 명사 앞에 씁니다.

수를 나타내는 형용사	의미	예
many	많은	I bought **many eggs**. 나는 많은 달걀을 샀다.
several	몇몇의	I bought **several eggs**. 나는 몇 개의 달걀을 샀다.
a few	약간의	I have **a few friends**. 나는 친구가 몇 명 있다.
few	거의 없는	I have **few friends**. 나는 거의 친구가 없다.

(2) 셀 수 없는 명사와 함께 쓰이는 형용사

양을 나타내는 형용사인 much, a little, little 등은 셀 수 없는 명사 앞에 씁니다.

양를 나타내는 형용사	의미	예
much	많은	I don't have **much money**. 나는 돈이 많지 않다.
a little	약간의	I have **a little money**. 나는 약간의 돈이 있다.
little	거의 없는	I have **little money**. 나는 돈이 거의 없다.

(3) 두 경우에 모두 쓰이는 형용사 표현

수와 양 모두 나타내는 형용사	의미	예
a lot of lots of	많은	I bought **lots** (**a lot**) **of apples**. 나는 많은 사과를 샀다. I bought **lots** (**a lot**) **of paper**. 나는 많은 종이를 샀다.
all	모든	I read **all books**. 나는 모든 책을 읽었다. I want **all information**. 나는 모든 정보를 원한다.
some	약간의	I need **some books**. 나는 책 몇 권이 필요하다. I need **some money**. 나는 약간의 돈이 필요하다.

GRAMMAR PRACTICE

A 다음 중 수와 양을 나타내는 형용사인 것을 고르세요.

(A) many   (B) number   (C) lot   (D) much
(E) amount   (F) few   (G) count   (H) nice
(I) some   (J) truly   (K) a little   (L) those
(M) sugar   (N) exciting   (O) little   (P) they
(Q) a few   (R) all   (S) water   (T) are

B 다음 중 맞는 표현을 고르세요.

1. (A) many boys   (B) much car   (C) many waters   (D) all orange
2. (A) many beer   (B) several desk   (C) much water   (D) a few air
3. (A) few advice   (B) all students   (C) a little pens   (D) much doors
4. (A) much ball   (B) some egg   (C) few bread   (D) a lot of doughnuts
5. (A) some teacher   (B) lots of book   (C) many milk   (D) some pens

C 괄호 안에 알맞은 수량형용사를 고르세요.

1. Eric eats very (many, much) meat.
2. There are (many, much) bottles.
3. We need (many, a lot of) money.
4. The children should read (much, a lot of) storybooks.
5. Jenny collects (much, lots of) cans every day.
6. There is too (many, much) information.
7. I bought (some, much) apples at the market.
8. You can see (lots of, little) visitors on the street.
9. David made (some, much) mistakes.
10. There are (much, many) beautiful parks in Korea.

VOCA   lot 한 무더기, 많은   amount 양   count 세다   truly 진실로   collect 모으다   visitor 방문객
make a mistake 실수하다

GRAMMAR IN SENTENCE

▶ 다음 문장에서 형용사를 찾고 해석하세요.

1. I watched an interesting movie.

2. People were disappointed with the result.

3. Students are surprised by the news.

4. I read a boring book yesterday.

5. I saw excited people in the park.

6. The children should read a lot of storybooks.

7. Jenny collects lots of cans every day.

8. There is too much information.

9. I bought some apples at the market.

10. The rainbow is beautiful.

 **Outro**

형용사

형용사는 사람이나 사물의 성질이나 상태를 표현하는 말입니다.

개념이해

초록(green)색 지붕과 빨간(red)색의 지붕을 가진 집이 있는 마을을 상상해 봅시다. 집 옆에는 아름다운(beautiful) 무지개가 떠 있네요. 무지개 옆에는 구름이 조금(some) 있습니다. 남자와 여자가 많은(many) 풍선들을 들고 계단을 올라가고 있습니다. 그 사람들은 행복해(happy) 보입니다.

개념정리

1. '빨간'(red), '초록'(green), '아름다운'(beautiful), '행복한'(happy) 등 형용사는 사람이나 사물의 성질이나 상태를 나타내는 말입니다.

2. '아름다운 무지개 (a beautiful rainbow)'또는 '무지개가 아름답다.(The rainbow is beautiful.)'라고 표현할 수 있듯이, 형용사는 명사 앞에서 꾸며줄 수도 있고 be동사를 써서 상태를 표현할 수도 있습니다.

3. 셀 수 있는 명사와 셀 수 없는 명사를 꾸밀 때는 각각 다른 형용사를 씁니다. '많은'이라는 뜻의 형용사를 사용할 때, 꾸밈을 받는 명사가 셀 수 있는 명사면 'many'를 사용하고, 꾸밈을 받는 명사가 셀 수 없는 명사면 'much'를 사용합니다.

UNIT 05 부사

◎ GRAMMAR POINT

부사는 형용사, 부사, 동사를 꾸며주는 말입니다.

① 부사의 형태와 종류

(1) 부사의 형태

모든 부사가 다 그러한 것은 아니지만 주로 형용사 뒤에 -ly 를 붙이면 부사가 됩니다.

부사의 형태	예
형용사 + ly	final + ly = finally 마침내 current + ly + currently 현재 rapid + ly + rapidly 빨리, 급속히 short + ly = shortly 곧
-le → e 삭제 후 y 삽입	simple + ly = simply 간단하게 flexible + ly = flexibly 유연하게
-y → ily	necessary + ly = necessarily 반드시 temporary +ly = temporarily 일시적으로

(2) 부사의 종류

1) 빈도부사

빈도부사는 '얼마나 자주'하는지 즉 회수를 나타내는 부사이며, be동사 뒤 일반 동사의 앞, 조동사와 일반 동사의 사이에 옵니다.

빈도	0%	10%	11 ~ 40%	41 ~ 70%	71~90%	100%
단어	never	rarely seldom	sometimes	often frequently	usually normally	always
뜻	결코 ~않는	거의 ~않는	가끔	자주	주로	항상

He is **never** late. 그는 절대 늦지 않는다.
He **sometimes** gets up late. 그는 가끔 늦게 일어난다.
He **always** tells a lie. 그는 항상 거짓말을 한다.

2) 시간, 장소, 정도, 방법 부사

부사가 형용사, 부사, 동사를 꾸며줄 때, 장소, 빈도, 때, 정도, 방법 등을 나타냅니다.

의미	예
장소	here 여기 there 저기 up 위 down 아래
시간	now 지금 soon 곧 currently 현재 early 일찍 already 이미
정도	very 매우 well 잘 quite 꽤 too 너무
방법	promptly 즉시 carefully 조심스럽게 fast 빠르게

GRAMMAR PRACTICE

A 다음 중 부사인 것을 고르세요.

(A) sky   (B) nice   (C) fast   (D) well
(E) yet   (F) fly   (G) flight   (H) high
(I) very   (J) airplane   (K) really   (L) soon
(M) sugar   (N) air   (O) go   (P) friendly
(Q) seldom   (R) current   (S) there   (T) prompt

B 우리말과 같은 뜻이 되도록 빈칸에 알맞은 말을 <보기>에서 골라 쓰세요.

보기) often   never   soon   always   rarely

1. 여름에는 자주 비가 내린다. → It _____ rains in summer.
2. Tom은 절대로 실수를 하지 않는다. → Tom _____ makes mistakes.
3. 아버지는 항상 바쁘다. → My father is _____ busy.
4. 곧 만나자. → See you _____.
5. Dr. Lee 는 거의 늦지 않는다. → Dr. Lee is _____ late

C 다음 중, 부사의 성격이 나머지와 다른 하나를 고르세요.

1. (A) here   (B) there   (C) usually   (D) up
2. (A) always   (B) often   (C) rarely   (D) now
3. (A) very   (B) well   (C) too   (D) never
4. (A) sometimes (B) always   (C) fast   (D) often
5. (A) now   (B) soon   (C) currently (D) down

D 괄호 안에 알맞은 형용사 또는 부사를 고르세요.

1. Nick is a (brave, bravely) student.
2. The bus goes (slow, slowly).
3. The street is (quiet, quietly).
4. Rosa can sing (beautiful, beautifully).
5. Tim speaks (loud, loudly).

(VOCA) well 잘   yet 아직도   high 높은, 높게   soon 곧   seldom 거의~않게   brave 용감한   quiet 조용한
quietly 조용하게   loud 소리가 큰   loudly 소리가 크게

◎ GRAMMAR POINT

② 형용사와 형태가 동일한 부사

부사 중에는 형용사와 뜻과 형태가 동일한 부사도 있습니다.

단어	뜻	단어	뜻
daily	매일(의)	early	이른, 일찍
weekly	매주(의)	long	오랜, 오래
monthly	매달(의)	fast	빨리, 빠른
quarterly	분기별(의)	far	멀리, 먼
yearly	매년(의)	near	가까이에, 가까운

I read a **daily** newspaper. (형용사) 나는 일간지를 읽는다.
I **read** a newspaper **daily**. (부사) 나는 매일 신문을 읽는다.

He is a fast runner. (형용사) 그는 빠른 선수다.
He runs fast. (부사) 그는 빨리 달린다.

③ 형용사, 부사 동형의 단어에 -ly를 붙여서 다른 뜻의 부사가 되는 경우

단어	품사	뜻	예시	단어	품사	뜻	예시
hard	부사	열심히	Tom **studies hard**. Tom은 열심히 공부한다.	hardly	부사	거의 ~ 않는	It **hardly rains** there. 그곳은 거의 비가 내리지 않는다.
	형용사	어려운, 힘든	This is a **hard work**. 이것은 어려운 일이다.				
high	부사	높이, 높게	Kites **fly high** in the sky. 연들이 하늘 높이 난다.	highly	부사	매우, 몹시	Australia is a **highly developed** country. 호주는 고도로 발전된 나라이다.
	형용사	높은	They climb a **high mountain**. 그들은 산을 등산한다.				
late	부사	늦게	Bob **gets up late**. Bob은 늦게 일어난다.	lately	부사	최근에	It **rained lately**. 최근에 비가 내렸다.
	형용사	늦은	Bob **was late** today. Bob은 오늘 늦었다.				
close	부사	가까이	They **sat close** to me. 그들은 나에게 가까이 앉았다.	closely	부사	면밀히, 상세히	They **looked** into the accident **closely**. 그들은 상세히 사건을 조사하였다.
	형용사	가까운	We are **close friends**. 우리는 가까운 친구다.				
	동사	닫다	**Close** the door. 문을 닫아라.				

GRAMMAR PRACTICE

A 보기의 단어를 형용사, 부사 그리고 형용사와 부사가 같은 형태인 것들로 분류하세요.

> 보기 well good early kind fast daily quiet always angry slowly long often

1. 형용사 : _____
2. 부사 : _____
3. 형용사와 부사 : _____

B 괄호 안에 알맞은 것을 고르고, 문장 속에서의 의미를 적으세요.

1. He went to bed (late, lately) last night.
2. This is a (hard, hardly) question for everyone.
3. Beth is a (high, highly) respected person.
4. The volume of the radio is too (high, highly).
5. That report is (hard, hardly) surprising.
6. The birds fly (high, highly) in the sky.
7. Could you (close, closely) the window?
8. I sat and read the report (close, closely) for a while.
9. The economy is (close, closely) to a recession.
10. They are (hard, hardly) workers.

GRAMMAR IN SENTENCE

▶ 다음 문장에서 부사를 찾고 해석하세요.

1. He went to bed late last night.

2. This is a hard question for everyone.

3. Beth is a highly respected person.

4. The volume of the radio is too high.

5. That report is hardly surprising.

6. The birds fly high in the sky.

7. Could you close the window?

8. I sat and read the report closely for a while.

9. The economy is close to a recession.

10. They are hard workers.

 **Outro**

부사

부사는 형용사, 부사, 동사를 꾸며주는 말입니다.

운동회가 열리고 있는 운동장을 상상해 봅시다. 선수들이 매우(very) 빠르게(fast) 달리다 마침내(finally) 결승선에 온 것 같습니다. 천천히(slowly) 달리는 여학생도 있고, 큰소리로(loudly)로 응원하는 여학생의 모습도 보이네요. 하늘에는 풍선이 높게(high) 날고 있습니다.

1. 위에서 천천히(slowly), 빨리(fast), 높이(high)와 같이 동사를 꾸며주는 말과 '매우(very)'와 같이 형용사와 부사를 꾸며주는 말이 있습니다. 이렇게 동사, 부사 또는 형용사를 꾸며주는 말을 부사라고 합니다.

2. 마침내(finally), 크게(loudly), 천천히(slowly) 등이 부사입니다. 여기서 finally는 형용사 final 뒤에 ly가, loudly는 형용사 loud 뒤에 ly가, slowly는 형용사 slow 뒤에 ly가 붙어 ly로 끝나는 형태의 부사입니다.

UNIT 06 전치사

GRAMMAR POINT

전치사는 (대)명사 앞에 붙어 시간, 위치, 장소 등을 나타내는 말입니다.

① 시간을 나타내는 전치사

(1) at, on, in

종류	뜻	예시
at + 짧은 시간 (분, 시, 밤, 새벽 등)	~에	at 10:00(10시에), at lunch time(점심 때), at midnight(한밤중에)
in + 긴 시간 (오전, 오후, 월, 연 등)		in the morning(아침에), in winter(겨울에), in 2030(2030년에)
on + 요일/ 특정한 날		on Sunday(일요일에), on my birthday(내 생일에)

(2) for, during

종류	뜻	예시
for + 숫자	~동안	for three years(3년 동안), for a week(1주 동안)
during + 특정명사		during the war(전쟁 중에), during the vacation(방학 중에)

(3) before / after

종류	뜻	예시
before	~ 전에	before lunch(점심식사 전에)
after	~ 후에	after dinner(저녁식사 후에)

(4) by / until

종류	뜻	예시
by	~까지	by 11 p.m.(11시까지)
until		until next Friday(다음 주 금요일까지)

Tip by 와 until은 우리말로는 '~까지'로 의미가 같지만 영어로 표현할 때는 명확하게 구별을 해야 합니다. by는 말한 시간까지 어떤 동작이나 상태가 완료된 것을 나타내고, until은 말한 시간까지 이미 하고 있던 동작이나 상태가 계속 된다는 뜻이라는 점을 유의해야 합니다.

- **by + 시점과 함께 써서** 동작의 완료를 나타내는 동사 : arrive(도착하다), finish (마치다), submit (제출하다)
- **until + 시점과 함께 써서** 상태의 계속을 나타내는 동사 : stay(머무르다), wait (기다리다), keep(지속하다)

I will be back **by** 11.p.m. 나는 오후 11시까지 돌아올 것이다.
I will do the work **until** next Friday. 나는 다음 주 금요일까지 그 일을 할 것이다.

GRAMMAR PRACTICE

A 다음 중 전치사인 것을 고르세요.

(A) in   (B) at   (C) the   (D) an   (E) go   (F) for
(G) and   (H) but   (I) to   (J) so   (K) of   (L) yet
(M) on   (N) into (O) ask   (P) by   (Q) her   (R) across
(S) because (T) with (U) far   (V) during (W) behind (X) really

B 다음 ( ) 안에 at, on, in 중에서 알맞은 전치사를 넣으세요.

(A) (　) Tuesday   (B) (　) January   (C) (　) my birthday
(D) (　) 2025   (E) (　) summer   (F) (　) 12 o'clock
(G) (　) October, 15th   (H) (　) December

C 다음 ( ) 안에 for, during 중에서 기간을 나타내는 알맞은 전치사를 넣으세요.

(A) (　) the class   (B) (　) an hour   (C) (　) the intermission
(D) (　) 30 minutes   (E) (　) one month   (F) (　) the holiday

D 다음 중 전치사가 잘못 들어간 것을 고르고, 바르게 고치세요.

(A) **at** midnight   (B) **on** Sunday   (C) **above** spring   (D) **in** the afternoon
(E) **in** Monday morning   (F) **at** 10 a.m.   (G) **in** 2026   (H) **at** five o'clock
(I) **on** Christmas Day   (J) **at** the moment   (K) **in** spring   (L) **at** April

E 다음 ( ) 안에 알맞은 전치사를 선택하세요.

1. Our school is far away (at, from) his house.
2. Let's have a meeting (on, before) dinner.
3. The bus will arrive (by, until) 9 o'clock.
4. I waited for him (by, until) 10 o'clock.
5. You should submit the report (by, until) tomorrow.

VOCA　intermission 휴식시간　holiday 휴일

◎ GRAMMAR POINT

② 장소를 나타내는 전치사

(1) at / in

종류	뜻	예시
at + 좁은 장소, 한 지점	~에서	at the bus stop(버스 정류장에서), at the door(그 문에서)
in + 넓은 장소		in Japan(일본에서), in the river(그 강에서)

(2) on / over / above

종류	뜻	예시
on(표면과 접촉)	~ 위에	on the desk(책상 위에), on the table(테이블 위에)
over(표면 바로 위)		over the river(강 위에), over the sea(바다 위에)
above(표면에서 높이 떨어져)		above the trees(나무 너머로), above the clouds(구름 위에)

(3) beneath / under / below

종류	뜻	예시
beneath(표면과 접촉)	~ 아래에	beneath the lake(호수 아래에), beneath the waves(파도 아래에)
under(표면 바로 아래)		under the table(테이블 아래에), under the tree(나무 아래에)
below (표면 아래에서 많이 떨어져)		below the bridge(다리 아래에), below the horizon(지평선 아래에)

③ 방향을 나타내는 전치사

(1) up / down

종류	뜻	예시
up	~ 위쪽으로	up the mountain(산 위로 - 오르고 있는 상황을 나타냄)
down	~ 아래쪽으로	down the stairs(계단 아래로 - 내려가고 있는 상황을 나타냄)

(2) from / to

종류	뜻	예시
from + 출발점	~로부터	from his house(그의 집으로부터)
to + 도착점	~으로	to the school(그 학교까지)

(3) into / out of

종류	뜻	예시
into	~안으로	into the bag(가방 안에), into the room(방 안에)
out of	~밖으로	out of my bag(내 가방에서), out of the room(그 방에서)

(4) along / through / across

종류	뜻	예시
along	~을 따라서	along the street 길을 따라서
through	~을 관통하여	through the tunnel 터널을 지나서
across	~을 가로질러	across the river 강을 가로질러

GRAMMAR PRACTICE

A 다음 ( ) 안에 **at, on, in** 중에서 알맞은 전치사를 넣으세요.

1. Students are studying _____ the classroom.

2. My office is _____ the third floor.

3. Jennifer cooks _____ the kitchen.

4. I live _____ a farm.

5. I'll wait for you _____ the station

B 괄호 안에 알맞은 전치사를 고르세요.

1. There are some boats (over, below) the bridge.

2. They are walking (along, over) the street.

3. The boys are jumping (under, over) the fence.

4. The train passes (on, through) the tunnel.

5. There is a computer (on, over) the desk.

6. Lamps are hanging (over, under) the table.

7. I will be (into, out of) town for a few days.

8. How far is it from here (up, to) your school?

9. The library is (across, over) the street.

10. The children are playing (on, down) the grass.

VOCA classroom 교실 office 사무실 floor 마루, 층 station 역, 정거장 boat 배 bridge 다리 lamp 램프
hang 매달다 seashore 해안가 grass 잔디

GRAMMAR IN SENTENCE

▶ 다음 문장에서 전치사를 찾고 해석하세요.

1. There are some boats below the bridge.

2. They are walking along the street.

3. The boys are jumping over the fence.

4. The train passes through the tunnel.

5. There is a computer on the desk.

6. Lamps are hanging over the table.

7. I will be out of town for a few days.

8. Tourists are walking along the seashore.

9. The library is across the street.

10. The children are playing on the grass.

 **Outro**

전치사

전치사는 (대)명사 앞에 붙어 시간, 위치, 장소 등을 나타내는 말입니다.

APRIL						
SUNDAY	MONDAY	TUESDAY	WEDNESDAY	THURSDAY	FRIDAY	SATURDAY
1	2	3	4	5	6	7
8	9 10:00 meet David	10	11	12	13	14
15	16 vacation	17 vacation	18 vacation	19 vacation	20 vacation	21

개념이해

여러분이 Jenny의 방안(in)을 살펴본다고 상상해 보겠습니다. 책상 위(on)에는 컴퓨터와 책들이 있습니다. 책상 옆(next to)에는 화분이 놓여 있군요. 그녀의 뒤(behind)에는 액자와 화분이 있습니다. 오른쪽에 있는 그녀의 4월 (in April)달력을 보면, 4월 9일 월요일(on Monday) 10시에 (at 10 o'clock)에 David와 약속이 있네요. 16일부터는 휴가입니다. 휴가동안(during vacation) 그녀는 무엇을 할 계획일까요?

개념정리

1. 전치사는 명사 혹은 명사의 성질을 갖는 말의 앞에 붙여 장소, 시간 등을 나타냅니다.
   장소를 나타내는 전치사에는 on(위에), in(안에), under(아래에), 옆에 (next to), 뒤에 (behind)등이 있습니다.

2. 시간을 나타내는 전치사에는 연도, 달, 계절 앞에 사용하는 in, 요일, 특정일 앞에는 on, 시간 앞에 쓰는 at 등이 있습니다. 전치사를 사용하여 기간을 표현할 수도 있습니다. 예를 들어 '월요일부터 금요일까지'는 'from Monday to Friday'로 씁니다. 기간을 나타내는 '휴가 동안'은 'during vacation'으로 숫자 표현과 더불어 쓰는 5일 동안은 'for 5 days' 라고 할 수 있습니다.

ACTUAL TEST 2

A 다음 빈칸에 들어갈 수 있는 것을 고르세요.

1 I met a -------- woman on the street.
(A) beauty (B) beautifully (C) beautify (D) beautiful

2 All of the employees are -------- thanks to the bonuses.
(A) happy (B) happiness (C) happily (D) happen

3 Beth made -------- mistakes yesterday.
(A) several (B) a little (C) much (D) little

4 I saw an -------- movie last night.
(A) excited (B) interesting (C) bored (D) exhausted

5 Our team holds a meeting -------.
(A) week (B) day (C) weekly (D) quarter

6 Those books are ------- recommended by experts.
(A) high (B) highly (C) higher (D) height

7 Ted will be back -------.
(A) short (B) shortly (C) shorten (D) immediate

8 Linda ------- goes to school by bus.
(A) lately (B) sometimes (C) well (D) easy

9 There is a big mirror ------- the wall.
(A) at (B) in (C) on (D) into

10 Kathy is standing -------- the subway station exit.
(A) in (B) at (C) on (D) over

11 Grace lives ------- Canada with her family.
(A) at (B) in (C) on (D) for

12 A man is using a phone --------- the door.
(A) above (B) beneath (C) in front of (D) over

B 다음 문장에서 틀린 부분을 찾아 바르게 고치세요.

1 Cerek runs very fastly.   (   ) → (   )

2 I was surprising at the news.   (   ) → (   )

3 Much books are on the bookshelves. (   ) → (   )

4 Mr. Lee is a good driver, so he drives safe. (   ) → (   )

5 Lucky, Ethan passed the final exam. (   ) → (   )

6 The kite flies highly in the sky. (   ) → (   )

7 Mr. Gregory walks slow in the park. (   ) → (   )

8 It's very cold at December.   (   ) → (   )

9 You should submit the report until Monday. (   ) → (   )

10 They are walking at the street.   (   ) → (   )

C 다음 밑줄 친 부분 중 어법상 틀린 것을 두 개 고르세요.

For this week only, all (1) <u>electronic</u> at Best Tech World will be on sale. Everything will be discounted up to 50% off! Come and choose from a wide selection of (2) <u>electronics</u>, including TVs, home stereos, and (3) <u>refrigerators</u>. Our store is located (4) <u>at</u> Washington Street. Just follow (5) <u>the</u> signs to "Best Tech World". Come soon before everything (6) <u>is</u> sold out.

MINI TEST 1

A 다음 빈칸에 들어갈 수 있는 것을 고르세요.

1. I saw a man and ---------- is sitting beside the table.
   - (A) a man
   - (B) the man
   - (C) men
   - (D) man

2. Linda loves -------- brother.
   - (A) her
   - (B) she
   - (C) herself
   - (D) herself

3. I don't know ------- name.
   - (A) he
   - (B) his
   - (C) him
   - (D) himself

4. Mike and I ---------- good friends.
   - (A) am
   - (B) are
   - (C) is
   - (D) be

5. The sun ---------- in the east.
   - (A) rise
   - (B) rises
   - (C) rose
   - (D) risen

6. Mike ---------- TV last night.
   - (A) watch
   - (B) watches
   - (C) watched
   - (D) will watch.

7. Birds -------------- in the sky.
   - (A) flies
   - (B) flied
   - (C) can fly
   - (D) is flied

8. Linda bought a ------- coat in a store.
   - (A) run
   - (B) blue
   - (C) tall
   - (D) newly

9. There is ------- cheese on the table.
   - (A) many
   - (B) a few
   - (C) several
   - (D) some

10. They study -------- in the library.
    - (A) hard
    - (B) hardly
    - (C) hardness
    - (D) quiet

11. I will visit London ------- summer vacation.
    - (A) on
    - (B) next to
    - (C) during
    - (D) for

12. We will take a midterm exam -------- October 20th.
    - (A) in
    - (B) at
    - (C) on
    - (D) for

B 다음 문장에서 틀린 부분을 찾아 바르게 고치세요.

1. I want to travel at the world. ( ) → ( )
2. You secretary took it to the repair shop. ( ) → ( )
3. They always look happily. ( ) → ( )
4. Ms. Rose like all kinds of flowers. ( ) → ( )
5. There is shop across the street. ( ) → ( )
6. Child are playing in a square. ( ) → ( )
7. Much boats are in the river. ( ) → ( )
8. The traffic on the street is very heavily. ( ) → ( )
9. He visit our factory tomorrow. ( ) → ( )
10. The tree have lost most of its leaves. ( ) → ( )

C 다음 공지를 읽고, 밑줄 친 부분 중 어법상 틀린 것을 두 개 고르세요.

> To All employees
>
> I just want to (1) <u>remind</u> everyone that (2) <u>constructive</u> of the new (3) <u>laboratory</u> is going to begin on Tuesday. The Facilities Department has just informed (4) <u>mine</u> that the north parking area will be (5) <u>closed</u> for the duration of the project. You'll have to use the east, west and south parking areas, so it will take longer to enter and (6) <u>exit</u> the company grounds. Thank you for your cooperation.

잉글리쉬앤 그래머 START

입문편

 코스

Unit 7 문장의 성분, 1형식
Unit 8 2형식 3형식
Unit 9 4형식 5형식

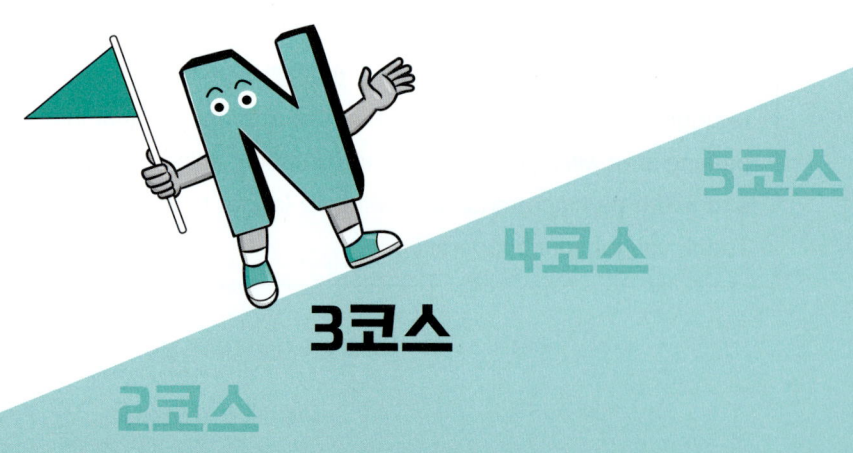

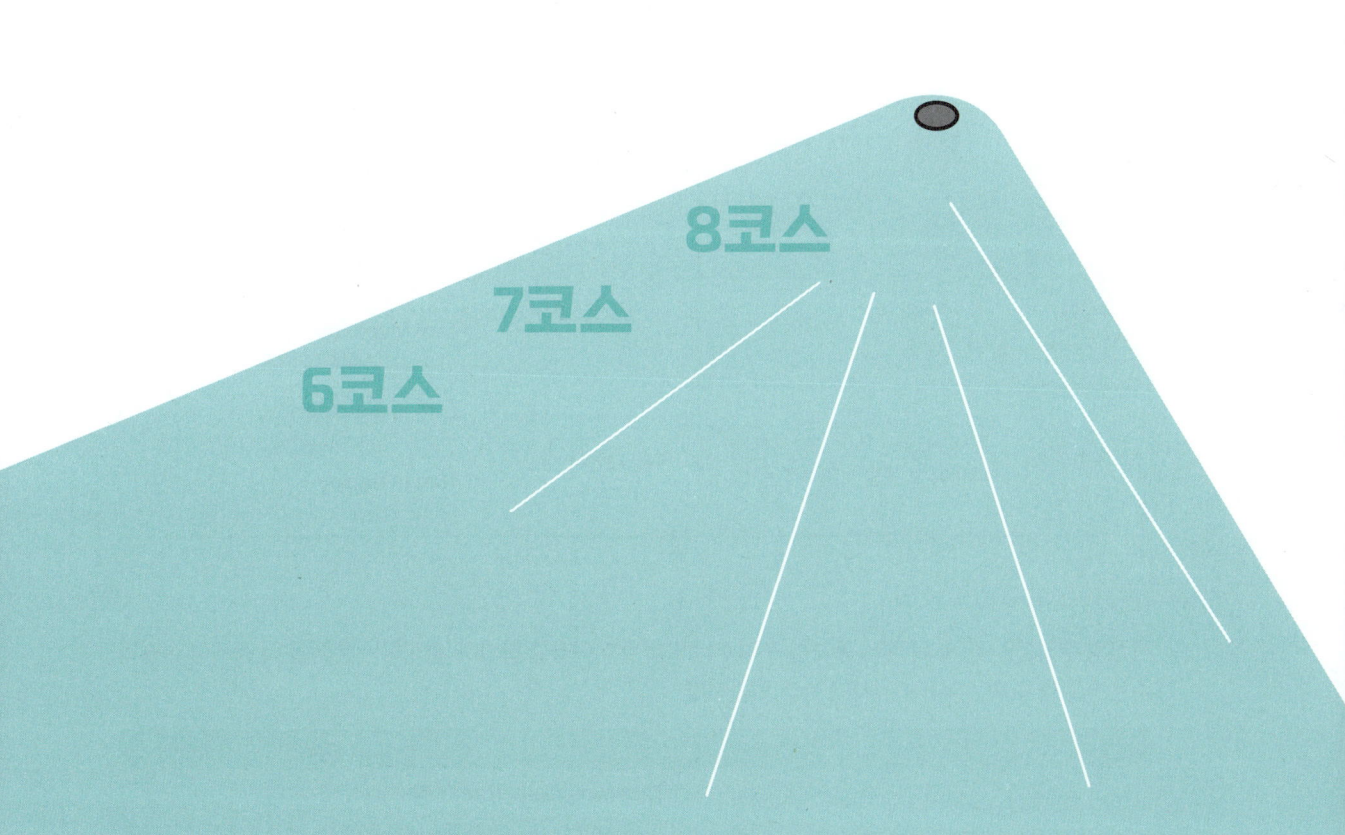

UNIT 07 문장의 성분, 1형식

GRAMMAR POINT

문장 성분은 문장을 구성하면서 일정한 역할을 하는 요소를 말합니다. 문장을 만드는 재료라고 할 수 있으며, 주어, 동사, 목적어, 보어가 있습니다.

① 문장 성분

(1) 주성분 : 주어, 동사, 목적어, 보어

문장 성분은 문장을 구성하면서 일정한 역할을 하는 요소를 말하며, 주요 문장 성분에는 주어, 동사, 목적어, 보어가 있습니다.

문장 성분	뜻	해당 품사	예시
주어	문장의 주체를 나타내는 말	명사, 대명사	**Tom** is a student. Tom은 학생이다. **He** has a car. 그는 자동차를 가지고 있다.
동사	주어의 동작이나 상태를 나타내는 말	동사	Tom **is** happy. Tom은 행복하다. He **has** a car. 그는 자동차를 가지고 있다.
목적어	주어의 대상이 되는 말	명사, 대명사	He has **a car**. 그는 자동차를 가지고 있다. Tom loves **her**. Tom은 그녀를 사랑한다.
보어	동사만으로는 뜻이 불충분하기 때문에 그 뜻을 보충해주는 말	명사, 대명사, 형용사	Tom is **a student**. Tom은 학생이다. Tom is **happy**. Tom은 행복하다.

(2) 부가적인 성분 : 수식어

문장의 주성분인 주어, 목적어, 동사를 꾸며주는 말을 수식어라고 합니다. 수식어는 문장을 더 상세히 설명해주는 역할을 하며, 부사, 전치사구 등이 있습니다.

수식어	역할
부사	Tom runs **fast**. Tom 은 빠르게 달린다. (부사인 fast 가 동사인 run을 수식)
전치사구(전치사 + 명사)	Linda lives **in Canada**. Linda는 캐나다에 산다. (전치사구인 in Canada가 동사인 live를 수식)

GRAMMAR PRACTICE

A 다음 문장을 주어, 동사, 목적어, 보어로 나누어 표시해 보세요.

〔보기〕 John has a sister.   John 주어 / has 동사 / a sister 목적어

1. Birds fly.

2. Linda is happy.

3. They have breakfast.

4. Children throw the ball.

5. The ball is white.

B 다음 밑줄 친 곳에 '주어, 동사, 목적어, 보어' 중 알맞은 것을 쓰세요.

1. **Dennis** is tall.
   (   )

2. Dennis plays **tennis**.
              (   )

3. Jenny is **beautiful**.
            (   )

4. He **loves her**.
      (   )(   )

5. We **finish the work**.
       (   ) (   )

C 다음 문장에서 수식어(구)를 골라 (   )를 하세요.

1. Tom makes dinner every day.

2. Susan studies very hard.

3. They live in Michigan.

4. Jenny sleeps at ten.

5. We swim in the river.

VOCA fly - flew - flown 날다   throw - threw - thrown 던지다   finish 마치다   swim 수영하다 - swam - swum

◎ GRAMMAR POINT

② 문장의 종류

동사에 따라 반드시 들어가야 하는 문장 성분이 있고, 반드시 들어가야 하는 문장 성분에 따라 문장의 종류를 구분한 것을 문장의 형식이라 합니다. 영어에서는 문장의 형식을 크게 다섯 가지로 분류합니다.

문장의 5 형식	문장의 구조
1형식	주어 + 동사 Mike works. Mike가 일합니다.
2형식	주어 + 동사 + 보어 Mike is a doctor. Mike는 의사입니다.
3형식	주어 + 동사 + 목적어 Mike loves his family. Mike는 그의 가족을 사랑합니다.
4형식	주어 + 동사 + 간접목적어 + 직접목적어 Mike gave his sister a book. Mike는 그의 여동생에게 책을 주었습니다.
5형식	주어 + 동사 + 목적어 + 보어 Mike makes his family happy. Mike는 그의 가족을 행복하게 해 줍니다.

③ 1형식 문장 : 주어(S) + 동사(V) (완전 자동사)

주어와 동사만으로도 충분히 의미를 전달할 수 있는 1형식 문장에서는 동사가 완전한 의미를 전달할 수 있기 때문에 문장 내에서 완전히 자립할 수 있는 동사라는 의미에서, '완전 자동사'라고 부릅니다.

1. Mike lives.   Mike는 살고 있다.   (1형식)
   주어 동사

2. Mike lives in Seattle.   Mike는 시애틀에 살고 있다.   (1형식)
   주어 동사 수식어구

3. Mike lives in Seattle with his family.   Mike는 그의 가족들과 함께 시애틀에 살고 있다.   (1형식)
   주어 동사 수식어구 수식어구

→ 위 문장 중에서 'Mike가 살고 있다'는 사실이 가장 중요하며, 문장의 최소단위가 됩니다. 시애틀에 살고 있다거나 그의 가족과 살고 있다는 말은 좀 더 문장의 뜻을 자세하게 전해주지만 문장이 성립하기 위해서 꼭 있어야 할 요소는 아닙니다.

> **Tip** 1형식 완전 자동사
> fall 떨어지다 work 일하다 walk 걷다 run 달리다 live 살다 sleep 자다 listen 듣다

GRAMMAR PRACTICE

A 다음 문장을 주어, 동사, 목적어, 보어로 나눈 후, 각 문장의 형식을 적으세요.

1. Mike works. _____

2. She has a dog. _____

3. He is a doctor. _____

4. They sleep. _____

5. They walk along the shore. _____

B 다음 문장의 형식을 쓰세요.

1. She sleeps at nine. (   )

2. Austin is very nice. (   )

3. Jenny likes apples. (   )

4. Austin gave Jennifer an apple. (   )

5. Austin made her angry. (   )

6. The leaves are falling on the street. (   )

7. David works on weekends. (   )

8. She reads a newspaper in the morning. (   )

9. Eric is handsome. (   )

10. They walk every day. (   )

VOCA give 주다 - gave - given   leaf(pl)leaves 잎   fall 떨어지다   handsome 잘생긴   walk 걷다

GRAMMAR IN SENTENCE

▶ 다음 문장에서 주어, 동사, 목적어, 보어 그리고 수식어구로 나눈 후, 해석하세요.
　주어는 S 동사는 V 목적어는 O, 보어는 C, 그리고 수식어구는 (　)를 해 주세요.

1. She sleeps at nine.

2. Austin is very nice.

3. Jenny likes apples.

4. Austin gave Jennifer an apple.

5. Austin made her angry.

6. The leaves are falling on the street.

7. David works on weekends.

8. She reads a newspaper in the morning.

9. Eric looks happy.

10. They walk every day.

 **Outro**

문장의 성분, 1형식

주어, 동사, 목적어, 보어는 문장을 만드는 데 필요한 주재료입니다.
'주어+동사'만으로 이루어진 문장을 1형식 문장이라고 합니다.

개념이해

회사원인 Tom을 주어로 하여 짧게 표현해 보겠습니다. Tom runs.(Tom은 달립니다.)에서 동사 'run'은 주어 외에 필요로 하는 것이 없네요. Tom is late.(Tom은 늦었습니다.)에서 동사 'is'는 'late'라는 형용사를 필요로 합니다. 이 때 be동사인 is 다음에 오는 late는 주어를 보충해 주는 보어라고 합니다. Tom meets a client. (Tom은 고객을 만난다.)에서 동사 'meet'은 주어 외에 'client'라는 명사를 목적어로 더 필요로 합니다. 동사에 따라 반드시 들어가야 하는 문장 성분인 주어, 동사, 목적어, 보어를 나열하여 문장의 종류를 구분한 것을 문장의 형식이라 합니다.

개념정리

1. 문장 성분은 문장을 구성하면서 일정한 역할을 하는 요소를 말합니다. 문장을 만드는 재료라고 할 수 있으며, 주어, 동사, 목적어, 보어가 있습니다.

2. 'Tom은 일한다.(Tom works)'와 같이, '주어+동사'만으로 이루어진 문장을 1형식 문장이라고 하며, 목적어가 필요 없이 스스로 자립하는 동사를 자동사라고 합니다.

UNIT 08 2형식, 3형식

◎ GRAMMAR POINT

2형식 문장 : 주어 + 동사 + 보어로 이루어진 문장을 2형식 문장이라고 합니다.
3형식 문장 : 주어 + 동사 + 목적어로 이루어진 문장을 3형식 문장이라고 합니다.

① 2형식 문장

be 동사, become, feel, seem, look 등의 동사는 뒤에서 주어를 설명하고 보충하는 주격 보어가 필요합니다. 이 때 주격보어 자리에 올수 있는 품사는 명사와 형용사입니다. 주어와 주격보어가 동격을 일 때는 명사가, 주어를 설명하고 꾸며주는 역할을 할 때는 형용사를 씁니다. seem, look과 같이 감각을 나타내는 동사는 보어자리에 명사를 쓸 때는 'like + 명사'형태로 써야 합니다.

2형식 동사	의미	예문
be 동사 become get	~이다 ~이 되다	He **is** nice. 그는 친절하다. He **is** a doctor. 그는 의사이다. He **became** a doctor. 그는 의사가 되었다.
look seem appear	(~처럼) 보이다	She **looks** happy. 그녀는 행복하다. She **looks like** a nurse. 그녀는 간호사처럼 보인다. He **seems** serious. 그는 심각해 보인다. He **seems like** a police officer. 그는 경찰처럼 보인다.
feel smell sound taste	(~처럼) 느끼다. (~처럼) 냄새가 나다 (~처럼) 들리다 (~한) 맛이 나다	I **feel** thirsty. 나는 목이 마르다. The cake **smells** good. 그 케이크의 향이 좋다. It **sounds** nice. 그거 좋을 것 같다. The pizza **tastes** great. 피자는 맛이 좋다.

② 3형식 문장

'주어 + 동사 + 목적어'의 형태로 이루어진 문장을 3형식 문장이라고 합니다. 이 때 동사는 목적어를 항상 필요로 하는 타동사가 옵니다. 대부분의 타동사는 3형식의 형태로 쓸 수 있습니다. 목적어 자리에는 명사, 대명사의 목적격이 올 수 있습니다.

3형식 동사	의미	예문
contact	연락하다	You can **contact** us anytime. 당신은 언제든지 우리에게 연락할 수 있다.
join	~에 합석하다	Could you **join** us at the party? 파티에 우리와 함께 할 수 있어요?
discuss	~에 대해 토론하다	We **discussed** the problem. 우리는 그 문제를 의논했다.
exceed	~를 능가하다	He **exceeded** the speed limit. 그는 제한 속도를 초과했다.
resemble	~를 닮다	Mary **resembles** her mother. Mary는 그녀의 어머니를 닮았다.

GRAMMAR PRACTICE

A 다음 문장에서 주격보어를 필요로 하는 2형식 동사를 찾아 밑줄을 그으세요.

1. The baby is cute.
2. The children are happy.
3. He looks sad.
4. They feel good.
5. They sing a song.
6. Tommy became a doctor.
7. She made some cookies.
8. She looks beautiful.
9. They discussed the problem.
10. Nick resembles his brother.

B 다음 ( ) 안에 알맞은 단어를 고르세요.

1. That food smells (good, well).
2. Tom looks (a poet, like a poet).
3. The flowers smell (nice. nicely).
4. It looks (a dinosaur, like a dinosaur bone).
5. The tigers looks (like cats, cats).

C 어법상 틀린 문장은 바르게 고치고, 틀린 부분이 없으면 O로 표시하세요.

1. The earth looks like beautiful.
2. The sun looks like a circle.
3. The people are happily.
4. The cake tastes well.
5. The moon looks like a half circle.

VOCA cute 귀여운 sad 슬픈 problem 문제 resemble 닮다 a poet 시인 dinosaur 공룡 bone 뼈
circle 원, 동그라미 half circle 반원

◎ GRAMMAR POINT

③ 자동사 vs 타동사

영어의 동사는 자동사와 타동사로 나뉘며, 그 구분은 목적어의 유무로 구분합니다. 자동사는 스스로 자립할 수 있는 동사로 절대로 뒤에 목적어를 갖지 않습니다. 반면, 타동사는 항상 목적어에 의지하는 동사입니다.

자동사 vs 타동사		문장의 구조
자동사	1 형식	주어 + 동사 He works hard.
	2 형식	주어 + 동사 + 주격보어 He looks angry.
타동사	3 형식	주어 + 동사 + 목적어 He loves **her**.
	4 형식	주어 + 동사 + 간접목적어 + 직접목적어 He gave **her a book**.
	5 형식	주어 + 동사 + 목적어 + 목적격보어 He makes **her happy**.

④ 태 (voice)

태는 동사를 나타내는 형태로, 주어가 동작을 일으키는 능동태와 주어가 동작의 대상이 되는 수동태가 있습니다. 그러므로 3, 4, 5형식의 문장은 수동태로 바꿀 수가 있습니다.

(1) 능동태 → 수동태로 전환하는 순서

1. 능동태의 주어는 수동태의 'by 목적격'으로
2. 능동태의 동사는 수동태의 be +p.p (과거분사)
3. 능동태의 목적어는 수동태의 주어로 한다.

(2) 시제에 따른 태의 변화

현재	People read the books. → The books **are read** by people.
미래	People will read the books. → The books **will be read** by people.
과거	People read the books. → The books **were read** by people. * read - read - read

GRAMMAR PRACTICE

A 다음 문장에서 목적어를 필요로 하는 3형식 동사를 찾아 밑줄을 그으세요.

1. The baby drinks milk.
2. They purchased a chair last weekend.
3. The movie made me sad.
4. He works hard.
5. This tea is great.
6. Tommy read a book.
7. The girl looks like an angel.
8. The man looks diligent.
9. My sister took a nap.
10. She painted the wall last month.

B 다음 문장에서 목적어를 찾아 밑줄을 그으세요.

(A) Justine reads a book every day.

(B) Kelly bought some bananas yesterday.

(C) Beth wrote an email last night.

C 다음 타동사로 쓰일 수 있는 동사를 고르세요.

(A) is	(B) make	(C) look	(D) read
(E) become	(F) walk	(G) give	(H) contact
(I) discuss	(J) work	(K) fall	(L) exceed
(M) resemble	(N) taste	(O) are	(P) join

D 다음 문장을 수동태로 바꾸세요.   * write – wrote – written

1. He writes a letter every day. → _____
2. He wrote a letter yesterday. → _____
3. He will write a letter tomorrow. → _____

VOCA drink 마시다 – drank – drunken   purchase 구매하다   tea 차   read 읽다 – read – read   diligent 부지런한
take a nap 낮잠을 자다   take – read – read – read 읽다   buy – bought – bought 사다
write – wrote – written 쓰다   is ~이다, 있다   make ~을 만들다   look ~처럼 보이다   read ~을 읽다
become ~이 되다   walk 걷다   give 주다   contact 연락하다   discuss 의논하다   work 일하다   fall 떨어지다
exceed ~을 능가하다   resemble ~을 닮다   taste ~한 맛이 나다   are ~이다, 있다   join ~에 합류하다

GRAMMAR IN SENTENCE

▶ 다음 문장에서 주어, 동사, 목적어, 보어 그리고 수식어구로 나눈 후, 해석하세요.
  주어는 S 동사는 V 목적어는 O (간접목적어 IO, 직접목적어 DO) 주격보어는 SC 목적격보어는 OC, 그리고 수식어구는 (　)를 해 주세요.

1. They discussed the problem.

2. Nick resembles his brother.

3. He will write a letter tomorrow.

4. Justine reads a book every day.

5. Kelly bought some bananas yesterday.

6. Beth wrote an email last night.

7. They purchased a chair last weekend.

8. The man looks very diligent.

9. The movie made me sad.

10. She painted the wall last month.

 **Outro**

2형식, 3형식

2형식 문장 : 주어 +동사+ 보어로 이루어진 문장을 2형식 문장이라고 합니다.
3형식 문장 : 주어 + 동사 + 목적어로 이루어진 문장을 3형식 문장이라고 합니다.

개념이해

Angela는 자신의 바람을 이루었습니다. Angela became a teacher.(Angela는 선생님이 되었습니다). Angela looks happy.(Angela는 행복해 보입니다.) 여기서 동사 become(~이 되다)과 look (~처럼 보이다) 만으로는 의미 전달이 불분명하므로 좀 더 구체적으로 주어의 상태나 성질을 나타내는 말로 보충을 해 주어야 합니다. '주어+동사+보어'로 이루어진 문장을 2형식 문장이라 합니다.

She reads a book. (그녀는 책을 읽고 있습니다.) She는 주어 read는 동사 a book 은 목적어입니다. 이렇게 목적어를 필요로 하는 동사를 타동사라고 합니다. 일반적으로 타동사가 사용된 문장은 '주어+동사+목적어'의 형태를 취하게 됩니다. 이렇게 '주어+동사+목적어'로 이루어진 문장을 3형식 문장이라고 합니다.

개념정리

1. '주어+동사+보어(주격 보어)'로 이루어진 문장을 2형식 문장이라고 합니다. 주격보어를 필요로 하는 동사로는 be동사, become, look, seem, appear, feel, smell 등이 있습니다. 주격 보어는 명사가 어떠한 것인지 보충 설명해 주거나 명사의 성질이나 상태를 보충 설명해 줍니다. 따라서 주격 보어의 자리에는 일반적으로 명사와 형용사가 들어갑니다.

2. '주어+동사+목적어'로 이루어진 문장을 3형식 문장이라고 합니다. 타동사는 목적어를 필요로 하는 동사입니다. 타동사에는 write(쓰다), join(연결하다), discuss(의논하다), await(기다리다), resemble(닮다) 등이 있습니다.

UNIT 09 4형식, 5형식

GRAMMAR POINT

4형식 문장은 '주어+동사+간접목적어+직접목적어'로
5형식 문장은 '주어+동사+목적어+보어'로 이루어집니다.

① 4형식 문장 : 주어+동사+간접목적어+직접목적어

4형식 동사, 즉 수여동사에서 직접 목적어와 간접 목적어가 같이 있을 때, 직접 목적어는 '~을(를)'에 해당하는 목적어이며, 간접 목적어는 '~에게'에 해당하는 목적어입니다.

4형식 동사 : 수여동사

주어	동사	간접목적어	직접목적어
	주다	(~에게)	(~을/~를)
	give 주다		
	send 보내다		
	show 보여주다		
	lend 빌려주다		
	offer 제공하다		
	award 수여하다		
	grant 수여하다		
	forward 보내다		

David gave **his sister a book**. David 는 그의 여동생에게 책 한권을 주었다.
　　　　　간접목적어　직접목적어

② 4형식 문장 → 3형식 문장

'~에게 ...해주다'로 표현 가능한 동사들(수여 동사)은 간접목적어와 직접목적어를 동시에 두 개 취하는 4형식과 직접 목적어만을 갖는 두 가지 형태가 동시에 가능합니다. 동사 뒤에 '~을/를'의 직접 목적어가 '~에게'의 간접 목적어보다 앞에 있으면 전치사 to 또는 for가 필요합니다.

4형식 → 3형식	주어 + 동사 + 간접목적어 + 직접목적어 → 주어 + 동사 + 직접목적어 (to/ for) + 간접목적어
to가 필요한 동사	give, send, lend, award, grant, forward, hand, offer, owe, write, show, teach, tell 등
	David gave his sister a book. → David gave a book **to** his sister. David는 그의 여동생에게 책 한권을 주었다.
for가 필요한 동사	make, buy, cook, find, get 등
	David bought his sister a book. → David bought a book **for** his sister. David는 그의 여동생에게 책 한권을 사 주었다.

GRAMMAR PRACTICE

A 다음 중 4형식 동사를 고르세요.

(A) give   (B) send   (C) look   (D) become   (E) do
(F) lend   (G) feel   (H) forward   (I) remain   (J) grant
(K) show   (L) smell   (M) offer   (N) appear   (O) award

B 다음 ( ) 안에 알맞은 것을 고르세요.

1. Mary sent (him an email / an email him).
2. I bought (a gift Tony / Tony a gift).
3. Jenny gave (him chocolates / chocolates him).
4. I will give (a hat her / her a hat).
5. Tom showed (me an album / an album me).

C ( ) 안에 **to** 와 **for** 중에서 알맞은 것을 넣으세요.

1. I showed album (   ) Beth.
2. I made some cake (   ) children.
3. My sister sent a message (   ) Linda.
4. Susan bought a bike (   ) his daughter.
5. They cooked a meal (   ) me.

D 다음에서 틀린 문장을 고르고, 바르게 고치세요.

1. My parents bought a pizza to me.
2. Mr. Johns sent his photo for me.
3. Can you lend the book for me?
4. Jenny will make a cake to you.
5. David gave me some flowers.

VOCA become - became - become ~이 되다   feel - felt - felt ~처럼 느끼다   smell - smelled - smelt 냄새가 나다
send - sent - sent 보내다   buy - bought - bought 사다   gave - gave - given 주다   album 앨범
make - made - made 만들다   message 메시지   lend - lent - lent 빌려주다

◎ GRAMMAR POINT

③ 5형식 문장 : 주어+동사+목적어+목적보어

5형식에서 목적보어가 명사인 경우 목적어와 같은 대상을 가리키고, 목적보어가 형용사인 경우 목적어의 성질이나 상태를 나타냅니다.

대표적인 5형식 동사			
주어	동사	목적어	목적보어
	make 만들다 find 발견하다 consider 간주하다 think 생각하다 deem 생각하다 keep 유지하다 leave 남겨두다 name 지명하다 call 부르다 elect 선출하다 appoint 임명하다		형용사 명사

You make **me happy**. 당신은 나를 행복하게 만들어 준다.
           목적어 목적보어

We elected **Tony the chairman**. 우리는 Tony를 회장으로 선출했다.
            목적어   목적보어

④ 4형식과 5형식 문장의 수동태

목적어가 둘이므로 수동태도 두 가지가 가능한데 간접 목적어가 주어가 되는 경우는 전치사가 필요 없지만 직접 목적어가 주어인 경우는 간접 목적어 앞에 to 또는 for의 전치사를 넣어주어야 합니다.

	3형식	4형식
능동태	David gave **a book to** his sister. David는 그의 여동생에게 책 한권을 주었다	David gave **his sister** a book. David는 그의 여동생에게 책 한권을 주었다
수동태	→ **A book** was given to his sister by David.	→ **His sister** was given a book by David.

	5형식
능동태	We elected **Tony the chairman**. 우리는 Tony를 회장으로 선출했다.
수동태	→ **Tony** was elected **the chairman** by us.

GRAMMAR PRACTICE

A 다음 중 5형식 동사를 고르세요.

(A) make   (B) give   (C) be   (D) consider
(E) sound   (F) call   (G) count (H) deem
(I) appoint (J) resemble (K) elect (L) send
(M) offer   (N) taste   (O) name (P) seem

B 다음 ( ) 안에 알맞은 것을 고르세요.

1. Terry made me (angry, angrily).
2. I found the test (difficulty, difficult).
3. Students found the midterm exam (easy, ease).
4. People called David (a genius, genuine).
5. People appointed Mr. Tomas (like the chairperson, the chairperson).

C 다음 ( ) 안에 알맞은 것을 고르세요.

1. A bicycle (gave / was given) to Linda.
2. Betty (sent / was sent) a letter to her boyfriend.
3. My mother (made / was made) us some cookies.
4. A man (named / was named) Aesop by people.
5. Jenny found her teacher (kind / kindly).

D 다음 능동태의 문장을 수동태로 바꾸세요.

1. Austin sent a letter to his brother.
   → _____
   → _____

2. People called the woman an angel.
   → _____

3. He gave a weekly report to me.
   → _____
   → _____

VOCA count 세다   deem 간주하다   appoint 임명하다   resemble 닮다   elect 선출하다   taste ~맛이 나다
name 지명하다   find 발견하다 - found - found   difficulty 어려움   difficult 어려운
think - thought - thought 생각하다   easy 쉬운   ease 편함   mid-term (학기 등의) 중간의   genius 천재
genuine 진짜의   chairperson 의장   weekly 매주의   report 보고서

GRAMMAR IN SENTENCE

▶ 다음 문장에서 주어, 동사, 목적어, 보어 그리고 수식어구로 나눈 후, 해석하세요.
주어는 S 동사는 V 목적어는 O (간접목적어 IO, 직접목적어 DO) 주격보어는 SC 목적격보어는 OC,
그리고 수식어구는 (   )를 해 주세요.

1. My parents bought a pizza for me.

2. Mr. Johns sent his photo to me.

3. Can you lend me the book?

4. Jenny will make you a cake.

5. David gave me some flowers.

6. Terry made me angry.

7. I found the test difficult.

8. Students found the mid-term exam easy.

9. People called David a genius.

10. People appointed Mr. Tomas the chairperson.

 **Outro**

4형식, 5형식

4형식 문장은 '주어+동사+간접목적어+직접목적어'로
5형식 문장은 '주어+동사+목적어+보어'로 이루어집니다.

개념이해

오늘은 Jina 의 졸업식입니다. 사람들이 Jina에게 다양한 선물을 주었습니다. (People gave Jina various presents.) 여기서 'Jina'는 받는 대상이며, 이를 간접목적어라고 합니다. 간접목적어는 우리말로 옮기면 '△△에게'에서 '△△'에 해당하는 말입니다. '주어+동사+직접목적어+간접목적어'로 이루어진 문장을 4형식 문장이라고 합니다.

Jina가 부모님을 기쁘게 해 드린 것 같네요. (Jina made her parents happy.) 2형식 문장에서 주격보어가 주어의 상태를 나타내듯이 앞 문장의 'happy'는 목적어의 상태를 나타냅니다. 이렇게 목적어의 상태나 성질을 나타내는 말을 목적보어라고 합니다.

개념정리

1. 주어+동사+간접목적어+직접목적어로 이루어진 문장을 4형식 문장이라고 합니다. 4형식 문장에 사용되는 동사를 수여동사라고 합니다. 수여동사에는 give(주다), send (보내다), show(보여주다), lend (빌려주다) 등이 있습니다.

2. 주어+동사+목적어+목적보어로 이루어진 문장을 5형식 문장이라 합니다. 5형식에서 목적보어가 명사인 경우 목적어와 같은 대상을 가리키고, 목적보어가 형용사인 경우 목적어의 성질이나 상태를 나타냅니다.

ACTUAL TEST 3

A 다음 빈칸에 들어갈 수 있는 것을 고르세요.

1. The car -------- down the hill.
   (A) run (B) ran (C) gives (D) gave

2. All employees ------- from Monday through Friday.
   (A) work (B) are (C) have (D) make

3. Tom ------- his girlfriend a ring yesterday.
   (A) was (B) loved (C) made (D) gave

4. My grandmother -------- the room warm last night.
   (A) were (B) liked (C) made (D) gave

5. Tommy -------- a new employee of the Sales Department.
   (A) is (B) runs (C) walks (D) drives

6. The bread on the table --------- good.
   (A) makes (B) are (C) smells (D) smells like

7. Our English teacher --------- really angry.
   (A) look (B) looks (C) is looked (D) look like

8. The man in the auditorium --------- a famous singer.
   (A) look (B) looks (C) looked (D) looks like

9. Our team will ------- the problem tomorrow.
   (A) feel (B) work (C) look (D) discuss

10. A professor -------- his students some questions to answer.
    (A) gave (B) found (C) kept (D) called

11. Jefferson wrote a letter --------- his girlfriend.
    (A) to (B) for (C) at (D) in

12. The movie --------- Matt Damon a big star.
    (A) made (B) gave (C) showed (D) sent

B 다음 문장에서 틀린 부분을 찾아 바르게 고치세요.

1 The birds fly high the sky.   (   ) → (   )

2 My sister is always happily.   (   ) → (   )

3 The cake tastes strangely.   (   ) → (   )

4 The baby looks an angel.   (   ) → (   )

5 The baseball player looks strongly.   (   ) → (   )

6 My boyfriend bought a jacket to me.   (   ) → (   )

7 He will lend some paper me.   (   ) → (   )

8 Mr. Lee sent a message for you.   (   ) → (   )

9 We should make our classroom cleans.   (   ) → (   )

10 Keep your body health.   (   ) → (   )

C 다음 밑줄 친 부분 중 어법상 틀린 것을 두 개 고르세요. (문자메시지)

Maria 1:11 p.m.	Hi, Bob. The air conditioner isn't working here.
Bob 1:13 p.m.	Okay. I'll send someone (1) <u>to</u> your office.
Maria 1:15 p.m.	Thanks. It's very (2) <u>uncomfortably</u> and (3) <u>hot</u>.
Bob 1:16 p.m.	(4) <u>Probable</u>, It is because the fan is (5) <u>old</u>, so we'll make it (6) <u>clean</u>.

잉글리쉬앤 그래머 START

입문편

4 코스

Unit 10 구
Unit 11 절
Unit 12 문장의 종류

UNIT 10 구

GRAMMAR POINT

구는 2개 이상의 단어가 모여 하나의 문장 성분 역할을 하는 것을 말합니다.
구는 문장에서 명사, 형용사, 부사로 쓰일 수 있습니다.

① 구의 정의

구는 두 개 이상의 단어가 모여 하나의 품사와 같은 구실을 하는 어군을 구라고 합니다. 구는 일반적으로 <전치사 + 명사(또는 대명사)>, <to + 동사원형>으로 되어 있습니다. 이러한 구가 문장에서 주어, 목적어, 보어로 쓰이면 명사구가 되고, 명사를 꾸며주거나 서술하면 형용사구, 그리고 동사나 형용사를 꾸며주거나, 상세히 설명하면 부사구가 됩니다.

품사	예	역할
명사	I want **a book**.	주어, 목적어, 보어 역할
명사구	I want **to buy a book**.	
형용사	The **beautiful** flower is mine.	명사를 꾸미거나 서술하는 역할
형용사구	The flower **in the vase** is mine.	
부사	Tom works **hard**.	동사, 형용사를 꾸며주는 역할
부사구	Tom works **to make money**.	

② 구의 종류

(1) 명사구(Noun Phrase)

명사처럼 주어, 목적어, 보어로 쓰입니다. <to + 동사원형>과 <동사 + -ing> 형태가 대표적인 명사구에 해당됩니다.

주어	**Speaking English** is not easy. 영어로 말하는 것은 쉽지 않다. (be동사 is의 주어) * 주어 자리에 <To 동사원형> 또는 <동사 + -ing> 오면 is, has 등의 단수동사를 씁니다. 이 때 주어자리에 <To 동사원형>은 자주 쓰는 표현은 아닙니다.
목적어	I want **to go to college**. 나는 대학교에 다니고 싶다. (타동사 want의 목적어)
보어	My plan is **to go to Europe**. 나의 계획은 유럽을 가는 것이다. (be동사 is의 보어)

GRAMMAR PRACTICE

A 주어진 동사를 이용하여 <보기>처럼 문장을 완성하고, 빈칸을 채우세요.

[보기] be : **She wants to be a singer**.   동사 : __wants__   목적어 : __to be__

1. go : They decided _____ on a picnic.
2. make : I need _____ money.
3. buy : He wants _____ some pork.
4. read : I plan _____ the book.
5. appear : Andy wants _____ on TV.

B 주어진 동사를 이용하여 <보기>처럼 문장을 완성하세요.

[보기] speak : **Speaking** Spanish is difficult.

1. go : _____ skiing is exciting.
2. sing : _____ a song is fun.
3. climb : _____ a mountain is hard.
4. jog : _____ in the morning is good for you.

C 괄호 안에 주어진 단어들을 적절히 배열하여 문장을 완성하세요.

1. (millionaire, be, to, a) My dream is _____.
2. (shopping, go, to) We plan _____.
3. (movies, watching) Karen loves _____.
4. (books, reading) Her hobby is _____.
5. (playing, games) _____ is fun.

VOCA decide 결정하다   pork 돼지고기   read - read - read 읽다   appear 나타나다   Spanish 스페인 말, 스페인 사람
skiing 스키타기   millionaire 백만장자

GRAMMAR POINT

(2) 형용사구(Adjective Phrase)

형용사처럼 명사를 수식하거나 보어로 쓰입니다.
명사를 직접 수식할 때는 일반적으로 명사의 바로 뒤에 놓입니다.

명사 대명사 수식	The books **on the desk** are mine. 책상 위에 있는 책들은 내 것이다. (바로 앞의 명사 books를 수식) I need something **to drink**. 나는 마실 것이 필요하다. (바로 앞의 대명사 something 수식)
명사 서술	This stick is **of no use**. 이 막대기는 쓸모가 없다. (be동사 is 의 보어) ▶ of no use 쓸모없는, 소용없는

(3) 부사구(Adverb Phrase)

부사처럼 동사나 형용사를 수식합니다.

동사수식	His house stands **on the hill**. 그의 집은 언덕 위에 서 있다. (바로 앞의 동사 stands를 수식)
형용사 수식	English is not easy **to learn**. 영어는 배우기가 쉽지 않다. (바로 앞의 형용사 easy를 수식)
이유, 목적	They study very hard **to pass the exam**. 그들은 시험에 통과하기 위하여 열심히 공부한다. (공부를 열심히 하는 이유, 목적 설명)

GRAMMAR PRACTICE

A 주어진 동사를 이용하여 <보기>처럼 문장을 완성하세요.

(보기) meet : Nice **to meet you**. 당신을 만나서 기쁘다.

1. make : They work hard _____ some money.

2. read : I went to the library _____ a book.

3. see : I came here _____ a doctor.

4. eat : I need something _____.

5. see : I'm happy _____ you.

B 주어진 구를 빈칸에 넣어서 문장을 완성하세요.

| in the room | to be a doctor | on the hill |
| to do his homework | learning English | |

1. Jenny wants _____.

2. The bag _____ is mine.

3. David stayed at home _____.

4. _____ is not hard at all.

5. The school is _____.

C 연결하여 문장을 완성하세요.

1. I went to bed early _____.   A. to be rich.

2. Tom works hard _____.   B. on the table

3. The ring _____ is hers.   C. to catch the train.

4. _____ is dangerous.   D. to get up early

5. I got up early _____.   E. swimming in this river

(VOCA) make - made - made 만들다   library 도서관   read - read - read 읽다   see - saw - seen 보다
eat - ate - eaten 먹다   dangerous 위험한

GRAMMAR IN SENTENCE

▶ 다음 문장에서 밑줄 친 구를 명사구, 형용사구, 부사구 중 알맞은 것을 넣은 후, 해석하세요.

1. Jenny wants <u>to be a doctor</u>.

2. The bag <u>in the room</u> is mine.

3. David stayed at home <u>to do his homework</u>.

4. I went to bed early <u>to get up early</u>.

5. The school is <u>on the hill</u>.

6. Tom works hard <u>to be rich</u>.

7. The ring <u>on the table</u> is hers.

8. <u>Swimming in this river</u> is dangerous.

9. I got up early <u>to catch the train</u>.

10. <u>Learning English</u> is not hard at all.

Outro

구

구는 2개 이상의 단어가 모여 하나의 문장 성분 역할을 하는 것을 말합니다.
구는 문장에서 명사, 형용사, 부사로 쓰일 수 있습니다.

개념이해

Bill과 Tom이 열심히 공부하고 있습니다. **Passing the exam** is difficult. (시험에 통과하는 것은 어렵다.)에서 'passing the exam'은 2개 이상의 단어가 모여 주어인 명사 역할을 하고 있습니다.

They study very hard **to pass the exam**. (그들은 시험에 통과하기 위하여 열심히 공부한다.) 여기서 'to pass the exam'도 2개 이상의 단어가 모여 부사 역할을 하고 있습니다. 특히 'to pass the bar exam'는 열심히 공부하는 목적을 나타냅니다.

또 다른 표현을 살펴봅시다. The books **on the desk** are theirs. (책상위에 있는 책은 그들의 것이다.) 여기서 'on the desk'는 2개 이상의 단어가 모여 앞의 the books라는 명사를 꾸며주는 형용사 역할을 하고 있습니다.

개념정리

1. 구는 문장 내에서 명사의 역할을 할 수 있습니다. 이렇게 문장 내에서 명사 역할을 하는 구를 명사구라고 합니다. 명사구는 명사와 같은 역할을 하기 때문에 문장에서 주어, 목적어, 보어의 자리에 올 수 있습니다.

2. 구는 문장 내에서 부사의 역할을 할 수 있습니다. 이렇게 문장 내에서 부사 역할을 하는 구를 부사구라고 합니다.

3. 구는 문장 내에서 형용사의 역할을 할 수 있습니다. 이렇게 문장 내에서 형용사 역할을 하는 구를 형용사구라고 합니다. 형용사구는 명사를 수식하거나 문장의 보어로 사용될 수 있습니다.

UNIT 11 절

◎ GRAMMAR POINT

절과 절을 연결할 때는 접속사가 필요합니다. 접속사는 낱말, 구, 절을 연결하는 품사로서 등위접속사(and, but, or, so)와 종속접속사(if, when, although, while, before, after, since, because, as, unless) 등이 있습니다.

① 절의 개념과 종류

(1) 절의 개념
두 개 이상의 단어가 '주어+ 동사'의 관계를 이루어 어떤 뜻을 나타낼 때, 이를 절이라고 합니다.

(2) 절의 종류

명사절	주어 역할	**That the earth is round** is an absolute truth. 지구가 둥글다는 것은 명백한 진리이다.
	목적어 역할	I believe **that he is honest**. 나는 그가 정직한다는 것을 믿는다.
	보어 역할	His problem is **that he is too lazy**. 그의 문제점은 그가 너무 게으르다는 것이다.
형용사절	형용사 역할	Jim is the one **who suggested the idea**. Jim이 그 아이디어를 낸 사람이었다.
부사절	시간	**When I was young**, I lived in Seoul. 내가 젊었을 때, 나는 서울에 살았다.
	조건	**If it rains tomorrow**, I won't go out. 내일 비가 오면 나는 외출을 안할 것이다.
	이유	**Because it is raining**, I can't go there. 비가 오기 때문에, 나는 그 곳을 갈 수가 없다.
	양보	**Although he is poor**, he spends a lot of money. 그는 가난하지만, 많은 돈을 쓴다.

GRAMMAR PRACTICE

A 다음에서 접속사를 찾으세요.

(A) the   (B) and   (C) she   (D) but
(E) although   (F) never   (G) because   (H) buy
(I) have   (J) if   (K) more   (L) that
(M) play   (N) so   (O) when   (P) while

B 주어진 절을 빈칸에 넣어서 문장을 완성하세요.

| because it snows a lot | that I read yesterday | |
| when I was young | who suggested the idea | that he is honest |

1. This is the book _____.
2. People think _____.
3. I can't go there _____.
4. Jack is the person _____.
5. I lived in California _____.

C 연결하여 문장을 완성하세요.

1. Her problem is   A. who is walking on the street
2. That the earth looks like a circle   B. we won't go on a trip
3. If it rains tomorrow   C. they spend too much money
4. Although they are poor   D. is true
5. I know the man   E. that she is too lazy

VOCA uggest 제안하다   honest 정직한   read - read - read 읽다   think - thought - thought 생각하다
problem 문제   circle 원   spend (돈을) 쓰다, 소비하다   lazy 게으른

◎ GRAMMAR POINT

② 접속사의 종류

(1) 접속사의 역할

접속사는 단어와 단어 구와 구, 또는 절과 절을 연결해 주는 말입니다. 접속사는 크게 등위접속사와 종속접속사로 나뉩니다.

문장의 일부분으로서 <주어 + 동사>의 관계를 가진 어군을 절이라 하며, 절은 하나의 품사와 같은 구실을 합니다. 문장 가운데서 중심이 되는 절을 주절이라고 하며, 주절에 딸린 절을 종속절이라 합니다.

(2) 등위 접속사

and 그리고	단어와 단어	Jenny is nice **and** beautiful. 제니는 멋지고 아름답다.
	구와 구	I like to swim **and** to play baseball. 나는 수영하는 것과 야구하는 것을 좋아한다.
	문장과 문장	He is handsome, **and** she is beautiful. 그는 잘생겼고, 그녀는 아름답다.
or 또는	단어와 단어	Do you want tea **or** coffee? 너는 차를 원하니? 커피를 원하니?
	구와 구	He will go to church by bus **or** by taxi. 그는 버스나 택시를 타고 교회를 갈 것이다.
	문장과 문장	Let's watch TV, **or** let's play a game. TV를 보거나 게임을 하자.
but 그러나	단어와 단어	He is poor **but** happy. 그는 가난하지만 행복하다.
	문장과 문장	She loves him, **but** he doesn't love her. 그녀는 그를 사랑하지만, 그는 그녀를 사랑하지 않는다.
so 그래서	문장과 문장	It was very cold, **so** I closed the window. 매우 추웠다. 그래서 내가 창문을 닫았다.

(2) 종속 접속사

종속접속사는 문장과 문장만을 연결합니다. 문장의 주요 문장을 주절, 접속사와 함께 쓰여서 주절을 설명해 주는 문장을 종속절이라고 합니다.

시간	when ~할 때 while ~하는 동안 before ~전에 after ~한 후에 since 과거에 ~한 이후로 줄곧
이유	because ~때문에 since ~이므로 as ~이므로
조건	if 만약 ~하면 unless 만약 ~하지 않으면
양보	although, even though, though ~에도 불구하고 whereas ~임에 반하여 even if 비록 ~일 지라도 while ~인 반면에

GRAMMAR PRACTICE

A 다음 접속사의 뜻을 쓰세요.

1. unless → _____
2. even though → _____
3. because → _____
4. whereas → _____
5. so → _____
6. while → _____
7. and → _____
8. since → _____
9. or → _____
10. even if → _____

B 다음 괄호 안에 알맞은 등위접속사 and, but, or, so를 골라 넣으세요.

1. Flowers are beautiful, (   ) they smell sweet.
2. Beth isn't beautiful, (   ) she is cute.
3. Which do you like better, spring (   ) fall?
4. I feel tired, (   ) let's go home now!
5. I bought a book yesterday, (   ) I didn't read it yet.

C 다음 문장을 주절과 종속절로 나누고, 접속사의 의미를 시간, 원인, 조건, 양보를 구별해서 쓰세요.

1. Before he went out, Tom took a shower. (   )
   주절 : _____
   종속절 : _____

2. Because he is poor, David cannot buy the car. (   )
   주절 : _____
   종속절 : _____

3. If it rains tomorrow, please call me. (   )
   주절 : _____
   종속절 : _____

4. Although he is poor, Robert is happy. (   )
   주절 : _____
   종속절 : _____

5. After he took a shower, Tom went to school. (   )
   주절 : _____
   종속절 : _____

VOCA sweet 달콤한   tired 피곤한   yet 아직도   go out 외출하다   take a shower 샤워하다

GRAMMAR IN SENTENCE

▶ 다음 문장에서 밑줄 친 절을 명사절, 형용사절, 부사절 중 알맞은 것을 넣은 후, 해석하세요.

1. <u>That the earth looks like a circle</u> is true.

2. People think <u>that he is honest</u>.

3. Her problem is <u>that she is too lazy</u>.

4. Jack is the person <u>who suggested the idea</u>.

5. <u>When I was young</u>, I lived in California.

6. <u>If it rains tomorrow</u>, we won't go on a trip.

7. <u>Because it snows a lot</u>, I can't go there.

8. <u>Although they are poor</u>, they spend too much money.

9. I know the man <u>who is walking on the street</u>.

10. This is the book <u>that I read yesterday</u>.

절

두 개 이상의 단어가 '주어+ 동사'의 관계를 이루어 어떤 뜻을 나타낼 때,
이를 절이라고 합니다.

개념이해

Tina의 학교생활을 살펴보겠습니다. Tina는 공부를 열심히 한 후, 친구와 이야기를 나누었습니다. (After Tina studied hard, she talked with a friend.)라는 문장에서, 접속사 After로 시작된 Tina studied hard는 시간을 나타내는 **부사절**이라고 하고, she talked with a friend.는 **주절**이라고 합니다.

점심시간으로 가 볼까요? Tina가 점심 식사를 하는 것은 건강에 좋습니다. (That Tina has lunch is good for health.)에서 That Tina has lunch가 is 의 주어로 쓰인 절로 **명사절**이라고 합니다. 야간 자율 학습 시간에 Tina 는 정말 공부를 열심히 하는군요. Tina 가 공부를 매우 열심히 하는 그 학생입니다. (Tina is the student who studies very hard.) 라고 하면, who studies very hard는 the student를 수식하는 **형용사절**이라고 할 수 있습니다.

개념정리

1. 절은 문장 내에서 명사의 역할을 할 수 있습니다. 이렇게 문장 내에서 명사 역할을 하는 절을 명사절이라고 합니다. 명사절은 명사와 같은 역할을 하기 때문에 문장에서 주어, 목적어, 보어의 자리에 올 수 있습니다.

2. 절은 문장 내에서 형용사의 역할을 할 수 있습니다. 이렇게 문장 내에서 형용사 역할을 하는 절을 형용사 절이라고 합니다. 다만 형용사절은 명사를 수식하는 역할만 합니다.

3. 절은 문장 내에서 부사의 역할을 할 수 있습니다. 이렇게 문장 내에서 부사 역할을 하는 구를 부사절이라고 합니다.

UNIT 12 문장의 종류

GRAMMAR POINT

문장에는 평서문, 부정문, 의문문, 명령문이 있습니다.

① be동사, 일반 동사의 부정문 만들기

be동사나 조동사 뒤에는 not만 붙이면 되고, 일반 동사는 do, does, did 다음에 not 을 붙여야 합니다. 일상생활에서는 대부분 괄호 안의 줄임말을 씁니다.

(1) be동사 부정문

수	주어	현재	과거	미래
한명, 하나	I	am not ('m not)	was not (wasn't)	will not be (won't be)
	You	are not (aren't)	were not (weren't)	
	He	is not (isn't)	was not (wasn't)	
	She			
	It			
두 명, 둘	We	are not (aren't)	were not (weren't)	
	You			
	They			

I am a student. → **I am not** a student. (= **I'm not** a student.) 나는 학생이 아니다.
They are nice. → They **are not** (**aren't**) nice. 그들은 친절하지 않다.
He was nice. → He **was not** nice. (= He **wasn't** nice.) 그는 친절하지 않았다.

(2) 일반 동사의 부정문

수	주어	현재	과거	미래
한명, 하나	I	do not (don't) + 일반동사의 원형	did not (didn't) + 일반동사의 원형	will not (won't) + 일반동사의 원형
	You			
	He	does not (doesn't) + 일반동사의 원형		
	She			
	It			
두 명, 둘 이상	We	do not (don't) + 일반동사의 원형		
	You			
	They			

I **play** tennis every day. → I **don't play** tennis every day. 나는 매일 테니스를 치지 않는다.
He **plays** tennis every day. → He **doesn't play** tennis every day. 그는 매일 테니스를 치지 않는다.
He **played** tennis yester day. → He **didn't play** tennis yester day. 나는 어제 테니스를 치지 않았다.

GRAMMAR PRACTICE

A 다음을 부정문으로 바꿔 쓰세요.

1. He is a student.
   → _____

2. They are nice.
   → _____

3. They found the bag.
   → _____

4. He does his homework every day.
   → _____

5. Jenny has lunch at noon.
   → _____

6. They will go on a picnic this weekend.
   → _____

7. Tom went shopping last Saturday.
   → _____

8. Tom and Jenny go to church every Sunday.
   → _____

9. Your dog is sleeping now.
   → _____

10. He hit the ball.
    → _____

B 다음을 부정문으로 바꿔 쓰세요.

1. I was late. → _____
2. We will play soccer tomorrow. → _____
3. I am a nurse. → _____
4. We had dinner together. → _____
5. We did our best. → _____

VOCA find - found - found 찾다   do one's homework 과제를 하다   go on a picnic 소풍을 가다
go shopping 쇼핑을 가다   hit - hit - hit 치다   do one's best 최선을 다하다

◎ GRAMMAR POINT

② 의문문 만들기

(1) be 동사의 의문문
be 동사나 조동사의 경우에는 'be동사/ 조동사 + 주어'의 어순이 되며, 일반동사의 경우에는 'Do, Does, Did + 주어'의 어순으로 쓰입니다.

종류	형태
평서문	주어 + be 동사 ~.
의문문	be동사 + 주어 ~?

He **is** a doctor → **Is** he a doctor? 그는 의사입니까?

(2) 일반 동사의 의문문

수		현재		과거		미래	
한명, 하나	Do	I	동사원형 +~?	I	동사원형 +~?	I	동사원형 +~?
		you		you		you	
	Does	he		he		he	
		she		she	Did	she	Will
		it		it		it	
두 명, 둘 이상	Do	we		we		we	
		you		you		you	
		they		they		they	

You **play** tennis every day. → **Do** you play tennis every day?
He **plays** tennis every day. → **Does** he play tennis every day?
He **played** tennis yesterday. → **Did** he play tennis yesterday?

③ 명령문
상대방에게 명령 할 때 쓰며, 주어 you 가 생략된 형태로 주어 없이 동사 원형으로 시작합니다.

Be quite ! 조용히 하세요!
Look at the beautiful girl. 저기 아름다운 소녀를 보아라.

> * 명령문의 부정 : 무조건 **Don't** 을 씁니다.
> **Don't be** late! 늦지 마세요!
> **Don't tell** a lie! 거짓말 하지 마라!

GRAMMAR PRACTICE

A 다음을 의문문으로 바꿔 쓰세요.

1. He is a student.
   → _____

2. They are nice.
   → _____

3. They found the bag.
   → _____

4. He does his homework every day.
   → _____

5. Jenny has lunch at noon.
   → _____

6. They will go on a picnic this weekend.
   → _____

7. Tom went shopping last Saturday.
   → _____

8. Tom and Jenny go to church every Sunday.
   → _____

9. Your dog is sleeping now.
   → _____

10. He hit the ball.
    → _____

B 다음 문장을 명령문으로 바꿔 쓰세요.

1. You should know yourself. → _____
2. You should not be selfish. → _____
3. You should look at yourself. → _____
4. You should not smoke here. → _____
5. You should be careful. → _____

VOCA selfish 이기적인   look at 보다   careful 주의깊은, 조심스러운

GRAMMAR IN SENTENCE

▶ 다음 문장에서 주어, 동사, 목적어, 보어 그리고 수식어구로 나눈 후, 해석하세요.
주어는 S 동사는 V 목적어는 O 보어는 C 그리고 수식어구는 ( )를 해 주세요.

1. He is a student.

2. They are nice.

3. They found the bag.

4. He does his homework every day.

5. Jenny has lunch at noon.

6. They will go on a picnic this weekend.

7. Tom went shopping last Saturday.

8. Tom and Jenny go to church every Sunday.

9. Your dog is sleeping now.

10. He hit the ball.

 **Outro**

문장의 종류

문장에는 평서문, 부정문, 의문문, 명령문이 있습니다.

	문장의 종류
평서문	앞에서 배운 1~5 형식 문장. Jenny is a student. 제니는 학생입니다. Jenny speaks English very well. 제니는 영어를 잘합니다.
부정문	**be 동사의 부정문** : 주어 + **be 동사** + **not**~~ Jenny is not a student. 제니는 학생이 아닙니다. **일반 동사의 부정문** : 주어 + **do/ does/ did/ will** + **not** + ~ Jenny does not speak English very well. 제니는 영어를 잘하지 못합니다.
의문문	**be 동사의 의문문** : **be 동사** + 주어 ~? Is Jenny a student? 제니는 학생입니까? **일반 동사의 의문문** : **Do/Does/Did/ Will** + 주어 + 동사원형 +~? Does Jenny speak English very well? 제니는 영어를 잘 합니까?
명령문	주어 + 동사원형! (주어를 쓰지 않고 동사원형으로 시작) Get up early! 일찍 일어나세요.

ACTUAL TEST 4

A 다음 빈칸에 들어갈 수 있는 것을 고르세요.

1 ------- Jenny wash her face every morning?
(A) Do (B) Did (C) Does (D) Has

2 Tom ------- a shower last night because he was too tired.
(A) doesn't take (B) don't take (C) didn't took (D) didn't take

3 Jenny -------- dinner because she wants to lose weight.
(A) have (B) don't have (C) doesn't have (D) didn't has

4 Mr Davidson ------- his new plan with his colleagues last night.
(A) discussed (B) talked (C) responded (D) reacted

5 ------- the truth is very important.
(A) Telling (B) Tells (C) Told (D) Have told

6 The flowers and trees in the field ------- very beautiful.
(A) is (B) was (C) has (D) are

7 My hobby is --------- horror movies.
(A) to watch (B) watch (C) watched (D) watches

8 I went to a Japanese restaurant -------- lunch.
(A) have (B) to have (C) having (D) has

9 Linda is nice, ------ her sister is polite.
(A) and (B) for (C) or (D) so

10 I was very busy, ------ I took a taxi.
(A) and (B) so (C) for (D) but

11 Is Tomorrow Thursday ----- Friday?
(A) and (B) but (C) or (D) so

12 ------ Beth is very nice, everybody likes her.
(A) And (B) Because (C) So (D) Although

98 잉글리쉬앤 그래머 START

B 다음 문장에서 틀린 부분을 찾아 바르게 고치세요.

1 I'll buy some milk but bread.　　　　　　　(　　) → (　　)

2 I had breakfast and I'm still hungry.　　　　(　　) → (　　)

3 Which do you prefer beef and chicken?　　(　　) → (　　)

4 Jenny go shopping every weekend.　　　　(　　) → (　　)

5 Does students go to school in August?　　(　　) → (　　)

6 This car don't look good.　　　　　　　　　(　　) → (　　)

7 Did you ordered some pizza?　　　　　　　(　　) → (　　)

8 You should bring your passport going abroad.　(　　) → (　　)

9 Although they are poor, they can't buy the car.　(　　) → (　　)

10 Mike and I goes to church every Sunday.　(　　) → (　　)

C 다음 밑줄 친 부분 중 어법상 틀린 것을 두 개 고르세요. (문자메시지)

Tina 10:09 a.m.	Donna! How (1) <u>was</u> your trip?
Donna 10:11 a.m.	Wonderful, thanks. I stayed at a small hotel with my family.
Tina 10:12 a.m.	Did you (2) <u>did</u> a lot of sightseeing?
Robin 10:14 a.m.	Only a bit. We (3) <u>were</u> (4) <u>interested</u> in lying on the beach in front of the hotel every day. I also went shopping (5) <u>because</u> bought something (6) <u>for</u> you.

MINI TEST 2

A 다음 빈칸에 들어갈 수 있는 것을 고르세요.

1. I have ---------- every morning.
   - (A) breakfast
   - (B) the breakfast
   - (C) a breakfast
   - (D) breakfasts

2. ------- are Tom's books.
   - (A) This
   - (B) That
   - (C) These
   - (D) It

3. Mr. Johns ------- a nice doctor.
   - (A) am
   - (B) are
   - (C) is
   - (D) be

4. I need something ------- to wear.
   - (A) newly
   - (B) new
   - (C) cloth
   - (D) clothing

5. The contracts are --------- kept in the safe.
   - (A) securing
   - (B) security
   - (C) secure
   - (D) securely

6. We passed -------- a long and huge tunnel.
   - (A) through
   - (B) at
   - (C) on
   - (D) during

7. Tom will finish his assignment ------- tomorrow.
   - (A) by
   - (B) for
   - (C) during
   - (D) at

8. Her voice is too -------.
   - (A) loudly
   - (B) loud
   - (C) highly
   - (D) noisily

9. He will ------- come today.
   - (A) hardly
   - (B) hard
   - (C) hardness
   - (D) harder

10. Ann -------- that she was late because of the bus strike.
    - (A) talked
    - (B) spoke
    - (C) complied
    - (D) explained

11. I will ----------- in the workshop in an hour.
    - (A) attend
    - (B) participate
    - (C) join
    - (D) contact

12. ------- you going to the laboratory this afternoon?
    - (A) Are
    - (B) Do
    - (C) Is
    - (D) Did

B 다음 문장에서 틀린 부분을 찾아 바르게 고치세요.

1 I'm surprising at her progress.　　　　　　　(　　　) → (　　　)

2 Does you know where I can get this film developed?　(　　　) → (　　　)

3 I take a lot of pictures yesterday.　　　　　　(　　　) → (　　　)

4 Him film was a box office hit.　　　　　　　(　　　) → (　　　)

5 I worked lately last night.　　　　　　　　(　　　) → (　　　)

6 I has been there for an hour.　　　　　　　(　　　) → (　　　)

7 I've already send her twenty roses.　　　　　(　　　) → (　　　)

8 I'm going to shopping.　　　　　　　　　(　　　) → (　　　)

9 I was very impressing.　　　　　　　　　(　　　) → (　　　)

10 Don't forgetting to sign your name.　　　　　(　　　) → (　　　)

C 다음 대화에서 밑줄 친 부분 중 어법상 틀린 것을 두 개 고르세요.

> M: Good afternoon, Can I help you?
>
> W: Yes, I'm having some (1) <u>problems</u> with my car. The engine is making some very (2) <u>strangely</u> noises. I think something is (3) <u>wrong</u> with the engine. Could you check it out for me?
>
> M: Sure. It's already Friday afternoon and we are closed on Saturday. You might have to wait (4) <u>by</u> next Monday or Tuesday to get your car back.
>
> W: Oh, that's fine. I'll leave it here and (5) <u>take</u> the subway. Thanks a lot.

FINAL TEST

A 다음 빈칸에 들어갈 수 있는 것을 고르세요.

1. ‑‑‑‑‑‑‑‑‑ was canceled last Friday.
   (A) Train
   (B) The train
   (C) The trains
   (D) Trains

2. Jenny isn't ‑‑‑‑‑‑‑‑‑ with her pay.
   (A) satisfy
   (B) satisfied
   (C) satisfying
   (D) satisfies

3. I think ‑‑‑‑‑‑‑‑‑ Mr. Dupont has a good chance.
   (A) that
   (B) and
   (C) because
   (D) but

4. ‑‑‑‑‑‑‑‑‑ you know who is working extra hours tonight?
   (A) Are
   (B) Is
   (C) Does
   (D) Do

5. I need to get a quick bite ‑‑‑‑‑‑‑‑‑ we go to the workshop.
   (A) or
   (B) for
   (C) before
   (D) until

6. I worked ‑‑‑‑‑‑‑‑‑ four in the morning due to the project.
   (A) on
   (B) to
   (C) until
   (D) in

7. My sister made me ‑‑‑‑‑‑‑‑‑ yesterday.
   (A) anger
   (B) angry
   (C) angered
   (C) to anger

8. The manager ‑‑‑‑‑‑‑‑‑ about going on a business trip.
   (A) talks
   (B) talked
   (C) were talking
   (D) talk

9. The president will ‑‑‑‑‑‑‑‑‑ his new plan with his employees next week.
   (A) discuss
   (B) talk
   (C) reply
   (D) speak

10. For help with your mortgage loan plans, ‑‑‑‑‑‑‑‑‑ our professional financial experts.
    (A) contacted
    (B) contacting
    (C) contact
    (D) contacts

11. All the employees ‑‑‑‑‑‑‑‑‑ the annual conference next month.
    (A) enrolled
    (B) will attend
    (C) have participated
    (D) will comply

12. All the employees in the Marketing Department should ‑‑‑‑‑‑‑‑‑ in group activities.
    (A) attend
    (B) participate
    (C) join
    (D) contact

B 다음 문장에서 틀린 부분을 찾아 바르게 고치세요.

1 It looks a good plan.   (   ) → (   )

2 He said he was interesting in sales.   (   ) → (   )

3 Do you still waiting for Mr. Buchanan to call?   (   ) → (   )

4 Do you have any idea how solve the problem?   (   ) → (   )

5 Did I get any phone calls if I was away?   (   ) → (   )

6 The new discovery will broad their previous knowledge.   (   ) → (   )

7 Let's care for the earth as well animals.   (   ) → (   )

8 The detective looked into the accident thorough.   (   ) → (   )

9 Do not disposing of trash, refuse or debris in front of my house.   (   ) → (   )

10 The collection consist of almost 500 paintings and sculptures.   (   ) → (   )

C 다음 대화에서 밑줄 친 부분 중 어법상 틀린 것을 두 개 고르세요.

> M: Hello. I'd like to mail (1) <u>this</u> package to California.
>
> W: Okay. Would you (2) <u>like</u> delivery confirmation on the package? It only (3) <u>cost</u> extra 3 dollars.
>
> M: Yes, that would be wonderful. And could you mark the package fragile?
>
> W: Of course. Your total is 20 dollars. Also, you (4) <u>need</u> to fill out a form for the delivery confirmation service (5) <u>if</u> you leave.

잉글리쉬앤 그래머 START

기본편

Unit 13 명사와 대명사
Unit 14 형용사와 부사
Unit 15 동사와 전치사

명사와 대명사

GRAMMAR POINT

① 명사의 형태

모든 명사가 다 그러한 것은 아니지만 명사는 일정한 형태가 있습니다.

어미 형태	단어
-tion	invitation 초대 production 생산
-sion	impression 인상 conclusion 결론
-ment	agreement 합의 development 개발
-ance	assistance 도움 attendance 출석
-al	arrival 도착 approval 승인 denial 거절
-ure	departure 출발 pressure 압력
-sis	analysis 분석 crisis 위기
-ness	effectiveness 효율성 happiness 행복
-ity	authority 권위 electricity 전기
-hood / -ship	childhood 어린 시절 leadership 지휘
-er, -ee, -ist, -ant -al	employer 고용자 employee 직원 applicant 지원자 scientist 과학자 accountant 회계사 professional 전문가

② 명사의 역할

(1) 주어 : 동사 앞에 오며 행위의 주체를 나타냅니다.
The president rejected the proposal. 사장은 제안을 거절했다.

(2) 보어 : 문장의 주체를 보충 설명합니다.
Tom is **a student**. 탐은 학생이다.
Everyone considered Tom **a genius**. 모든 사람들은 탐을 천재라고 생각했다.

(3) 타동사의 목적어 : 동사 뒤에 나오며, 행위의 대상을 나타냅니다.
We usually eat **lunch** at 1 p.m. 우리는 주로 오후 1시에 점심식사를 한다.

(4) 전치사의 목적어 : 전치사 뒤에 옵니다.
The building is under **construction**. 그 건물은 공사 중이다.

③ 명사가 들어가는 위치

(1) 형용사 + 명사
The company needs competitive **applicants**.   그 회사는 경쟁력이 있는 지원자들을 필요로 한다.

(2) 소유격 + 명사
My **supervisor** asked a contractor to submit an estimate.
나의 상관이 계약자에게 견적서를 제출하도록 요구했다.

(3) a(n) / the (+ 부사 + 형용사) + 명사
This is a newly purchased **computer**. 이것은 새로 구입한 컴퓨터이다.

GRAMMAR PRACTICE

A 다음 동사의 명사형을 쓰세요

1. invite _____
2. conclude _____
3. develop _____
4. attend _____
5. approve _____
6. depart _____
7. analyze _____
8. impress _____
9. agree _____
10. produce _____

B 괄호 안에 알맞은 것을 고르세요.

1. The (manager / manage) attended the meeting.
2. They elected Mr. Johns (president / presidential).
3. Mr. Johnson has a (property / proper) in the country.
4. The (construction / constructive) of the building is interesting.
5. This book will provide a very persuasive (argue / argument).

C 어법상 틀린 문장은 바르게 고치고, 틀린 부분이 없으면 O로 표시하세요.

1. All the residents filed a complain due to the noise.
2. Our company needs knowledgeable apply.
3. The first impressing is very important to everyone.
4. The price seldom directly reflects the cost of deliver.
5. Despite his denial that he robbed the bank, he was found guilty.

VOCA rob 강탈하다　guilty 유죄의　invite 초대하다　conclude 결론을 내리다　develop 발전시키다　attend 출석하다　approve 찬성하다　depart 출발하다　analyze 분석하다　impress 감동시키다　agree 동의하다　produce 생산하다　manage 관리하다　persuasive 설득력 있는　resident 거주자　complain 불평하다　due to ~ 때문에　knowledgeable 지식이 있는　directly 직접　reflect 반영하다

GRAMMAR POINT

④ 인칭대명사의 종류

	인칭	주격	소유격	목적격	소유대명사	재귀대명사
단수	1인칭	I	my	me	mine	myself
	2인칭	you	your	you	yours	yourself
	3인칭	he	his	him	his	himself
		she	her	her	hers	herself
		it	its	it	X	itself
복수	1인칭	we	our	us	ours	ourselves
	2인칭	you	your	you	yours	yourselves
	3인칭	they	their	them	theirs	themselves

⑤ 인칭대명사와 재귀대명사 역할과 쓰임

(1) 소유격과 소유대명사의 구분

소유격 형용사 뒤에는 명사가 와서 대명사가 명사를 수식하는 '형용사' 구실을 하지만, 소유대명사 뒤에는 명사가 올 수 없고, 스스로 '~의 것'이라는 의미를 가지고 있는 대명사입니다.

This is **my computer** = This computer is **mine**.
This is **his office** = This office is **his**.

(2) 재귀대명사

문장의 주어와 목적어가 같은 경우에 목적어 자리에 재귀대명사를 씁니다.

> Tip 재귀대명사 관용 표현 **by oneself** = **on one's own** 혼자서
> Hillary finished the report **by herself**. 힐러리는 혼자서 보고서를 마쳤다.
> = Hillary finished the report **on her own**.

⑥ 지시대명사 that, those

(1) that of와 those of

비교급 문장에서 앞에 나온 명사(비교 대상)를 받을 때는 that/those가 쓰입니다.
비교 대상이 단수 명사일 때는 that을, 복수 명사일 때는 those로 받습니다.

The new **policy** is more efficient than **that** of the previous year.
이 새로운 정책은 지난해 것보다 더 효율적이다.

(2) those who ~: ~하는 사람들

Those who are responsible for the event will arrive here at 1 o'clock.
이 행사에 책임이 있는 사람들이 이곳에 1시까지 도착할 것이다.

GRAMMAR PRACTICE

A 괄호 안의 두 단어 중 알맞은 것을 고르세요.

1. Richard told me that (he, his) can help us.

2. Austin started learning Korean by (him, himself).

3. The new policy is more efficient than (that, those) of the previous year.

4. The book on the table is (me, mine.)

5. (Anyone, Those) who apply for the position should fill out this form.

B 빈칸에 밑줄 친 부분을 대신하는 알맞은 대명사를 쓰세요.

1. Jenny and I went to the park. _____ had a good time.

2. Jenny is pretty and nice. I like _____.

3. Sled dogs are pulling a sled. Santa Claus is riding _____.

4. I bought this shirt yesterday, but _____ size is too big for me.

5. Guide dogs help blind people. The dogs always walk with _____.

C 어법상 틀린 문장은 바르게 고치고, 틀린 부분이 없으면 O로 표시하세요.

1. His hat is blue, and she is orange.

2. Their ball is yellow. Look at them!

3. You should always love and take care of yourself.

4. Those who are interested in music will go there.

5. Jenny just finished the project on his own.

VOCA previous 이전의　policy 정책　apply for 지원하다　position 직책　fill out 채워 넣다　have a good time 좋은 시간을 보내다　sled 썰매　ride 타다　too 너무 ~하게　guide 안내자　blind 눈먼　take care of 돌보다, 처리하다

GRAMMAR IN SENTENCE

▶ 의미 단위로 문장을 끊어 읽고, 해석하세요.

1. All the residents filed a complaint due to the noise.

2. Our company needs knowledgeable applicants.

3. The first impression is very important to everyone.

4. The price seldom directly reflects the cost of delivery.

5. Despite his denial that he robbed the bank, he was found guilty.

6. Richard told me that he can help us.

7. Austin started learning Korean by himself.

8. The new policy is more efficient than that of the previous year.

9. Jenny just finished the project on her own.

10. Those who apply for the position should fill out this form.

명사

명사는 문장에서 주어, 목적어, 보어로 쓰입니다.

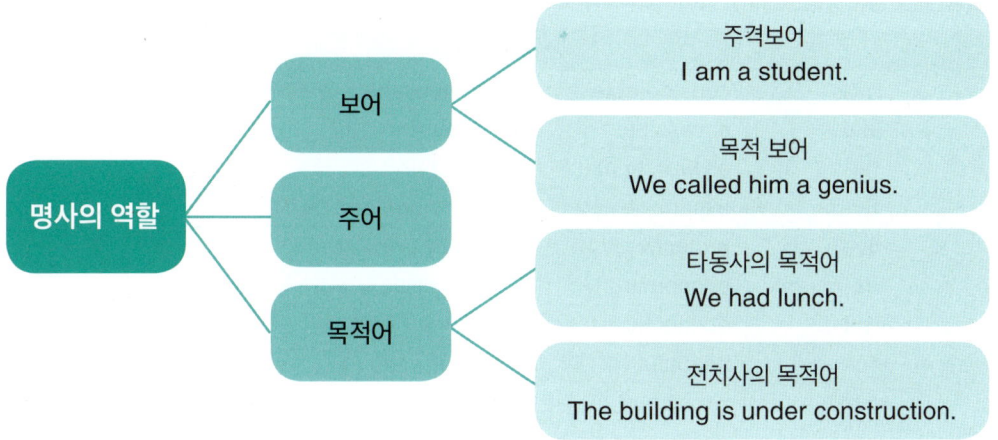

대명사

명사의 반복을 피하기 위해 사용하는 것이 대명사입니다.

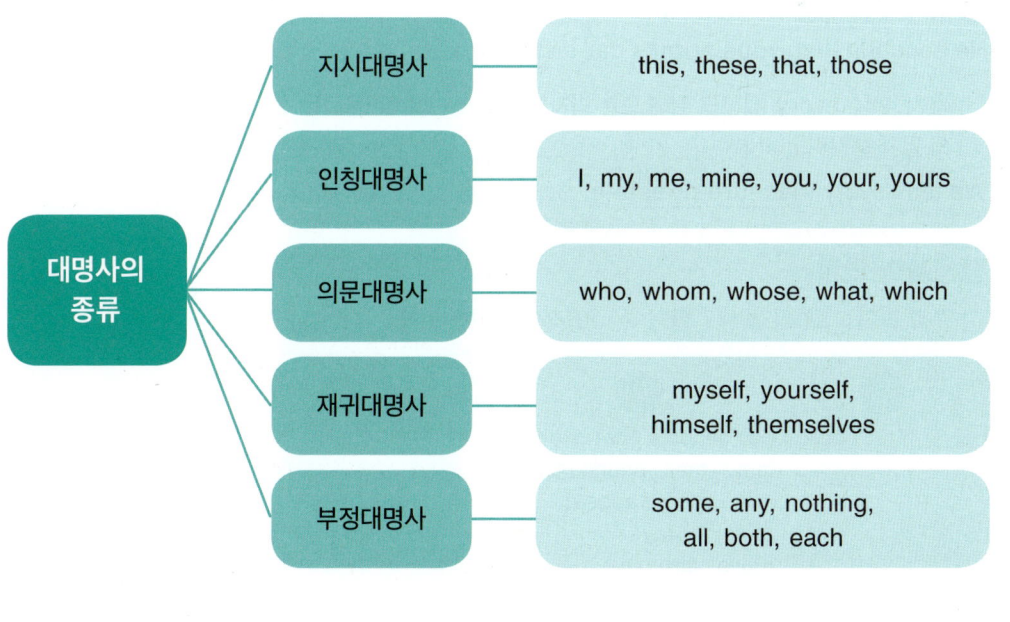

UNIT 14 형용사와 부사

◎ GRAMMAR POINT

① 형용사의 형태

형용사는 '명사 또는 동사 + 접미사'의 형태로 만들어 진 것이 많습니다.

어미 형태	단어
-able	considerable 상당한, 중요한　payable 지불해야 할
-ible	accessible 이용할 수 있는　possible 가능한
-al	environmental 환경의　formal 공식적인
-sive	expansive 광대한, 확장적인　impressive 인상적인
-tive	protective 보호하는　attractive 마음을 끄는
-ic	economic 경제의, 경제학의　realistic 실제적인, 현실주의
-ical	economical 절약하는　historical 역사에 관한
-ful	beautiful 아름다운　respectful 공손한
-ous	conscious 알고 있는　numerous 다수의, 수많은
-ent	confident 확신하는, 자신만만한　different 다른
명사 + ly	costly 비용이 드는　friendly 친절한　timely 적시의

② 형용사의 위치

(1) 관사 + 형용사 + 명사

the **beautiful girl** 아름다운 소녀

(2) 명사 수식: 형용사 + 복합명사

He bought a **luxurious sports car** last month. 그는 지난달에 호화로운 스포츠카 한 대를 샀다.

(3) 후치 수식: every, 최상급 뒤에 오는 명사를 -able, -ible로 끝나는 형용사가 수식하는 경우, 뒤에서 앞의 명사를 꾸며줍니다.

We took every **measure possible**. 우리는 가능한 모든 조치를 취했다

③ 형용사의 역할

(1) 주격 보어 - 2형식 동사 + 형용사: 대표적인 불완전 동사

He **looks happy**. 그는 행복해 보인다.

GRAMMAR PRACTICE

A 다음 동사 또는 명사의 형용사형을 한글 뜻에 맞게 쓰세요

1. consider _____ 상당한
2. pay _____ 지불할 만한
3. access _____ 이용할 수 있는
4. impress _____ 인상적인
5. protect _____ 보호하는
6. environment _____ 환경의
7. economy _____ 경제의
8. history _____ 역사에 관한
9. cost _____ 비용이 드는
10. friend _____ 친절한

B 괄호 안에 알맞은 것을 고르세요.

1. They looked very (friend, friendly).
2. The puppy seems (happy, happily).
3. The mask is so (colorful, colorfully).
4. The man looks (angry, angrily).
5. The cake tastes (sweet, sweetly).

C 어법상 틀린 문장은 바르게 고치고, 옳은 문장에는 표시 (O) 하세요

1. The driver of the bus had seriously injuries.
2. Mr. Smith is responsibility for hiring the staff.
3. Mr. Glee is interested in environment issues.
4. Everything possibly should be done to help you.
5. The policeman made a timely appearance on the scene.

VOCA consider 숙고하다　pay 지불하다　access 접근, 접근하다　protect 보호하다　economy 절약, 경제
injury 상해, 부상　hire 고용하다　issue 문제　appearance 출연　scene 현장

GRAMMAR POINT

(2) 목적격 보어 - 5형식 동사 + 목적어 + 형용사: 대표적인 불완전 타동사

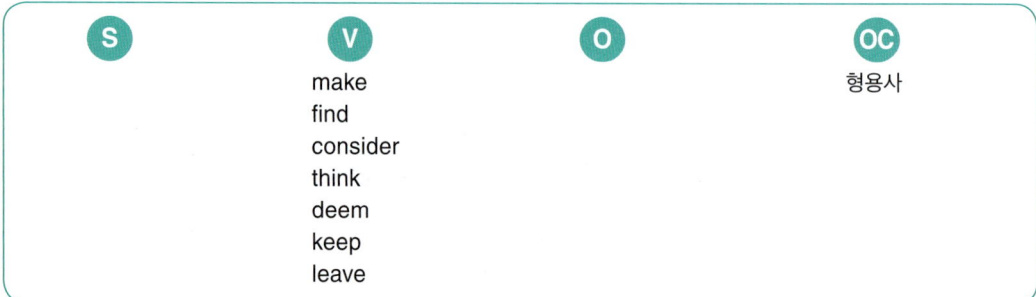

I found **the game interesting**. 난 그 게임이 흥미로운 걸 알았다.

④ 부사의 역할과 위치

부사는 우리말의 '어떻게'에 해당하는 정보를 지닌 말로서 동사, 형용사, 또 다른 부사, 문장 전체를 수식하는 수식어입니다. 영어의 부사는 주로 형용사에 -ly를 붙여서 만듭니다.

▪ have + 부사 + p.p.	ABC, Inc. has **voluntarily** recalled some products. ABC 사는 제품을 자발적으로 회수하고 있다.
▪ be + 부사 + -ing/p.p.	People were **completely** satisfied with the results. 사람들은 그 결과에 완전히 만족했다.
▪ to + 동사원형 + 부사	Staff members are trained to react **calmly**. 직원들은 침착하게 대응하도록 교육받고 있다.
▪ 부사 + 형용사 + 명사	an **increasingly** competitive global market. 점점 더 경쟁이 심해지는 국제 시장
▪ be동사 + 부사 + 형용사	They are **usually** busy in the morning. 그들은 아침에 주로 바쁘다.
▪ 부사 + 종속절/ 전치사구	**Shortly** after the meeting, I'll get back to you. 회의가 끝난 직후에, 다시 연락할게요.

☑ '약, 대략'이라는 의미의 부사

almost = **approximately** = **nearly** = **around** = **about** 거의

It's **almost** 10 o'clock. 거의 10시이다.

GRAMMAR PRACTICE

A 괄호 안에 알맞은 것을 고르시오.

1. You should keep it (secret, secretly).

2. The restaurant makes its customers (happy, happily).

3. Since last year, the net profit has (significant, significantly) increased.

4. Smoking in the room is (absolute, absolutely) forbidden.

5. The profit has increased by (approximate, approximately) ten percent.

B 주어진 표현을 활용하여 문장을 완성하시오.

1. I believe that my parents are _____ right. (absolute)

2. _____ these things have changed quickly over time. (Apparent)

3. The cost has been reduced _____. (considerable)

4. Everyone in the audience found the opera _____. (impress)

5. The committee _____ agreed to expand into a new market. (final)

C 어법상 틀린 문장은 바르게 고치고, 옳은 문장에는 표시 (O) 하세요.

1. Personally, I agree complete with the author.

2. Everything seems to be convenient set up for people.

3. Managers are asked to regularly check the attendance rates of their employees.

4. All the staff members have been trained extensive by professional instructors.

5. Recent, there have been many car thefts in the area.

VOCA customer 고객   net   profit 순수익   be forbidden 금지되다   increase 증가하다   absolute 절대적인
apparent 명백한   considerable 상당한   audience 청중   committee 위원, 위원회   expand into ~로 확장하다
personally 개인적으로   complete 완전한   author 저자   convenient 편리한   set up 설치하다
set - set - set   regularly 정기적으로   attendance 출석   extensive 광대한, 넓은   professional 전문적인
instructor 강사   recent 최근의   theft 도둑

GRAMMAR POINT

⑤ 비교급과 최상급의 형태와 변화

(1) 비교급과 최상급의 형태 : 규칙변화

	원급	비교급	최상급
1. 기본원칙	high	higher	highest
2. -e로 끝나는 단어 → -r 또는 -st 만 붙임	large	larger	largest
3. '단모음 +단자음'으로 끝나는 단어 → 자음을 하나 더 쓰고 -er, -est 붙임.	big	bigger	biggest
4. 자음으로 끝나는 단어 → y를 i로 고치고 -er, -est 붙임.	busy	busier	busiest
5. 일부의 2음절 단어 또는 3음절 이상인 단어 → more, most 붙임.	important	more important	most important

보통 형용사 또는 부사 뒤에 비교급은 -er, 최상급은 -est 를 붙입니다. 단어가 길 경우 형용사 또는 부사 앞에 비교급은 more, 최상급은 most를 붙입니다.

(2) 비교급과 최상급의 형태 : 불규칙변화

형용사와 부사의 비교급과 최상급이 불규칙한 형태로 변하는 단어들이 있습니다. 이러한 단어들의 비교급과 최상급 형태는 별도로 기억해 두어야만 합니다.

⑥ 동등 비교 : 원급을 이용한 비교

두 사람이나 두 개의 사물이 서로 얼마나 같은지 비슷한지를 비교하는 표현입니다. 이때, as 형용사 또는 부사 as 형태로 씁니다. 이때 형용사 또는 부사가 원래 형태인 원급형태를 써야합니다.

형태	의미	예
as 원급 as	~만큼 ~하게	Mike is **as tall as** Jenny. Mike 는 Jenny 만큼 키가 크다.
the same ~ as Just as ~ as	~와 똑같은	Mike is **the same** age **as** Jenny. Mike와 Jenny는 나이가 똑같다. Mike is **just as** busy **as** Jenny. Mike는 Jenny만큼이나 바쁘다.
not as(so) 원급 as	~만큼~하지 않은	Mike is **not as tall as** his brother. Mike는 그의 형만큼 키가 크지 않다.
as 원급 as possible	가능한 ~하게	Mike walked **as fast as possible**. Mike는 가능한 빨리 걸었다.

⑦ 비교급, 최상급을 이용한 중요 표현

비교급 문장에서 비교급 다음에는 than 을 써야 합니다.
명사를 수식하는 형용사에 대한 최상급은 앞에 정관사 the를 붙여야 합니다.

형태	의미	예
비교급 ~ than	~보다 ~하다	A basketball is **bigger than** a baseball. 농구공이 야구공보다 크다.
the 최상급 in 장소 (of 복수명사)	가장 ~한	Mike is **the tallest** boy **in his class**. Mike가 교실에서 가장 크다.

GRAMMAR PRACTICE

A 다음 표의 빈칸에 알맞은 것을 쓰세요.

원급	비교급	최상급
strong		
nice		
hot		
pretty		
confident		

B 다음 표의 빈칸에 알맞은 것을 쓰세요.

원급	비교급	최상급
good		
much		
badly		
little		
late (순서)		

C 다음 주어진 단어를 활용하여 **as ~ as** 표현을 완성하세요.

  보기   Linda speaks Chinese **as well as** Tom. (well)

1. Mike is _____ Jenny. (tall)
2. The weather today is _____ the weather yesterday. (nice)
3. This book is _____ that book. (just / thick)
4. Mike came back home _____. (soon)

D -er -est 또는 more most를 넣어서 다음의 문장을 완성하세요.

1. Beth is _____ than her sister. (happy)
2. Jenny is _____ girl of all the students. (smart)
3. Mathematics is _____ than English to me. (difficult)
4. This is the _____ car in the parking lot. (expensive)

VOCA strong 강한   nice 훌륭한   hot 더운   pretty 예쁜   confident 확신하는   badly 나쁘게   thick 두꺼운   soon 곧
mathematics 수학   difficult 어려운   expensive 비싼   parking lot 주차장

GRAMMAR IN SENTENCE

▶ 의미 단위로 문장을 끊어 읽고, 해석하세요.

1. You should keep it a secret.

2. The restaurant makes its customers happy.

3. Since last year, the net profit has significantly increased.

4. Everything possible should be done to help you.

5. The policeman made a timely appearance on the scene.

6. Personally, I agree completely with the author.

7. Everything seems to be conveniently set up for people.

8. Managers are asked to regularly check the attendance rates of their employees.

9. All the staff members have been trained extensively by professional instructors.

10. Mathematics is more difficult than English for me.

형용사

형용사는 명사를 직접 수식하거나, 보어 자리에 놓여 명사를 설명하는 역할을 합니다.

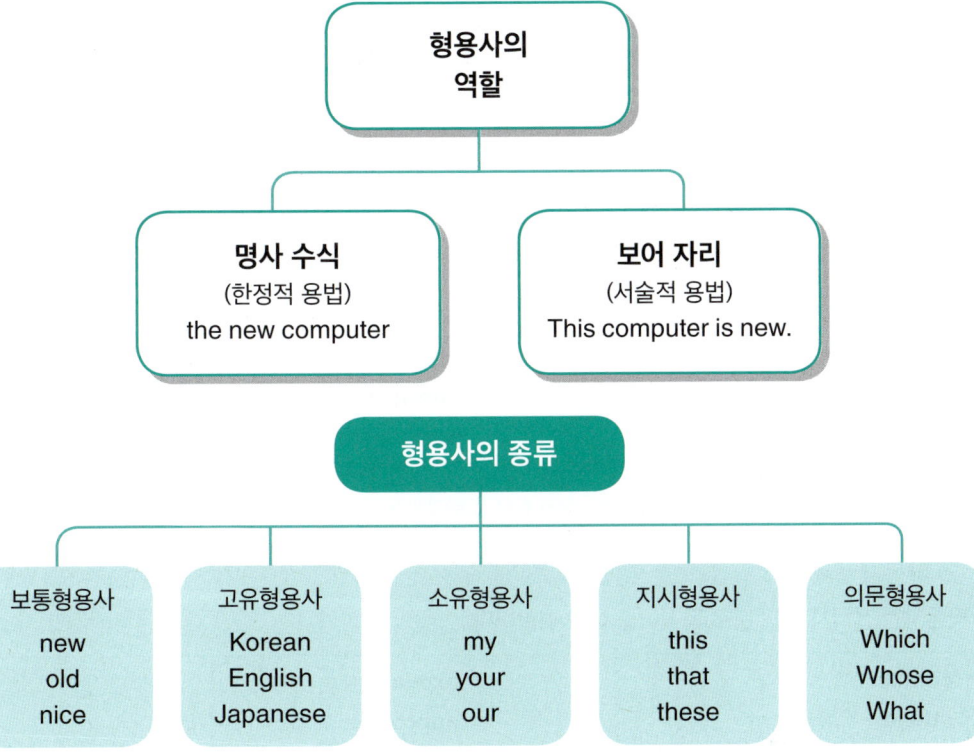

부사의 위치

have + 부사 + p.p.	have **voluntarily** recalled 자발적으로 회수하다.
be + 부사 + -ing/p.p.	were **completely** satisfied 완전히 만족하다.
to + 동사원형 + 부사	to react **calmly** 침착하게 대응하도록
부사 + 형용사 + 명사	an **increasingly** competitive global market 점점 더 경쟁이 심해지는 국제 시장
be동사 + 부사 + 형용사	are **usually** available 대개 이용이 가능하다.
부사 + 종속절/ 전치사구	**shortly** after 직후에

UNIT 15 동사와 전치사

◎ GRAMMAR POINT

① 동사의 종류

자동사는 스스로 자립할 수 있는 동사로 절대로 뒤에 목적어를 갖지 않습니다. <자동사 + 전치사 + 전치사의 목적어>가 기본적인 형태입니다. 반면, 타동사는 목적어에 의지하는 동사이며, 능동태의 경우 타동사는 반드시 목적어가 있어야 합니다.

(1) 자동사 + 전치사 + 목적어

자동사는 목적어를 취하지 않지만 의미상 목적어를 필요로 하는 경우가 많습니다. 이럴 땐 자동사와 목적어 사이에 전치사를 넣습니다.

agree with ~에 동의하다	**speak to** ~와 이야기하다
comply with ~에 따르다	**deal with** ~를 다루다
interfere with ~를 방해하다	**enroll in** ~에 등록하다
look into ~ ~을 조사하다	**participate in** ~에 참석하다

Our team **agreed with** the topic. 우리 팀은 그 주제에 동의했다.

(2) 타동사 + 목적어

타동사는 전치사 없이 바로 목적어를 항상 취합니다.

contact ~에 연락하다	**exceed** ~를 능가하다
attend ~에 참석하다	**approach** ~에 접근하다, 다가가다
access ~에 접근[접속]하다, 사용하다	**arrange** ~를 정돈하다, 처리하다
disclose ~를 폭로하다	**join** ~에 합석하다, 합류하다

We **discussed** the problem. 우리는 그 문제를 의논했다.

(3) 유사 의미 자동사와 타동사 구별하기

의미	자동사 + 전치사 + 목적어	타동사 + 목적어
질문에 답하다	**respond to** the question **reply to** the question	**answer** the question
문제를 의논하다	**talk about** the problem	**discuss** the problem
결과를 설명하다	**account for** the results	**explain** the results
생각에 반대하다	**object to** the idea	**oppose** the idea

Our team **talked about** the problem. 우리 팀은 그 문제에 대해 이야기했다.

Our team **discussed** the problem. 우리 팀은 그 문제를 의논했다.

GRAMMAR PRACTICE

A 괄호 안에 알맞은 것을 고르시오.

1. You can't (access to, access) the building without a permit.

2. We must (comply, comply with) the terms of the contract.

3. Lisa is not able to (deal, deal with) the problem.

4. May I (speak, speak to) John, please?

5. Kimberly can (discuss, deal) with the problem.

6. Linda decided to (comply, join) our team.

7. Jenny will (answer, reply) the question.

8. I (talked, explained) the schedule to her.

9. No one will (object, oppose) changing the law.

10. Managers should (contact to, contact) their local business office.

B 어법상 틀린 문장은 바르게 고치고, 옳은 문장에는 표시 (O) 하세요

1. Mike contacted with his supervisor immediately.

2. Don't interfere our conversation.

3. Do not exceed the daily dose.

4. The manager is talking the phone now.

5. If you accept to the position, we would appreciate it.

VOCA permit 허가증 terms of the contract 조항 계약서 decide to V ~을 결정하다 truth 진실성 falsehood 거짓
local 지방의 supervisor 관리 감독자 immediately 즉시 conversation 대화 anger 노여움 control 통제
position 자리, 직책 appreciate 감사하다

◎ GRAMMAR POINT

② 이유와 양보를 나타내는 전치사

~ 때문에	because of due to owing to on account of	**Because of** the bad weather, the game was canceled. 나쁜 날씨 때문에 그 경기는 취소되었다.
~에도 불구하고	in spite of despite	**In spite of** his age, he is still in good health. 나이에도 불구하고, 그는 여전히 건강하다.

③ 혼동되는 전치사들

(1) by / until (~까지)
- **by** + 시점 동작의 완료를 나타내는 동사 arrive, pay, complete, finish, submit, return 등과 쓰입니다.
- **until** + 시점 상태의 계속을 나타내는 동사 postpone, stay, remain, last, continue, wait, keep 등과 쓰입니다.

He will have **finished** his work **by** Wednesday. 그는 그의 보고서를 수요일까지 마칠 것이다.
You can **stay** here **until** tomorrow. 당신은 내일까지 여기 머물 수 있다.

(2) for / during (~동안)
- **for** + 불특정 기간 for 뒤에는 주로 시간 표현의 숫자가 오며, '얼마나 오랫동안 지속되었는지'를 표현합니다.
- **during** + 특정 기간 during 뒤에는 행사, 사건 등이 와서 특정 기간을 나타냅니다.

He has lived in Chicago **for ten years**. 그는 10년째 시카고에 살고 있다.
I fell asleep **during the film**. 나는 영화를 보다가 잠이 들었다.

(3) throughout / upon / over
- **throughout** ~동안 내내, ~전역을 거쳐서(시간 및 장소 표현과 모두 함께 쓸 수 있음)
- **upon** ~하자마자
- **over** ~에 걸쳐서, ~동안에

He has worked for CNN **over** the last ten years. 그는 지난 10년 동안 CNN에서 일하고 있다.
Upon arrival in Paris, I called on him. 파리에 도착하자마자 나는 그를 찾아갔다.
The restaurant is known **throughout** the city. 그 레스토랑은 도시 전역에 알려져 있다.
Rain is expected to fall **throughout** the week. 비는 이번 주 내내 계속될 것으로 예상됩니다.

(4) within / in
- **within** + 기간 ~기간 이내에
- **in** + 기간 ~기간 지나서

You should pay your bill **within** three days. 귀하는 청구서 금액을 3일 내에 지불하셔야 합니다.
You'd better pay your bill **in** three days. 귀하는 청구서 금액을 3일 후에 지불하셔야 합니다.

GRAMMAR PRACTICE

A 괄호 안에 알맞은 것을 고르시오.

1. The plane was delayed (because of, because) the weather.

2. They love him (in spite, despite) his faults.

3. You can play a game (for, during) one hour

4. I can stay in Seoul (by, until) tomorrow.

5. Bob has lived here (during, for) ten years.

6. I was asleep (throughout, for) the class.

7. Jenny is very busy (for, during) the festival.

8. I watched TV (during, for) two hours last night.

9. We have to arrive at home (by, until) 10 o'clock.

10. It snowed a lot (for, during) the night.

B 어법상 틀린 문장은 바르게 고치고, 옳은 문장에는 표시 (O) 하세요

1. You need to submit this report until Wednesday.

2. I'll call you back in 10 minutes.

3. I have to finish this project by this Friday.

4. I stay in bed by late afternoon on Saturday.

5. An epidemic spread throughout the country.

VOCA delay 미루다, 연기하다　fault 결점　fall asleep 잠들다　fall - fell - fallen　festival 축제　submit 제출하다
epidemic 전염병　spread - spread - spread

GRAMMAR IN SENTENCE

▶ 의미 단위로 문장을 끊어 읽고, 해석하세요.

1. Mike contacted his supervisor immediately.

2. Don't interfere with our conversation.

3. Do not exceed the daily dose.

4. You can't access the building without a permit.

5. We must comply with the terms of the contract.

6. The plane was delayed because of the weather.

7. They love him despite his faults.

8. Managers should contact their local business office.

9. An epidemic spread throughout the country.

10. You need to submit this report by Wednesday.

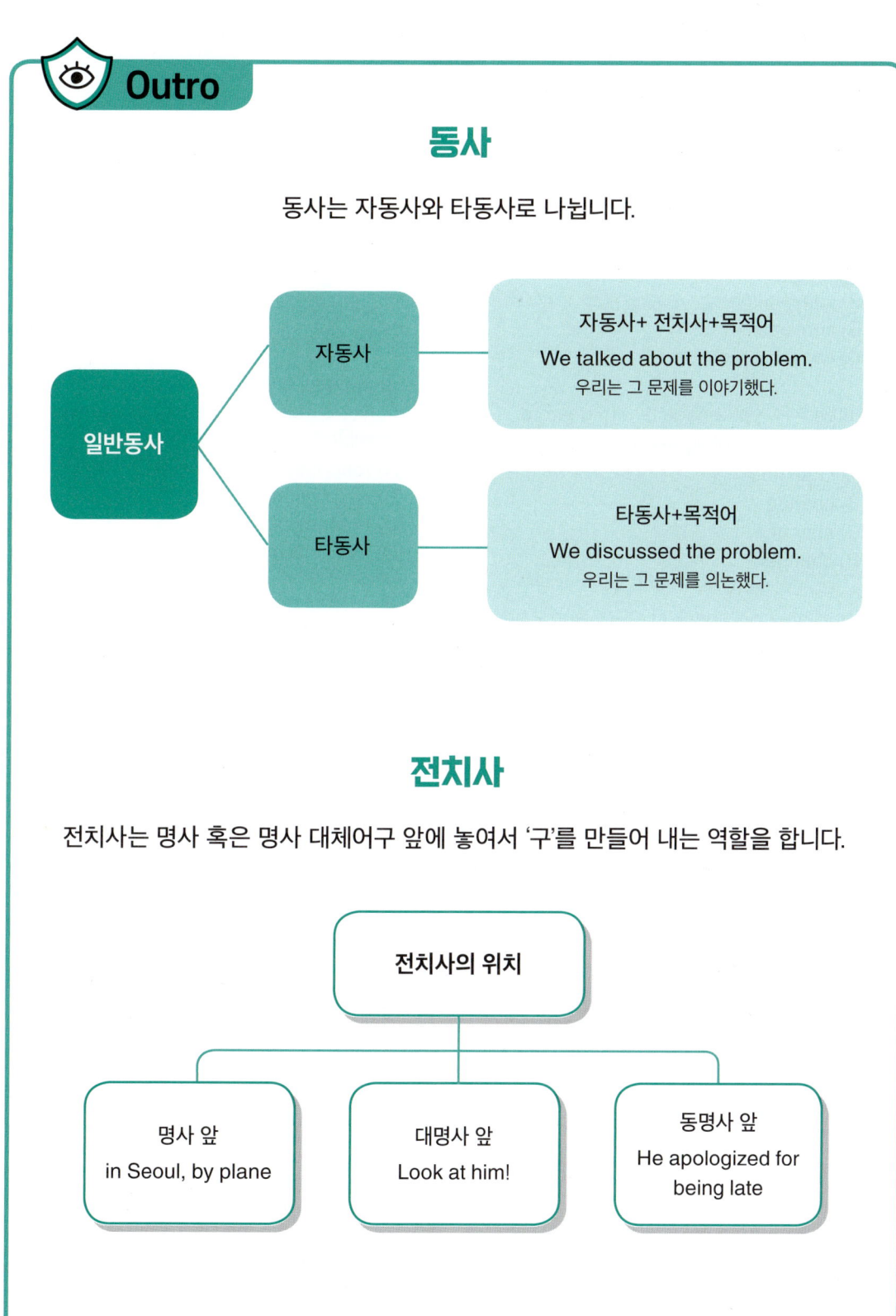

ACTUAL TEST 5

A 다음 빈칸에 들어갈 수 있는 것을 고르세요.

1. For your --------, we have these two large tables in the center of the room.
   (A) convenient
   (B) convenient
   (C) convene
   (D) convenience

2. Three ------- proposed by the board of directors are highlighted in blue.
   (A) changing
   (B) change
   (C) changes
   (D) changed

3. Dr. Hatley will speak in ------- about how this building came to be.
   (A) depth
   (B) deep
   (C) deepen
   (D) deeply

4. The --------- for the summer festival was made a year in advance.
   (A) reserve
   (B) reserved
   (C) reservation
   (D) reserves

5. All passengers are advised to secure all -------- valuables in their carry-on baggage.
   (A) they
   (B) them
   (C) their
   (D) theirs

6. ------- who want to continue their contracts will have their fringe benefits renewed each year.
   (A) They
   (B) One
   (C) Anyone
   (D) Those

7. ABC, Inc. provides -------- products that revolutionize business operations for our customers.
   (A) innovator
   (B) innovate
   (C) innovative
   (D) innovation

8. Employees are -------- for making LED monitors that have the highest quality possible.
   (A) responsibility
   (B) responsibly
   (C) responsible
   (D) responsive

9. ------- the tight deadline for the project, the staff needs to work overtime this week.
   (A) Therefore
   (B) Moreover
   (C) Because of
   (D) Nevertheless

10. ------- the one-year contract period, replacement parts will be provided free of charge.
    (A) During
    (B) Before
    (C) Between
    (D) Beyond

11. A number of middle school students in the city --------- in the special event held by Dell this weekend.
    (A) participates
    (B) are participated
    (C) is participating
    (D) are participating

12. You can find books on analysts who are ------- recommended by Adam Smith, an economist.
    (A) height
    (B) higher
    (C) highest
    (D) highly

B 다음 빈칸에 들어갈 수 있는 것을 고르세요.

Questions 13-18 refer to the following article.

Seattle Times

Next week, almost 5,000 students are expected to **13** -------- the Winter Career Fair.

More than 100 companies in Washington **14** --------- to set up booths at the fair, and expect to fill over 1,000 intern positions **15** ---------- the winter vacation. This is the first year that the Winter Career Fair is being held. However, if it is a success, the fair is expected to be a **16** ------- occurrence in Seattle every December, and it will expand to other university cities **17** -------- the United States.

Doors open at 9:00 A.M., and the fair will **18** ------- at 5:00 P.M.

Entrance is free for all students, but a valid student card must be presented at the door.

---

13 (A) enroll
 (B) take part
 (C) attend
 (D) go

14 (A) register
 (B) registration
 (C) has registered
 (D) have registered

15 (A) during
 (B) for
 (C) to
 (D) on

16 (A) regulate
 (B) regulation
 (C) regular
 (D) regularly

17 (A) throughout
 (B) by
 (C) at
 (D) over

18 (A) close
 (B) closed
 (C) closing
 (D) closure

잉글리쉬앤 그래머 START

기본편

Unit 16 시제
Unit 17 수일치
Unit 18 태

5코스
4코스
3코스
2코스
1코스

UNIT 16 시제

GRAMMAR POINT

① 단순시제

영어 문장에서 가장 기본적인 시제는 현재, 과거, 미래를 나타내는 단순 시제입니다.

(1) 현재 시제

현재 시제는 불변의 진리, (일정 기간) 변함없는 사실, 습관, 반복을 나타내는 경우에 씁니다. 주로 every day, each month, often, frequently, usually 등과 함께 씁니다. 주어가 3인칭 단수인 경우에는 동사 뒤에 -(e)s를 붙여 써야 합니다.

불변의 진리	The sun **rises** in the east. 태양은 동쪽에서 뜬다.
현재의 사실이나 상태	I **live** in Seoul. 나는 서울에 산다.
현재의 습관, 반복되는 행위	I **get up** at 6:00 every morning. 나는 매일 아침 6시에 일어난다.

(2) 과거 시제

과거 시제는 이미 끝난 과거의 동작이나 상태를 나타냅니다. 과거 시제와 함께 쓰이는 표현으로는 last year, two years ago 등이 있습니다.

He **played** tennis **yesterday**. 그는 어제 테니스를 쳤다.

(3) 미래 시제: will + 동사원형

미래 시제는 <will + 동사원형>이 가장 기본적인 형태이며, 미래의 상황에 대한 추측이나 의지를 나타냅니다. <be going to + 동사원형> 또는 <be + -ing> 형태도 미래를 나타냅니다. **tomorrow**, **next year** 등과 함께 씁니다.

He **will play** tennis **tomorrow**. 그는 내일 테니스를 칠 것이다.

② 진행시제

현재, 과거, 미래의 각 시점에서 진행 중인 동작이나 상황을 나타낼 때 쓰이는 시제입니다.

(1) 현재 진행: am/is/are + -ing

현재 시점에 진행되고 있는 일을 나타 낼 때 쓰며, **now**, **currently** 등과 함께 씁니다.

He **is playing** tennis **now**. 그는 지금 테니스를 치고 있다.

(2) 과거 진행: was/were + -ing

특정한 과거 시점에 진행되고 있었던 일을 표현할 때 씁니다.

He **was playing** tennis then. 그는 그 당시에 테니스를 치던 중이었다.

(3) 미래 진행: will be + -ing

특정한 미래 시점에 진행되고 있을 일을 표현할 때 씁니다.

He **will be playing** tennis **after work tomorrow**. 그는 내일 일을 마친 후에 테니스를 치고 있을 것이다.

GRAMMAR PRACTICE

A 괄호 안에 알맞은 것을 고르시오.

1. Tommy (goes, went) to school every day.
2. He is currently (attended, attending) the workshop.
3. Water (is boiling, boils) at 100 degrees Celsius.
4. The water (is boiling, boils) now.
5. Jenny (attends, will be attending) the meeting at 3:00 p.m. tomorrow.
6. Banks (will open, open) at 9:00 every morning.
7. Tom always (keeps, kept) promises.
8. Mr. Lee (attends, will attend) the workshop next week.
9. He (played, plays) baseball with his friend yesterday.
10. I (have, had) breakfast with my family every weekend.

B 어법상 틀린 문장은 바르게 고치고, 옳은 문장에는 표시 (O) 하세요.

1. Nurses take care of patients in hospitals.
2. The water boils now, so can you turn it off?
3. I see Lisa downtown last weekend.
4. Ann listens to music when the phone rang.
5. Sally works in her office at 3 o'clock tomorrow.

VOCA currently 현재 boil 끓다 degree 도 Celsius 섭씨 always 항상 promise 약속 nurse 간호사 take care of 돌보다 patient 환자 turn off 끄다 downtown 시내 ring 울리다 - rang - rung

GRAMMAR POINT

③ 완료 시제
완료 시제란 어떤 시점에서 어떤 시점까지 계속되거나 끝난 일을 나타낼 때 쓰는 시제를 말합니다.

(1) 현재 완료: **have** + 과거분사 (**p.p.**)
과거에 일어난 동작이나 상태가 지금까지 계속되거나 끝났을 때 쓰는 표현입니다. <since + 과거 시점>, <for + 기간>, in the past ~ years 등과 함께 씁니다.

He **has played** tennis **since last year**. 그는 작년부터 테니스를 쳐오고 있다.
He **has just finished** his homework. 그는 숙제를 막 마쳤다.

☑ **have been** to ~해 본 적이 있다 vs **have gone** to ~ 가버리고 이곳에 없다.
 I **have been** to New York. 나는 New York에 가본 적이 있다.
 Tina **has gone** to New York. Tina는 New York 으로 떠나 버렸다.

(2) 과거 완료: **had** + **p.p**.
과거의 어떤 시점을 기준으로 그 이전에 일어난 동작이나 상태가 그 과거 시점까지 계속되거나 이미 끝났을 때 쓰는 표현입니다. 그러므로 과거 시제와 함께 사용하는 경우가 많습니다.

We *had already played* tennis when it *started* to rain.
(비가 내리기 시작한 과거 시점을 기준으로 해서 이전에 이루어진 일이 테니스 친 일이라는 것을 알 수 있음)
비가 내리기 시작했을 때 우리는 이미 테니스를 치고 있었다.

(3) 미래 완료: **will have** + **p.p**.
과거에 일어난 어떤 사건이나 동작이 미래의 특정한 시점까지 계속되거나 완료될 때 쓰는 표현입니다.
즉, 과거에 시작된 동작이 현재를 지나 미래의 특정한 시점에 완료될 때 사용하기 때문에 상당한 기간을 의미합니다. 주로 <by + 미래 시간의 부사구>와 함께 쓰이거나, 또는 <By the time S2 + V2(현재시제), S1 + V1(will + have + p.p.)>의 형태로 많이 쓰입니다.

I **will have read** the books by tomorrow. 나는 내일까지 그 책을 다 읽을 것이다.
(과거부터 현재까지 책을 계속 읽어왔으며, 내일까지 책 읽는 것을 끝내겠다는 사실을 나타냄)

He **will have played tennis** 30 times by next month.
(이전부터 치기 시작했던 테니스가 다음 달이 되면 30번이 됨을 나타냄)
그는 다음 달까지면 테니스를 30번치는 것이 될 것이다.

By the time he **retires**, he **will have worked** for 20 years.
그가 은퇴할 때까지면, 그는 20년 동안 일한 것이 된다.

④ 시간, 조건의 부사절
시간이나 조건의 부사절에서는 미래 시제 대신에 현재 시제를 쓴다.

☑ 시간이나 조건의 부사절을 이끄는 접속사

> 시간: when, while, before, after, until, as soon as, by the time
> 조건: as long as, if, unless, once

When you meet Jenny tomorrow, please give her this book. (시간 부사절)
내일 Jenny를 만나면, 이 책을 주세요.

GRAMMAR PRACTICE

A 괄호 안에 알맞은 것을 고르시오.

1. I (have known, knew) Sandra since she was a child.

2. We (lived, have lived) in London three years ago.

3. We (lived, have lived) in London for three years.

4. Tony (will have played, had played) the game when I visited him.

5. I (will have attended, attended) the seminar 10 times by next year.

6. I (didn't see, haven't seen) Fredrik since last Tuesday.

7. Rachel (were waiting, has been waiting) for an hour.

8. I (lost, have lost) my key yesterday.

9. They (will have left, had left) home by the time we arrive.

10. He (will meet, will have met) his girlfriend tomorrow.

B 어법상 틀린 문장은 바르게 고치고, 옳은 문장에는 표시 (O) 하세요

1. Did you ever been to Paris?

2. Tourists have just arrived at the hotel.

3. It was cold since yesterday, so I bought a coat.

4. I will have read the books by tomorrow.

5. As long as you will love me, I can do everything for you.

VOCA buy - bought - bought 사다   as long as ~하는 한

GRAMMAR IN SENTENCE

▶ 의미 단위로 문장을 끊어 읽고, 해석하세요

1. Nurses take care of patients in hospitals.

2. The water is boiling now, so can you turn it off?

3. I saw Lisa downtown last weekend.

4. Ann was listening to music when the phone rang.

5. Sally will be working in her office at 3 o'clock tomorrow.

6. I have known Sandra since she was a child.

7. Tony had played the game when I visited him.

8. I will have attended the seminar 10 times by next year.

9. They will have left home by the time we arrive.

10. As long as you love me, I can do everything for you.

# Outro

시제

주어의 동작이나 상태를 시간과 연관 지어 나타내는 말을 시제라고 합니다.

	시제의 종류	
기본시제	과거	과거 ●──────── 현재 ──────── 미래
	현재	과거 ●════════ 현재 ════════ 미래
	미래	과거 ──────── 현재 ──────── ● 미래
진행시제	과거진행	● 과거 ──────── 현재 ──────── 미래
	현재진행	과거 ──────── ● 현재 ──────── 미래
	미래진행	과거 ──────── 현재 ──────── ● 미래
완료시제	과거완료	대과거 ●════ 과거 ──────── 현재 ──────── 미래
	현재완료	과거 ●════════ 현재 ──────── 미래
	미래완료	과거 ●════════ 현재 ════════ 미래

기본

UNIT 17 수일치

GRAMMAR POINT

① 단수 주어 + 단수 동사 / 복수 주어 + 복수 동사

단수 동사에는 is/was, has 등이 있고, 일반 동사는 현재 시제일 경우에 동사 뒤에 -(e)s를 붙입니다.
복수 동사에는 are/were, have 등이 있고, 일반 동사일 경우에는 동사원형을 씁니다.

Ms. Smith takes the bus every day. Smith 씨는 매일 버스를 탄다.
　주어 (단수)　동사 (단수)

There are many people in the auditorium. 강당에 많은 사람들이 있다.
　　동사(복수)　　주어(복수)

② 주어 + (수식어구) + 동사

주어와 동사 사이에 수식어구가 있을 때, 그 수식어구를 생략하면 주어와 동사를 쉽게 찾을 수 있습니다.

Linda, together with her family, goes to church every Sunday.
주어 (단수)　　　　　　　　　동사 (단수)
Linda와 그녀의 가족은 매주 일요일 교회에 간다.

③ 구나 절이 주어 자리에 올 때 : 단수 취급

구나 절이 주어 자리에 오면 동사 자리에는 단수 동사를 씁니다.

Skiing in this area is very dangerous. 이 지역에서 스키 타는 것은 매우 위험하다.
　주어 (명사구)　　　동사 (단수)

What I want to know is if Ted will come here tonight.
　주어 (명사절)　　동사 (단수)
내가 알고 싶은 것은 Ted가 오늘밤 여기에 오는지의 여부이다.

④ 유도부사 there

'~가 있다'는 뜻으로 뒤의 명사의 수에 맞추어 be 동사의 수를 정합니다.

There + 동사(be동사, remain, exist, live) + 명사
　　　　　　　　　　　　　　　　　　　　　주어

There are twenty offices on this floor. 이 층에는 20개의 사무실이 있다.
　　be동사　　주어

GRAMMAR PRACTICE

A 괄호 안에 알맞은 것을 고르시오.

1. Mark (go, goes) swimming every morning.

2. All the books on the desk (is, are) mine.

3. Swimming in this river (was, were) funny.

4. Tom and Jenny (is, are) good friends.

5. James (attend, attends) the meeting every month.

6. What the teacher said (was, were) absolutely true.

7. When you meet people, being polite (is, are) important.

8. The president, together with his employees, (is, are) dining here tonight.

9. There (is, are) many books on the shelves.

10. Running every day (help, helps) you keep healthy

B 어법상 틀린 문장은 바르게 고치고, 옳은 문장에는 표시 (O) 하세요

1. There is a lot of people in the square.

2. The clerks in this store works overtime every Monday.

3. What the president said were true.

4. Eating breakfast every day are good for your health.

5. Why Tom left Jenny is still unknown.

VOCA polite 예의바른 president 사장 employee 직원 dine 식사하다 shelf 선반 - (pl.) shelves healthy 건강한
square 광장 clerk 점수 work overtime 초과 근무를 하다 president 사장 health 건강
leave 떠나다 - left - left still 여전히 unknown 알려지지 않은

GRAMMAR POINT

⑤ 그 외에 주어를 단수 취급하는 경우

(1) 시간, 거리, 금액, 무게

Thirty kilometers is too far to walk. 30km는 걷기에는 너무 멀다.

(2) one/each of the 복수명사 + 단수동사

One of the students is looking at the window. 학생 중의 한명이 창문을 바라보고 있다.

(3) -s로 끝나는 학문명 국가명, 병명

mathematics(수학), economics(경제학), physics (물리학), diabetes(당뇨병), the Philippines (필리핀), the United States (미국)

⑥ The number of vs. A number of

The number of ~는 항상 단수 취급하기 때문에 이 표현이 주어로 오면 동사는 단수가 되어야 하고, A number of ~는 복수 명사를 수식하는 수식어일 뿐 주어는 of 뒤의 복수 명사이므로 동사는 복수형이 되어야 합니다.

> **The number of** + 복수 명사 → 단수 동사: ~의 수
>   주어
>
> **A number of** + 복수 명사 → 복수 동사: 많은 ~
>   주어

The number of our employees **is** 1000. 우리 직원들의 수는 1000명이다.
   주어   단수 동사

A number of our employees **were** interested in the new policy.
            주어   복수 동사

우리 직원들 중에서 많은 사람들이 새 정책에 관심이 있었다.

⑦ 수량과 수일치

many(a) few, several a number of, a variety of	가산명사 (복수)	복수 동사
each, every, another	가산명사 (단수)	단수 동사
much, (a) little a large/small amount of a great deal of	불가산명사	단수 동사
some, any, all, most a lot of = lots of, plenty of	가산 명사(복수)	복수 동사
	불가산 명사	단수 동사

GRAMMAR PRACTICE

A 괄호 안에 알맞은 것을 고르시오.

1. The number of people (is, are) unexpected.

2. A number of car drivers (is, are) tired at night.

3. (All, Each) of the students attend the workshop every month.

4. Economics (is, are) difficult to study.

5. One of my friends (live, lives) in California.

6. Each of the designers (is, are) planning to attend the seminar.

7. Most of the classrooms (is, are) under construction.

8. Twenty years (is, are) such a long time.

9. Some of the books (was, were) written in the 1900s.

10. All the supervisors (is, are) required to submit reports every day.

B 괄호 안에 알맞은 것을 고르세요.

1. Linda did not eat (many, much, a few) meat.

2. They need (a lot of, many, a number of) money.

3. The students want to buy (some, each, a little) books.

4. There is (a few, a little, several) juice left in the glass.

5. I want to ask you (much, several, another) questions.

VOCA tired 피곤한　economics 경제학　difficult 어려운　under construction 공사 중인
write - wrote - written 쓰다　require ~을 요구하다　submit 제출하다　meat 고기　leave 남다 - left - left

GRAMMAR IN SENTENCE

▶ 의미 단위로 문장을 끊어 읽고, 해석하세요

1. What the teacher said was absolutely true.

2. When you meet people, being polite is important.

3. The president, together with his employees, is dining here tonight.

4. There are many books on the shelves.

5. Running every day helps you keep healthy.

6. Each of the designers is planning to attend the seminar.

7. There is a little juice left in the glass.

8. Twenty years is such a long time.

9. Some of the books were written in the 1900s.

10. All the supervisors are required to submit reports every day.

 **Outro**

수일치

문장에서 주어와 동사는 수를 일치시켜야 합니다. 기본적으로 주어가 단수이면 동사도 단수, 주어가 복수이면 동사도 복수가 와야 합니다.

be 동사의 수일치

수	주어	현재	과거	현재완료	미래
한 명, 하나	I	am	was	have been	will be
	You	are	were		
	He	is	was	has been	
	She				
	It				
두 명, 둘 이상	We	are	were	have been	
	You				
	They				

일반 동사의 수일치

수	주어	현재	과거	현재완료	미래
한 명, 하나	I	동사원형	동사원형 + ed / 또는 과거형 (불규칙 동사)	have p.p.	will 동사원형
	You				
	He	동사원형 + -s(-es)		has p.p	
	She				
	It				
두 명, 둘 이상	We	동사원형		have p.p	
	You				
	They				

UNIT 18 태

GRAMMAR POINT

① 수동태의 기본 형태

> 능동태의 동사는 수동태의 be +p.p. (과거분사)
> 능동태의 목적어는 수동태의 주어가 된다.

현재	능동	She writes a letter every day.
	수동	A letter **is written** every day (by her).
미래	능동	She will write a letter tomorrow.
	수동	A letter **will be written** tomorrow (by her).
과거	능동	She wrote a letter yesterday.
	수동	A letter **was written** yesterday (by her).
현재완료	능동	She has written a letter since last month.
	수동	A letter **has been written** since last month (by her).
미래완료	능동	She will have written a letter by 8:00 in the evening.
	수동	A letter **will have been written** by 8:00 in the evening (by her).
과거완료	능동	She had written a letter when I arrived at home.
	수동	A letter **had been written** when I arrived at home (by her).
현재진행	능동	She is writing a letter now.
	수동	A letter **is being written** now (by her).
과거진행	능동	She was writing a letter when I called her yesterday.
	수동	A letter **was being written** when I called her yesterday (by her).

② 다양한 형태의 수동형

수동태 뒤에는 목적어가 오지 않는 것이 일반적입니다. 그러나 by 이외의 전치사를 쓰는 관용적인 수동태 구문과 수동태 뒤에도 명사가 오는 4형식과 5형식 동사들도 확인해야 합니다.

(1) 수동태 뒤에 명사가 올 수 있는 경우

① 4형식 동사

'~에게 ~을 주다'라는 의미를 가진 수여동사인 give, send, show, lend, offer, award, grant 등은 4형식으로 쓸 수 있습니다. 이 때 수동태로 만들면, 수동태 뒤에 능동태의 직접 목적어였던 명사가 올 수 있습니다.

수여동사의 3형식

(능동) I sent a letter to my parents. → (수동) A letter was sent to my parents.
나는 부모님께 편지를 보냈다. 부모님께서는 편지 한통을 받으셨다.

수여동사의 4형식

(능동) I sent my parents a letter. → (수동) My parents were sent a letter (by me).
나는 부모님께 편지를 보냈다. 직접 목적어는 그대로 위치합니다.
 부모님께서는 편지 한통을 받으셨다.

GRAMMAR PRACTICE

A 빈칸을 채워 다음 문장을 수동태로 바꾸어 쓰시오.

1. 현재   능동   He takes a picture every day.
         수동   A picture _____.

2. 미래   능동   He will take a picture tomorrow.
         수동   A picture _____.

3. 과거   능동   He took a picture yesterday.
         수동   A picture _____.

4. 현재완료   능동   She has taken these pictures since yesterday.
         수동   These pictures _____.

5. 미래완료   능동   She will have taken these pictures by tomorrow.
         수동   These pictures _____.

6. 과거완료   능동   She had taken these pictures when I called her.
         수동   These pictures _____.

7. 현재진행   능동   He is taking some pictures now.
         수동   Some pictures _____.

8. 과거진행   능동   She was taking some pictures when I arrived there.
         수동   Some pictures _____.

B 다음 문장을 수동형으로 바꾸세요.

1. They are painting the wall.
   → _____

2. They will clean the room tomorrow.
   → _____

3. They built the old house in 1960.
   → _____

4. Many people love the movie.
   → _____

5. The company gave all the employees computers.
   → _____
   → _____

VOCA take a picture 사진을 찍다(take – took – taken)   paint 페인트칠하다   clean 청소하다   build – built – built 짓다

GRAMMAR POINT

② 5형식 동사

make, find, consider, think, deem, call, appoint, elect 등은 수동태 뒤에 목적 보어인 명사가 올 수 있습니다.

(능동) Employees **considered** the president a great leader.
직원들은 그 사장님이 훌륭한 지도자라고 여겼다.

(수동) The president **was considered** a great leader by employees.
　　　　　　　　　　　　　　　　명사나 형용사 형태의 목적보어는 그대로 위치합니다.
그 사장은 직원들에 의해 훌륭한 지도자라고 여겨졌다.

③ 감정동사의 능동태, 수동태 구별

감정을 나타내는 타동사는 주어가 감정을 느끼는 주체가 되면 수동태를, 주어가 감정의 원인이면 능동태를 씁니다.

☑ 감정동사의 수동태 관용표현

be interested in ~에 관심이[흥미가] 있다	be pleased with ~에 기쁘다
be tired of ~에 싫증나다	be surprised at ~에 놀라다
be amazed at ~에 놀라다	be frightened at ~에 두려움을 느끼다, 깜짝 놀라다
be disappointed at ~에 실망하다	be satisfied with ~에 만족하다

People **were interested in** the game. (주어가 감정을 느끼는 주체)
사람들은 게임에 흥미가 있었다.

The game **was interesting**. (주어가 감정의 원인)
게임은 흥미진진하다.

④ by 이외의 전치사를 쓰는 관용적 표현

be covered with ~로 덮여있다	be crowded with ~로 붐비다
be located in(on) ~에 위치해 있다	be filled with ~로 채워져 있다.

The mountain **is covered with** snow. 그 산은 눈으로 덮여 있다.

GRAMMAR PRACTICE

A 다음 문장을 수동형으로 바꾸세요.

1. People call these houses igloos.
   → _____.

2. They will appoint Mr. Lee the president tomorrow.
   → _____.

3. His attitude made the woman angry.
   → _____.

4. The movie made the actor popular.
   → _____.

5. You should keep your passwords secret.
   → _____.

B 괄호 안에 알맞은 것을 고르시오.

1. Tim (elect, was elected) chairperson.
2. The history of the museum is (amazing, amazed)
3. The test result made our team (satisfactory, satisfied).
4. People were (surprising, surprised) at the news.
5. I'm (interesting, interested) in the managerial position.

C 어법상 틀린 문장은 바르게 고치고, 옳은 문장에는 표시 (O) 하세요.

1. Ted was called a genius by people.
2. Pets do not allow in this restaurant.
3. The bottles are filled by water.
4. The conference held every month.
5. The town is crowded by many tourists.

VOCA igloo 이글루   attitude 태도   actor 배우   popular 인기 있는   password 암호   secret 비밀의   chairperson 의장   history 역사   managerial position 관리직   genius 천재   pet 애완동물   allow 허락하다   bottle 병   conference 회담   tourist 관광객

GRAMMAR IN SENTENCE

▶ 의미 단위로 문장을 끊어 읽고, 해석하세요.

1. The old house was built in 1960.

2. The movie is loved by many people.

3. The company gave all the employees computers.

4. All the employees were given computers by the company.

5. Computers were given to all the employees by the company.

6. His attitude made the woman angry.

7. The woman was made angry by his attitude.

8. You should keep your passwords secret.

9. Your passwords should be kept secret by you.

10. Pets are not allowed in this restaurant.

 **Outro**

태

일반적으로 주어가 동작을 하는 주체이면 능동태,
주어가 동작의 대상이 되면 수동태를 씁니다.

능동태	주어 + **타동사** + **목적어**
	a/the/소유격 + (형용사) + 명사
	this/that + (형용사) + 명사
	명사s
	형용사 + 명사

수동태	주어 + **be동사 + p.p.** + 전치사/부사

능동태   주어 + 타동사 + 목적어

수동태   주어 + be 동사 + p.p. + 전치사 + 목적어

(능동태) They <u>accepted the proposal</u>. 그들은 그 제안을 받아들였다.
        타동사   목적어(the + 명사)

(수동태) The proposal <u>was accepted</u> <u>(by</u> them). 그 제안은 그들에 의해 받아들여졌다.
        be + p.p.   전치사

ACTUAL TEST 6

A 다음 빈칸에 들어갈 수 있는 것을 고르세요.

1. All application forms should --------- by email by the end of this month.
   (A) send
   (B) are sending
   (C) be sent
   (D) have sent

2. The Maintenance Department ----------- with new computers last month.
   (A) was equipped
   (B) equipped
   (C) equips
   (D) was equipping

3. Because the new system ---------- last month, we can work effectively.
   (A) installed
   (B) was installed
   (C) is installed
   (D) has been installed

4. The floor plan -------- a gorgeous fireplace as the focal point of the living room.
   (A) featuring
   (B) features
   (C) is featured
   (D) feature

5. The design specifications for the convention center ------- very strict.
   (A) were
   (B) was
   (C) is
   (D) has been

6. The number of freelance writers --------- remarkably in recent years.
   (A) have increased
   (B) increasing
   (C) are increased
   (D) has increased

7. Almost all of the people in this area ------- their electricity from hydoelectric power plants.
   (A) is gotten
   (B) has gotten
   (C) gets
   (D) get

8. Royal, Inc. ------- a wide range of environmentally friendly products in Iowa.
   (A) offers
   (B) offer
   (C) is offered
   (D) offering

9. The freshness of the bread served at this restaurant -------- a great deal depending upon the time.
   (A) vary
   (B) varies
   (C) varying
   (D) to vary

10. All employees ------- a coffee break between 3:30 and 4:00 p.m every working day.
    (A) take
    (B) took
    (C) takes
    (C) was taken

11. According to the news, the rate of inflation ------- by 7.5 percent last quarter.
    (A) rises
    (B) rose
    (C) has risen
    (D) rise

12. This year, the gourmet restaurant ------- over 100,000 new customers, which is the highest number record in its history.
    (A) was attracted
    (B) has attracted
    (C) had attracted
    (D) has been attracted

B 다음 빈칸에 들어갈 수 있는 것을 고르세요.

Questions 13-18 refer to the following guarantee.

GUARANTEE

Magic Cooker **13** ---------- against defective material or workmanship. The two-year guarantee entitles owners to receive replacements. Damage due to accidents or abuse by the user **14** ---------- . It doesn't cover normal wear over the years. If Magic Cooker **15** ---------- commercially, the warranty **16** ---------- to six months. After examination, if parts are considered **17** ---------- , delivery **18** ---------- .

---

13 (A) guarantee
(B) is guaranteed
(C) guaranteed
(D) has guaranteed

14 (A) are not covered
(B) did not cover
(C) does not cover
(D) is not covered

15 (A) is used
(B) are used
(C) uses
(D) use

16 (A) limits
(B) are limited
(C) is limited
(D) had been limited

17 (A) defect
(B) defected
(C) defective
(D) defection

18 (A) will repay
(B) repaid
(C) was repaid
(D) will be repaid

MINI TEST 3

A 다음 빈칸에 들어갈 수 있는 것을 고르세요.

1. The company have spent --------- time and money developing new products.
   (A) consider
   (B) considered
   (C) considerable
   (D) consideration

2. The directors --------- arguing among themselves about the new proposal yesterday.
   (A) was
   (B) were
   (C) is
   (C) are

3. No --------- would be made without a proper assessment of the return.
   (A) investment
   (B) invest
   (C) investing
   (D) invested

4. You should submit --------- about the sales figures by tomorrow morning.
   (A) reporting
   (B) reported
   (C) the report
   (D) report

5. The flight was delayed by the late arrival of some --------- and was finally cleared for takeoff at 5:15 p.m.
   (A) luggages
   (B) luggage
   (C) bag
   (D) baggages

6. Real estate agencies have more information about available housing than you could have ---------.
   (A) itself
   (B) himself
   (C) yourself
   (D) myself

7. FTD will conduct an --------- search in order to find a manager to be in charge of the Accounting Department.
   (A) extensive
   (B) extension
   (C) extend
   (D) extensively

8. The Department of Health has a --------- website providing a good deal of information.
   (A) use
   (B) usably
   (C) useful
   (D) using

9. --------- international pressure , the government decided not to follow the agreements.
   (A) According
   (B) Whenever
   (C) Unless
   (D) In spite of

10. --------- new employees are encouraged to get a complete physical examination.
    (A) All
    (B) Little
    (C) Less
    (D) Much

11. World Architecture decided to build the most --------- responsible office building in the country.
    (A) environmental
    (B) environment
    (C) environmentally
    (D) environmentalist

12. Openings are available for --------- all of the courses offered on the company webpage.
    (A) nearly
    (B) nearer
    (C) nearest
    (D) nearing

13 Sales of luxury goods have risen recently --------- the recession.
(A) According
(B) Whenever
(C) Unless
(D) In spite of

14 The offices are closed --------- the inclement weather and a corporation-wide strike.
(A) due to
(B) while
(C) since
(D) as if

15 Everyone in the office --------- overtime to meet the deadline today.
(A) has worked
(B) have worked
(C) has been worked
(D) have been worked

16 Every applicant will --------- a written notification with the results of their applications.
(A) receive
(B) receives
(C) be received
(D) received

17 The entire staff in the marketing division needs to --------- the annual conference next month.
(A) enroll
(B) attend
(C) participate
(D) comply

18 The number of Koreans traveling overseas --------- twenty percent over last year.
(A) has increased
(B) have increased
(C) increase
(D) are increased

19 Flight attendants should confirm and announce the estimated time of --------- in Chicago.
(A) arrival
(B) arriving
(C) arrive
(D) arrived

20 Effective next year, a subway pass --------- you a 30% discount off the regular city subway fare.
(A) give
(B) will give
(C) gives
(D) gave

21 As the new air filtration system --------- last month, we can work effectively.
(A) installed
(B) was installed
(C) has installed
(D) installs

22 Every candidate's application should --------- by email by the end of next month after the candidates fill in the blanks.
(A) send
(B) be sent
(C) sent
(D) be sending

23 All of the employees --------- a coffee break between 3:30 p.m and 4:00 p.m. every working day.
(A) take
(B) took
(C) taken
(D) had taken

24 According to the news, the rate of inflation --------- by 7.5 percent last quarter.
(A) rises
(B) rose
(C) risen
(D) wil rise

25 The company --------- bonuses to its employees at the end of each year.
(A) gave
(B) is given
(C) give
(D) will give

Mini Test 3 **151**

MINI TEST 3

B 다음 빈칸에 들어갈 수 있는 것을 고르세요.

Questions 26-31 refer to the following advertisement.

Are you looking for the perfect place to live ?

Are you interested in a **26** ---------- and quiet house? This apartment is a must-see. It **27** ---------- in a suburban area of Kingston Mountain and features three large bedrooms, each with its own full bathroom. The **28** ---------- kitchen includes all essential appliances. Included in the unit **29** ---------- a washing machine and a dryer for your laundry needs. The combined **30** ---------- living room and dining room is a must-see. This condo has a beautiful view of Kingston Mountain. If you **31** ---------- a perfect and quiet living space, this is what you should get.

---

26 (A) privacy
 (B) private
 (C) privately
 (D) privates

27 (A) locates
 (B) located
 (C) will locate
 (D) is located

28 (A) convenient
 (B) convenience
 (C) convene
 (D) conveniently

29 (A) is
 (B) are
 (C) has
 (D) have

30 (A) probable
 (B) potential
 (C) foreseeable
 (D) spacious

31 (A) needs
 (B) are needed
 (C) need
 (D) will need

Questions 32-37 refer to the following email.

To : Sandra Stones

From : Mary Johns

Subject : The job offer

I'm writing **32** ---------- you email regarding the job offer you got from Sigma Inc. It seems that they want you to work as their new accounting **33** ---------- as soon as possible. However, you are having a hard time **34** ---------- on this matter, so you'd like some **35** ---------- from me. I suggest that you move to the new company since Sigma Inc. is offering you a great **36** ----------. Also, I think you should tell this to your boss as soon as possible so that he will have **37** ---------- time to find some to replace you. This would be a good chance for your future. Good luck!

---

32 (A) return
(B) returning
(C) to return
(D) returned

33 (A) manage
(B) manager
(C) managing
(D) managed

34 (A) decide
(B) to decide
(C) decided
(D) deciding

35 (A) advice
(B) advise
(C) advisor
(D) advices

36 (A) dealer
(B) dealing
(C) deals
(D) deal

37 (A) so
(B) too
(C) enough
(D) very

잉글리쉬앤 그래머 START

기본편

 코스

Unit 19 부정사
Unit 20 동명사
Unit 21 분사

UNIT 19 부정사

GRAMMAR POINT

① to 부정사의 개념과 역할

to부정사는 동사 앞에 to를 붙여서 '~는 것', '~할', '~하기 위하여' 등의 의미를 나타내며, 문장 내에서 명사, 형용사, 부사의 역할을 할 수가 있습니다.

(1) 명사적 역할

명사는 문장에서 주어, 목적어, 보어로 쓰입니다. 그러므로 명사적 역할을 하는 to 부정사도 문장에서 주어, 목적어, 보어로 쓰일 수 있습니다.

① 주어 역할 (~하는 것은)

to 부정사가 주어자리에 올 수도 있지만, 대부분 가짜주어 it을 씁니다. 주어 자리에 to 부정사가 오면, 보통 주어 자리에 it을 쓰고 to 부정사는 뒤로 보냅니다.

> **To be honest** is important. 정직한 것은 중요합니다.
> = **It** is important **to be honest**.
> 가짜주어   진짜주어

② 목적어 역할 : (~하는 것을) to부정사를 목적어로 취하는 동사들이 있으며, 미래의 할 일을 나타내는 경우가 많습니다.

plan to V	~할 계획이다.	I **plan to study** abroad. 나는 유학 갈 계획이다.
want to V hope to V	~ 하기를 원한다.	I **want to go** on a trip. 나는 여행가기를 원한다.
decide to V	~ 하기로 결정하다	I **decided to tell** the truth. 나는 진실을 말하기로 결정했다,
agree to V	~하는 것에 동의하다.	I **agreed to go** together. 나는 함께 가는 것에 동의했다.

③ 주격 보어 역할 : to 부정사가 주격보어 자리에 올 수 있습니다.

주로 be 동사, seem 등의 2형식 자동사 뒤에 보어가 오는 자리에 to 부정사를 써서, '~하는 것이다.'라는 의미를 나타냅니다.

be to V	~하는 것이다.	My dream **is to become** a singer. 나의 꿈은 가수가 되는 것이다.
seem to V	~처럼 보인다.	Ann **seems to be** sick. Ann이 아파보인다.

④ 목적격 보어 역할 : to 부정사가 목적격 보어 자리에 올 수 있습니다.
<동사 + 목적어 + to부정사> 형태로 목적어로 하여금 ~하게 하다'라는 의미를 갖고 있습니다.

ask A **to** do **tell** A **to** do	A에게 ~하라고 요청하다 A에게 ~하라고 말하다	She **asked** me **to clean** the room. 그녀는 나에게 방을 청소하고 요청했다.
advise A **to** do **allow** A **to** do	A에게 ~하라고 조언하다 A에게~하는 것을 허락하다	He **advised** me **to eat** vegetables. 그는 나에게 야채를 먹으라고 조언했다.

GRAMMAR PRACTICE

A 주어진 동사를 이용하여 <보기>처럼 It ~ to 부정사 구문으로 완성하세요.

보기) good / see : It is good **to see** you again.
　　　　　　　　　　당신을 다시 만나서 기쁘다.

1. hard / fix : It is _____ the broken machine.
2. difficult / learn : It is not _____ English.
3. fun / make : It is _____ cookies.
4. dangerous / ski : It's _____ here.
5. hard / understand : It's _____ my sister.

B 주어진 표현과 to 부정사를 함께 사용하여 문장을 완성하세요.

| A. want, buy　B. decide, stay　C. plan, study　D. plan, save　E. hope, see　F. agree, sell |

보기) F : I <u>agree to sell</u> the new dish.

1. It's raining, so did you _____ at home?
2. I _____ English in the United States.
3. The children _____ their parents soon.
4. My car is too old, so I _____ a new one.
5. We _____ money to buy a house.

C 연결하여 문장을 완성하세요.

1. I have gained weight. My plan is　　　　　　　A. to go there
2. My room was dirty. My mom advised me　　　 B. to get out
3. It's cold. I asked my sister　　　　　　　　　C. to close the window
4. Lisa was angry with John. She told him　　　 D. to clean the room
5. I wanted to travel to Italy. My parents allowed me　E. to lose weight

VOCA) hard 어려운　fix 고치다　difficult 어려운　dangerous 위험한　understand 이해하다　save 절약하다
　　　gain weight 살이 찌다, 몸무게가 늘다　get out 나가다　dirty 더러운　lose weight 살이 빠지다

GRAMMAR POINT

(2) 형용사적 역할
명사 뒤에 to 부정사를 써서 명사를 수식할 수 있습니다.

형용사 역할	something을 수식하는 역할	I need **something to drink**. 나는 마실 것이 필요하다.
	time 을 수식하는 역할	I don't have **time to do my homework**. 나는 숙제를 할 시간이 없다.
	homework를 수식하는 역할	I have lots of **homework to do**. 나는 해야 할 숙제가 많다.

(3) 부사적 역할
to 부정사가 부사로서 형용사를 꾸며주거나, 동사의 목적을 나타내는 역할을 할 수 있습니다.

부사역할		예문
형용사 수식	형용사 glad 수식하는 역할	I am **glad to see you**. 너를 만나서 기쁘다.
동사 수식	동사 work 수식하는 역할	He **works** hard **to study abroad**. 유학가기 위해서 열심히 일한다

☑ **in order to 동사원형 = so as to 동사원형**

목적 (~하기 위하여)이나 이유를 나타내며 문장 맨 앞이나 뒤에 위치합니다.

I got up early (in order) **to catch the train**.
= (In order) **To catch the train**, I got up early.
나는 기차를 타기 위하여 일찍 일어났다.

② 의문사 + to 동사원형

의문사 뒤에 to 부정사를 써서, 명사 자리에 쓰입니다.

what to V	무엇을 V 해야 할지	I don't know + What should I do? = I don't know **what to do**. (목적어) 나는 무엇을 해야 할지 모르겠다.
when to V	언제 V해야 할지	I wonder + When should I go there? I wonder **when to go there**. (목적어) 언제 그곳에 가는지 궁금하다
how to V	어떻게 V 해야 할지	I learned + How should I drive? I learned **how to drive**. (목적어) 나는 운전하는 방법을 배웠다

GRAMMAR PRACTICE

A 주어진 동사와 to 부정사를 함께 사용하여 문장을 완성하세요.

| eat | drink | help | talk | go |

1. I've just finished my work. I have time _____ with you.
2. I have few friends, so I have no one _____ me.
3. I'm thirsty. I need something _____.
4. He's hungry. He wants something _____.
5. I have plans _____ to London.

B 다음 두 문장을 to 부정사를 이용하여 만드세요.

1. Olivia went to the store. She wanted to buy new pants.
   → _____
2. Tom practices all day. He wants to win at the Olympics.
   → _____
3. My family went to the restaurant. We wanted to eat some delicious food.
   → _____
4. I go to the library I want to read books.
   → _____
5. I ran. I want to catch the bus.
   → _____

C 다음 두 문장을 "의문사 to 부정사"구문을 이용하여 한 문장으로 만드세요.

1. I asked him. + Where should I go?
   → _____
2. I don't know. + What should I do?
   → _____
3. Please tell me. + Where should I put these things?
   → _____
4. I can't decide. + What should I wear for my birthday party
   → _____
5. I want to learn. + How should I use this machine?
   → _____

VOCA finish 끝내다   thirsty 목마른   hungry 배고픈   pants 바지   practice 연습하다   delicious 맛있는   machine 기계

GRAMMAR IN SENTENCE

▶ 의미 단위로 문장을 끊어 읽고, 해석하세요.

1. It is hard to fix the broken machine.

2. It's hard to understand my sister.

3. The children hope to see their parents soon.

4. My mom advised me to clean the room.

5. I asked my sister to close the window.

6. My parents allowed me to go there.

7. I've just finished my work. I have time to talk with you.

8. Tom practices all day to win at the Olympics.

9. I can't decide what to wear for my birthday party.

10. I want to learn how to use this machine.

 **Outro**

부정사

동사의 원형에 to 만 붙였을 뿐인데 명사, 형용사, 부사의 역할을 다 할 수 있습니다.

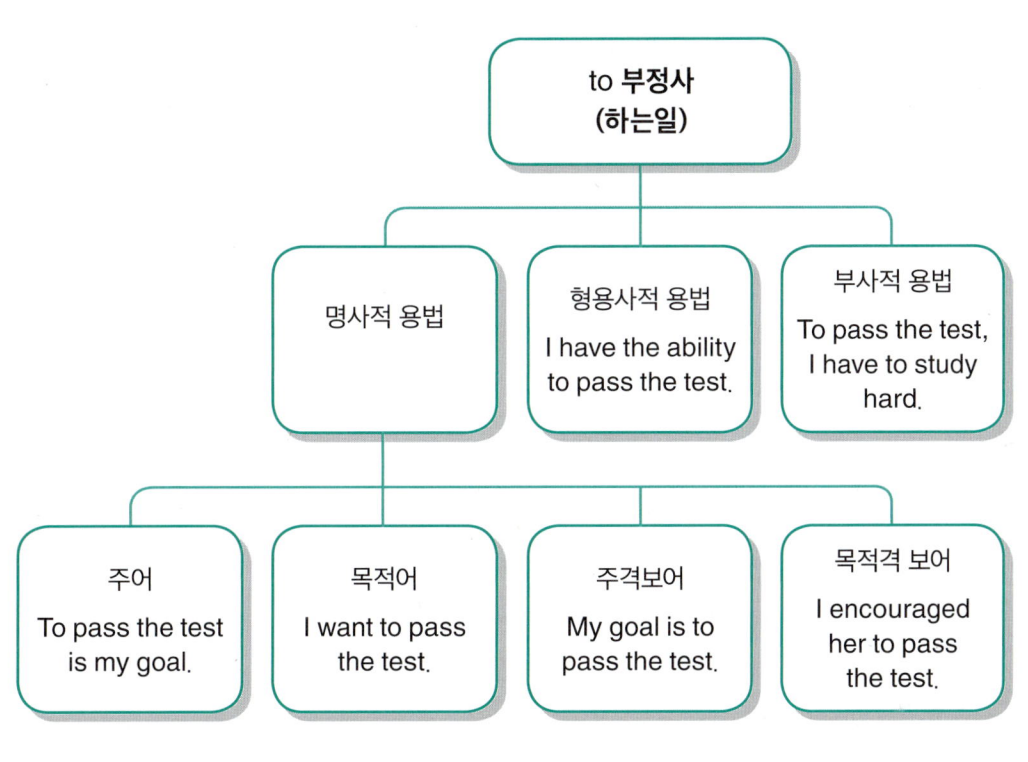

UNIT 20 동명사

GRAMMAR POINT

① 동명사의 역할

'동사원형 + ~ing' 형태로 쓰이는 동명사는 문장에서 주어, 목적어, 보어로 쓰여 명사역할을 합니다.

역할	의미	예문
주어	~하는 것은	**Studying** English is important. 영어를 공부하는 것은 중요하다.
목적어	~것을	Tom likes **swimming**. Tom은 수영하는 것을 좋아한다.
보어	~하는 것이다.	My hobby is **taking** pictures. 나의 취미는 사진을 찍는 것이다.

② 동명사 vs to 부정사

(1) 동명사를 목적어로 취하는 동사

정지형	**stop** 멈추다 **quit** 그만두다 **finish** 마치다 **give up** 포기하다 **discontinue** 중단하다
연기형	**delay** 미루다 **put off** 연기하다 **postpone** 연기하다
고민, 추천형	**consider** 고려하다 **recommend** 추천하다 **suggest** 제안하다
부정형	**mind** 꺼리다 **deny** 부인하다 **avoid** 피하다 **escape** 달아나다 **resist** 저항하다
기타	**enjoy** 즐기다 **anticipate** 학수고대하다

Mike **finished** <u>**reading**</u> the report. Mike는 그 소설을 읽는 것을 마쳤다.

(3) to 부정사를 목적어로 취하는 동사

원하다	**want to** 원하다 **wish to** 바라다 **hope to** 희망하다 **expect to** 예상하다
(앞날을) 계획하고 제안하고 약속하다	**plan to** 계획하다 **promise to** 약속하다 **decide to** 결정하다 **offer to** 제공하다 **propose to** 제안하다 **agree to** 동의하다
~을 거절하다 ~하지 못하다	**refuse to** 거절하다 **fail to** 실패하다

Jenny **wants** <u>**to lose**</u> her weight. 나는 몸무게를 줄이기를 원한다.

GRAMMAR PRACTICE

A 주어진 동사를 이용하여 <보기>처럼 동명사 구문으로 완성하세요.

　보기　see : **Seeing** is believing.

1. fix : _____ the broken machine is hard.

2. learn : _____ English is not difficult.

3. make / fun : _____ cookies is _____.

4. ski / dangerous : _____ here is _____.

5. hard / understand : _____ my sister is not _____.

B ( ) 안에서 알맞은 것을 고르세요.

1. Mike (wanted, avoided) talking about it.

2. Our team failed (to go, going) to the final.

3. I finished (to read, reading) a novel.

4. My sister (refused, denied) to lend me her car.

5. John gave up (to jog, jogging) every morning.

6. Tom suggested (to master, mastering) a foreign language.

7. They promised (to visit, visiting) their hometown.

8. He quit (to smoke, smoking) last month.

9. He refused (to join, joining) their party.

10. Kathy enjoys (to listen, listening) to music.

VOCA　broken 망가진, 고장 난　machine 기계　difficult 어려운　dangerous 위험한　final 결승　novel 소설
　　　foreign 외국의　language 언어　hometown 고향

◎ GRAMMAR POINT

(2) 동명사와 to 부정사를 모두 목적어로 취하는 타동사

like prefer	좋아하다 더 좋아하다	I like swimming. = I like to swim. 나는 수영하는 것을 좋아한다.
begin start	시작하다 출발하다	She started crying. = She started to cry. 그녀는 울기 시작했다.
hate love	싫어하다 사랑하다	I love dancing = I love to dance. 나는 춤을 추는 것을 좋아한다.
continue	계속하다	They continued to talk. = They continued talking. 그들은 계속해서 이야기를 했다.

③ 명사 vs 동명사

(1) 동명사는 목적어나 보어를 취할 수 있습니다.

I received a letter of **acceptance.** 나는 수락의 편지를 받았다.

He sent a letter of **accepting** my offer. 그는 나의 제안을 받아드리는 편지를 보냈다.

(2) 동명사 앞에는 관사가 올 수 없습니다.

They are interested in the **development** of natural resources.
그들은 천연자원의 개발에 관심이 있다.

They are interested in **developing** natural resources.
그들은 천연자원을 개발하는 것에 관심이 있다.

④ 명사나 동명사를 목적어로 취하는 전치사

📝 to + 명사/ -ing형

be accustomed to -ing ~에 익숙하다	be used to -ing ~에 익숙하다
be devoted to -ing ~에 몰두하다	be committed to -ing ~에 헌신하다
be dedicated to -ing ~에 전념하다	look forward to -ing ~을 기대하다
when it comes to -ing ~에 관해서는	as opposed to -ing ~에 반대해서, ~이 아니라
object to -ing ~에 반대하다	be subject to -ing ~될 수 있는

We **are accustomed to jogging** every day. 우리는 매일 조깅하는 것에 익숙하다.

GRAMMAR PRACTICE

A 밑줄 친 부분을 동명사로 고쳐서 이용하여 같은 의미로 바꾸세요.

1. I will continue **to study** English. = I will continue _____ English.
2. Lisa likes **to watch** movies. = Lisa likes _____ movies.
3. Kent hates **to speak** loudly. = Kent hates _____ loudly.
4. Tomas loves **to play** basketball. = Tomas loves _____ basketball.
5. They will continue **to create** new products.
   = They will continue _____ new products.

B 괄호 안에 알맞은 것을 고르시오.

1. I always use this brush for (wash, washing) the dishes.
2. She has to wear glasses for (reading, read).
3. Laura wanted (getting, to get) a rest.
4. We are looking forward to (see, seeing) you soon.
5. Tom is skilled at (use, using) all the equipment.

C 어법상 틀린 문장은 바르게 고치고, 옳은 문장에는 표시 (O) 하세요.

1. I am used to jogging every morning.
2. Do you mind to open the window?
3. They are dedicated to preserve natural resources.
4. He is accustomed to work in dangerous environments.
5. They are committed to preventing accidents.

VOCA loudly 크게　create 만들다　product 제품　brush 솔, 브러시　wash the dishes 설거지하다　take a rest 쉬다　equipment 장비　preserve 보존하다　natural resources 천연자원　dangerous 위험한　environment 환경　prevent 예방하다　accident 사고

GRAMMAR IN SENTENCE

▶ 의미 단위로 문장을 끊어 읽고, 해석하세요.

1. Learning English is not difficult.

2. Skiing here is dangerous.

3. Mike avoided talking about it.

4. I always use this brush for washing the dishes.

5. Tom is skilled at using all the equipment.

6. I am used to jogging every morning.

7. Do you mind opening the window?

8. They are dedicated to preserving natural resources.

9. He is accustomed to working in dangerous environments.

10. They are committed to preventing the accident.

 **Outro**

동명사

동사에 ~ing를 붙여 명사로 변한 것이 동명사입니다.
태생을 버리지 못해 동사의 성격(목적어, 보어수반 가능, 부사의 수식도 받을 수 있음)도 가지고 있습니다.

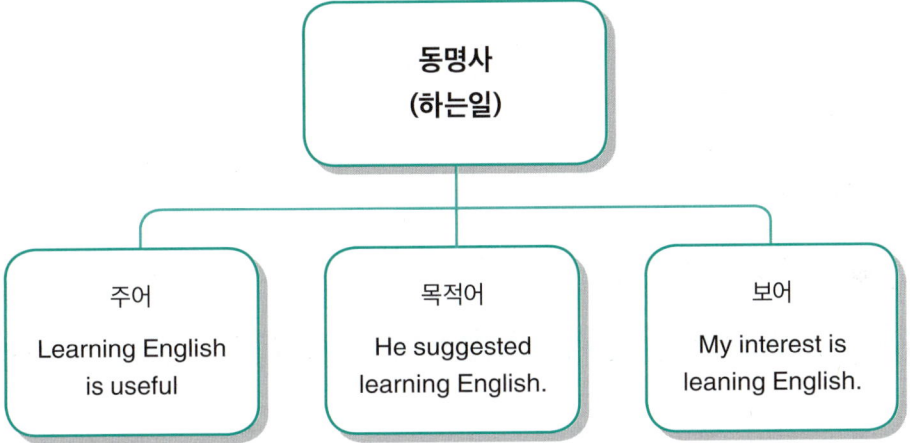

UNIT 21 분사

GRAMMAR POINT

① 분사의 개념과 역할

분사란 동사의 원형에 ing를 붙이거나 동사의 형태를 과거분사인 형태로 변화시켜 문장에서 형용사의 역할을 수행하는 것을 말합니다.

(1) 분사의 개념: 분사에는 현재분사와 과거분사가 있습니다.

	현재분사	과거분사
형태	동사원형 + -ing	p.p. (동사원형 +-ed 또는 불규칙 변화)
해석	'~하고 있는', '~하게 하는'	'~해진(당한)', '~한'
의미	능동 또는 진행의 의미	수동 또는 완료의 의미
예	**boiling** water 끓고 있는 물 **falling** leaves 떨어지고 있는 나뭇잎들	**boiled** water (이미) 끓은 물 **fallen** leaves 떨어진 나뭇잎들

(2) 분사의 역할: 분사는 동사에서 만들어졌지만, 문장에서 단독으로는 본동사로 쓰일 수 없습니다. 분사는 형용사 역할을 하므로 명사의 앞이나 뒤에서 명사를 수식하고, 보어 자리에 쓰일 수 있습니다.

역할	형태	예문
진행형 만들 때	is (was) -ing are(were) -ing	Children **are playing** baseball. 아이들이 야구를 하고 있다.
완료형 만들 때	have (has) p.p	They **have finished** the report. 그들은 보고서를 마쳤다.
수동형 만들 때	be p.p	The bag **was stolen**. 그 가방을 도난당했다.
명사 수식 (앞에서)	-ing/p.p + 명사	Linda found a **broken window**. 린다는 깨어진 창문을 발견했다.
명사 수식 (뒤에서)	명사 +-ing/p.p	The **boy playing baseball** is my son. 야구를 하고 있는 소년이 나의 아들이다.
보어 역할	주어 동사 -ing/ p.p	The vase **was broken**. 화병이 깨어졌다.

② 감정동사의 현재분사 vs 과거분사

excite, bore, tire, impress, satisfy 등과 같이 감정을 나타내는 동사는 분사형으로 자주 쓰입니다. '~한 감정을 느끼게 만드는'의 능동의 뜻일 때는 현재분사를 쓰고 '~한 감정을 느끼는'의 수동의 뜻을 때에는 과거분사를 씁니다.

	감정을 유발하는 현재분사 (-ing)	감정을 나타내는 과거분사 (p.p)
interest	interesting games 재미를 불러일으키는 경기	interested spectators 재미를 느끼는 관객들
excite	an exciting movie 흥미를 불러일으키는 영화	excited people 흥미를 느끼는 사람들
shock	shocking news 충격적인 소식	shocked people 충격을 받은 사람들
bore	a boring class 지루함을 느끼게 하는 수업	bored students 지겨워하는 학생들

GRAMMAR PRACTICE

A 주어진 단어를 현재 분사형으로 고치고, 한글로 해석하세요.

1. Let's listen to the _____ birds. (sing)

2. Look at the _____ leaves. (fall)

3. I saw her _____ face. (smile)

4. History is an _____ subject. (interest)

5. The eggs are _____ now. I like to eat boiled eggs. (boil)

B 주어진 단어를 과거 분사형으로 고치고, 한글로 해석하세요.

1. Kathy found her _____ purse. (steal)

2. Look at the _____ leaves. (fall)

3. I bought some _____ chairs. (paint)

4. These are _____ dishes. (break)

5. I'm not _____ in science. (interest)

C ( ) 안에 알맞은 분사의 형태를 고르세요.

1. The concert was (disappointing, disappointed), so he was (disappointing, disappointed).
2. I saw a (boring, bored) movie yesterday, so I was (boring, bored).
3. The game was (exciting, excited), but the players were (tiring, tired).
4. I heard some (surprising, surprised) news, so everyone was (shocking, shocked).
5. Laura called me late last night and I was (annoying, annoyed). I think Laura is a such an (annoying, annoyed) girl.

VOCA fall - fell - fallen 떨어지다   history 역사   subject 과목   steal - stole - stolen 훔치다
break – broke - broken 깨지다   disappoint 실망시키다   annoy 상가시게 굴다

◎ GRAMMAR POINT

③ 분사 구문 : 주절과 시제가 일치할 때

분사를 이용하여 부사절을 간단히 부사구로 고친 것으로, 그 구가 주절을 부사적으로 수식할 때 이를 분사 구문이라고 하며, 때(시간), 이유·원인, 조건, 양보, 부대 상황(동시 동작, 연속 동작)을 표시하는 접속사의 뜻이 내포되어 있습니다.

● 분사 구문 만드는 요령
① 접속사를 생략합니다.
② 분사 구문으로 변형시킬 종속절의 주어가 주절의 주어와 같을 때는 분사 구문에 따르는 주어를 생략합니다.
③ '능동과 수동'을 따져서 종속절의 동사를 현재 분사나 과거 분사로 바꿉니다.

(1) 시제 일치, 능동

While she was walking along the street, Lisa **met** an old friend.
→ **Walking** along the street, Lisa **met** an old friend. Lisa는 길을 따라 걷다가 옛 친구를 만났다.

(2) 시제 일치, 수동

As she was tried, Lisa **went** to bed early
→ **Tired**, Lisa **went** to bed early. Lisa는 피곤해서 잠자리에 일찍 들었다.

④ 완료 분사 구문 : 주절과 시제가 일치하지 않을 때

<having + p.p.>의 형태를 취하는 완료 분사 구문은 주절의 시제보다 앞선 시제를 나타내게 됩니다.

(1) 한 시제 앞설 때, 능동

After they had finished the report, the entire staff **had** dinner
→ **Having finished** the report, the entire staff **had** dinner.
완료 분사 구문(보고서를 마친 게 저녁식사를 한 것보다 앞선 일임을 나타냄)

모든 직원들은 보고서를 마친 후에 저녁식사를 했다.

(2) 한 시제 앞설 때, 수동

After he had been advised to lose weight by his doctor, he **began** to diet.
→ **Having been advised** to lose weight by his doctor, he **began** to diet.
완료 분사 구문(의사에게 조언을 들은 게 식이요법 시작보다 앞선 일임을 나타냄)

그는 의사로부터 몸무게를 줄여야만 한다는 충고를 받고 난 후에 식이요법을 시작했다.

⑤ 부대 상황을 나타내는 분사 구문

분사 구문을 이용하면 '~하면서, ~한 채'라는 의미의 동시 동작이나 부대 상황을 간단히 표현할 수 있습니다.

Saying "*Good-bye*," he went out of the house. 작별 인사를 하면서 그는 집 밖으로 나갔다.
= He went out of the house as he said "*Good-bye*."

GRAMMAR PRACTICE

A 다음 종속절을 분사구문으로 바꾸세요.

1. As he was sick, Mike went to bed early.
   → _____, Mike went to bed early.
2. When she was left alone, Jenny began to cry.
   → _____, Jenny began to cry.
3. After he had eaten lunch, Tony started to work.
   → _____, Tony started to work.
4. After he had been advised not to be late, he went to work early.
   → _____, he went to work early.
5. I'm taking that class because I'm interested in history.
   → I'm taking that class, _____.

B 다음 밑줄 친 분사구문을 '접속사 주어 동사'로 바꾸세요.

1. Having Finished the project, we had a party.
   → _____, we had a party.
2. Interested in the game, I bought some tickets.
   → _____, I bought some tickets.
3. Applying for the position, you must submit a letter of recommendation.
   → _____, you must submit a letter of recommendation.
4. Unemployed, Mike doesn't have much money.
   → _____, Mike doesn't have much money.
5. Living in the city, I don't know about country life.
   → _____, I don't know about country life.

C 괄호 안에서 알맞은 것을 고르시오.

1. He bought a (using, used) car last month.
2. I heard some (surprising, surprised) news from my cousin yesterday.
3. The baby (sleeping, slept) in the bed is my daughter.
4. (Fall, Fallen) leaves on the ground make me sad all the time.
5. Sprint.com tries to make the customers (satisfying, satisfied).

VOCA a letter of recommendation 추천서   unemployed 실직한   ground 땅

GRAMMAR IN SENTENCE

▶ 의미 단위로 문장을 끊어 읽고, 해석하세요.

1. Having finished the project, we had a party.

2. Interested in the game, I bought some tickets.

3. Applying for the position, you must submit a letter of recommendation.

4. Unemployed, Mike doesn't have much money.

5. Living in the city, I don't know about country life.

6. He bought a used car last month.

7. I heard some surprising news from my cousin yesterday.

8. The baby sleeping in the bed is my daughter.

9. Fallen leaves on the ground make me sad all the time.

10. Sprint.com tries to make its customers satisfied

 **Outro**

분사

동사에 ~ing 또는 -ed(과거분사)가 붙어 형용사화 된 것을 분사라고 합니다.
~ing(현재분사)가 붙으면 능동, 진행의 의미,
-ed(과거분사)가 붙으면 수동, 완료의 의미입니다.

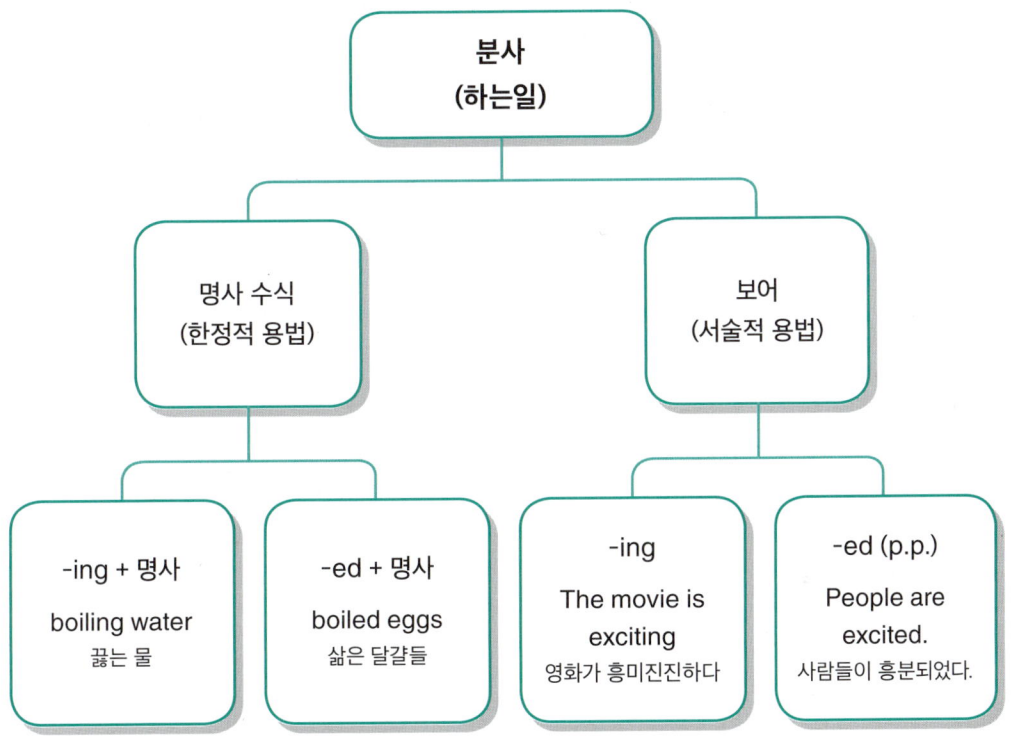

ACTUAL TEST 7

A 다음 빈칸에 들어갈 수 있는 것을 고르세요.

1. The government plans -------- the environmental policies.
   (A) following
   (B) to follow
   (C) followed
   (D) to following

2. All the residents in this area are opposed --------- the building.
   (A) to construct
   (B) to constructing
   (C) constructing
   (D) constructed

3. The supervisor offered --------- some schedules for the team members.
   (A) rearranging
   (B) to rearrange
   (C) to rearranging
   (D) rearranges

4. Staff members are allowed --------- in the lot downstairs starting next week.
   (A) to parking
   (B) park
   (C) to park
   (D) parking

5. The education grant will be used in order ------- the school with new computer. equipment
   (A) to providing
   (B) provide
   (C) providing
   (D) to provide

6. David Russel, the president of the company, has announced that it is going to discontinue ------- its unprofitable pagers.
   (A) make
   (B) making
   (C) to make
   (D) to making

7. According to the booklet, this furniture is on sale for a ------- period of time.
   (A) limiting
   (B) limits
   (C) limited
   (D) limit

8. Most participants were ----------- that the workshop had been canceled without any explanation.
   (A) disappointing
   (B) disappointed
   (C) to disappoint
   (C) to disappointing

9. --------- a walk in the park yesterday, Mr. Conner met a colleague of his.
   (A) Taken
   (B) Taking
   (C) To be taken
   (D) To taking

10. Nowadays, most people prefer small cars because of the -------- cost of gasoline.
    (A) rising
    (B) risen
    (C) rose
    (D) rise

11. People --------- in joining the baseball club should contact Mr. Clarkson.
    (A) interesting
    (B) interest
    (C) interested
    (D) interests

12. Applications -------- after September 10 will not be considered for the program.
    (A) arriving
    (B) arrived
    (C) arrive
    (D) to be arrived

B 다음 빈칸에 들어갈 수 있는 것을 고르세요.

Questions 13-18 refer to the following letter.

Dear Phillip Greg

Hello, My name is Jim Bright. I am one of the people participating in the upcoming job expo **13** --------- in Chicago. Susan Williams and I were supposed **14** --------- the job fair together. We **15** --------- many things for this event starting two months ago. As you had determined, I was going to give an introduction of our company and conduct interviews and with individuals **16** ---------- in our company for potential employment, However,

However, Susan cannot come and **17** --------- me because of the flu. Without her, I cannot do anything. I need your help in **18** --------- a solution to this matter. Thank you.

13 (A) hold
    (B) holding
    (C) held
    (D) was held

14 (A) to take part in
    (B) taking par in
    (C) to be taken part in
    (D) take part in

15 (A) have been prepared
    (B) have been preparing
    (C) are prepared
    (D) prepared

16 (A) interesting
    (B) interest
    (C) interests
    (D) interested

17 (A) assists
    (B) assist
    (C) assisted
    (D) assisting

18 (A) finding
    (B) find
    (C) found
    (D) to find

잉글리쉬앤 그래머 START

기본편

Unit 22 접속사 1
Unit 23 접속사 2
Unit 24 관계사

UNIT 22 접속사 I

◎ GRAMMAR POINT

① 등위접속사 : and, but, or, so, for

등위접속사와 상관접속사는 접속사를 중심으로 앞뒤에 문법적으로 같은 구조가 와야 한다는 특징이 있습니다. 등위접속사 and, but, or는 앞뒤를 대등하게 연결합니다. 즉, 앞뒤가 명사-명사, 구-구, 절-절 등과 같이 문법적으로 같은 구조를 취해야 합니다.

단, so와 for는 오직 절과 절을 연결할 수 있으며, 단어나 구는 연결하지 못합니다.

단어 / 구 / 절	and 그리고 but (= yet) 그러나 or 또는	단어 / 구 / 절
절 (주어 + 동사)	so 그래서 for 왜냐하면	절 (주어 + 동사)

Mike raised his hand **and** waved. (raised her hand = waved) 마이크는 손을 들고 흔들었다.

Do you like oranges **or** bananas? (명사 or 명사) 오렌지를 좋아하세요, 바나나를 좋아하세요?

It was very cold, **so** I closed the window. (절 so 절) 날씨가 너무 추워서, 문을 닫았다.

② 등위상관접속사

등위상관접속사는 반드시 짝을 맞춰 같이 쓰며, A와 B는 같은 문법 구조를 갖습니다.

상관 접속사의 수일치	
either A or B A 또는 B neither A nor B A도 B도 아닌 not only A but also B = B as well as A A뿐만 아니라 B도 not A but B A가 아니라 B	B에 동사 수일치
both A and B A와 B 둘 다	항상 복수 동사

Neither my sister **nor** I **am** a student. 여동생도 나도 모두 학생은 아니다.

Both Linda **and** John **are** smart 린다와 존 모두 똑똑하다

GRAMMAR PRACTICE

A 보기와 같이, 다음 주어진 등위접속사를 연결하여, 하나의 문장으로 만드세요.
단, 각 등위접속사는 각 문항에 한번만 사용할 수 있습니다.

| for   so   and   but   or |

보기) They ate dinner. + They talked for a while.
→ They ate dinner and talked for a while.

1. The baseball game was interesting. + It was exciting.
→ _____

2. I bought a book yesterday. + I haven't read it yet.
→ _____

3. Will you hang out with me? + Will you stay at home?
→ _____

4. It was very hot. + I opened the window.
→ _____

5. He should stay at home. + He is sick.
→ _____

B 다음 빈칸에 등위접속사 **and, but or, so, for**을 알맞게 넣으세요.
단, 각 등위접속사는 각 문항에 한번만 사용할 수 있습니다.

1. Flowers are beautiful, (　　) they smell sweet.
2. Beth isn't beautiful, (　　) she is cute.
3. Which do you like better, spring (　　) fall?
4. I feel tried, (　　) let's go home now!
5. I have to buy an umbrella, (　　) it is raining.

C 괄호 안에 알맞은 것을 고르세요.

1. Either a bus (or, nor) a taxi is available at the airport.
2. Both Jenny (and, but) Mike are intelligent.
3. Neither my parents (or, nor) my sister likes meat.
4. Mr. Tucker speaks not only Chinese (but also, as well as) Spanish very well.
5. He did not come on Monday night (and, but) on Tuesday morning.

VOCA   **for a while** 한동안   **available** 이용할 수 있는   **intelligent** 영리한   **hang out with** ~와 시간을 보내다

Unit 22 | 접속사 I | 179

GRAMMAR POINT

③ 명사절을 이끄는 접속사
문장에서 명사절을 만들어 주어, 목적어, 보어의 역할을 하는 문장을 이끕니다.

(1) 명사절을 이끄는 접속사 that
접속사 that이 이끄는 명사절은 <주어 + 동사 + 보어> 또는 <주어 + 동사 + 목적어>의 완전한 문장 구조를 갖습니다.

I believe **that John is honest**. (목적어) 나는 존이 정직하다는 것을 믿는다.

(2) 명사절을 이끄는 접속사 if나 whether
if나 whether는 명사절을 이끌어 '~인지 아닌지'의 의미를 나타내며 주어, 보어, 목적어로 쓰입니다.
명사절을 이끄는 if 는 주어 자리나 전치사의 목적어로는 사용하지 않습니다.

I wanted to see **if you had any questions**. (목적어) 당신이 질문이 있으신지 궁금했습니다.

④ 명사절을 이끄는 접속사 what
what은 명사절을 만들어 주어, 목적어, 보어의 역할을 합니다.
what이 이끄는 명사절은 주어, 목적어 중 한 가지 필수성분이 없는 불완전한 문장 구조를 갖습니다.

What he wants is unclear. 그가 원하는 것이 불분명하다.
(주어로 쓰임. 타동사 want 뒤에 목적어가 없음)

I want to know **what makes you so happy**. 나는 무엇이 너를 행복하게 만드는지 알고 싶다.
(타동사 know에 대한 목적어로 쓰임. what 뒤에 주어가 없음)

That is **what he checked at the meeting**. 그것은 그가 회의에서 확인한 것이다.
(is의 보어로 쓰임. checked 뒤에 목적어가 없음)

⑤ 명사절 that, if, whether, what 구별하기
that, if, whether가 이끄는 명사절에서는 완전한 절이 오지만, what이 이끄는 명사절에서는 주어나 목적어가 빠진 불완전한 절이 옵니다. 명사절 that절 뒤에는 확실한 사실이, if나 whether절 뒤에는 불확실한 사실을 나타내는 문장이 옵니다.

What I want right now is your advice. 내가 지금 원하는 것은 너의 충고다.

I know **that** the convention is very important. 나는 그 집회가 매우 중요하다는 것을 알고 있다.

We don't know **whether** (**if**) they will sign the contract. 그들이 계약서에 서명할지 안 할지 알 수 없습니다.

GRAMMAR PRACTICE

A 다음 밑줄 친 부분 that의 쓰임을 찾아 번호를 쓰세요.

① 주어 ② 목적어 ③ 보어

1. I think that the problem is serious.

2. That Jane loves David is secret.

3. The problem is that you were late for the meeting.

4. I didn't know that Ben is a singer.

5. His wish is that he gets well soon.

B 괄호 안에서 알맞은 것을 고르세요.

1. I didn't know (that, what) Linda was a teacher.

2. (That, What) I want now is your help.

3. I cannot be sure (that, whether) he will attend the meeting or not.

4. It is certain (that, what) he is innocent.

5. I wonder (whether, what) he is at home or at the office.

C 어법상 틀린 문장은 바르게 고치고, 틀린 부분이 없으면 O로 표시하세요.

1. That I need right now is your report.

2. I'm not sure whether he is Korean or not.

3. What I want to know is that you like.

4. If I can finish this project is another matter.

5. It is not clear whether he will accept the offer or not.

VOCA serious 심각한   get well 건강해지다   innocent 결백한   matter 문제   offer 제안   accept 받아들이다

GRAMMAR IN SENTENCE

▶ 의미 단위로 문장을 끊어 읽고, 해석하세요.

1. I didn't know that Linda was a teacher.

2. What I want now is your help.

3. I cannot be sure whether he will attend the meeting or not.

4. It is certain that he is innocent.

5. I wonder whether he is at home or at the office.

6. What I need right now is your report.

7. I'm not sure whether he is Korean or not.

8. What I want to know is what you like.

9. Whether I can finish this project is another matter.

10. It is not clear whether he will accept the offer or not.

 **Outro**

접속사 I

접속사는 단어와 단어, 구와 구, 절과 절을 연결시키는 기능을 할 수 있습니다.

```
                접속사의 종류 I
                       |
      ┌────────────────┼────────────────┐
   등위접속사         상관접속사       명사절 접속사
  대등하게 연결해야   짝을 이루는 접속사   주어, 목적어, 보어로
      할 때                              쓰임
                     both A and B
   and, but, or,     either A or B     that, whether,
    yet, so 등       neither A nor B    if what 등
```

단어 + 단어	**You and your friend** should study hard. 너와 너의 친구는 공부를 열심히 해야 한다
구 + 구	I like **to read books and watch TV**. 나는 책 읽는 것과 TV보는 것을 좋아한다.
절 + 절	**I am poor, but he is rich.** 모든 가난하지만, 그는 부자이다.

UNIT 23 접속사 II

GRAMMAR POINT

1 부사절 접속사

부사절이란 하나의 절(주어와 동사를 갖춤)이 시간, 이유, 조건, 양보, 목적 등을 나타내는 부사로 쓰이는 것을 말합니다. 부사절은 <부사절 접속사 + 주어 + 동사>로 이루어집니다.

의미	부사절 접속사		
시간	**when** ~할 때 **before** ~전에 **since** ~이래로	**while** ~하는 동안 **after** ~한 후에 **as soon as** ~하자마자	**until** ~할 때까지 **by the time** ~할 때까지는
조건	**if** 만약 ~하면 **once** 일단 ~하면	**unless** 만약 ~하지 않으면 **in case** ~, **in the event (that)** ~한 일이 일어날 경우에	**as long as** ~하는 한
양보	**although, even though, even if, though, whereas** 비록 ~이지만		
이유	**because** ~때문에 **since** ~이므로 **as** ~이므로 **now that** 이제 ~이니까		
목적	**so that** S + **may(can)** ~ , **in order that** ~ ~하기 위해서		

Before he went out, Tom took a shower (시간)
그가 외출하기 전에, Tom은 샤워를 했다.

If it rains tomorrow, please call me. (조건)
내일 비가 오면, 나에게 전화해 줘.

Although he is poor, Mark is happy (양보)
Mark는 가난함에도 불구하고, 행복하다.

Because he is poor, David cannot buy the car (이유)
David는 가난하기 때문에, 그 자동차를 살 수 없다.

Richard studies hard **so that** he may pass the examination. (목적)
Richard는 시험에 합격하려고 열심히 공부한다.

2 시간, 조건의 부사절

시간이나 조건을 나타내는 부사절에서는 현재시제 또는 현재완료시제가 미래를 나타냅니다. 이때 주절은 will, can, may, should 등의 조동사와 함께 미래 시제 쓰거나 또는 명령문을 씁니다.

시간	before, after, when, until, while, by the time, as soon as
조건	if, unless, as long as, once (일단~하면)

If you need money, Andrew will lend you some. 당신이 돈이 필요하면 Andrew 가 빌려줄 거 에요.

GRAMMAR PRACTICE

A 연결하여 문장을 완성하세요.

1. Because she is very nice
2. If you meet Tom
3. After I finish the work
4. While you are waiting
5. While I sleep

A. please give him this book
B. everyone likes her
C. you can play the game
D. I dream a lot.
E. I will go to bed

B 괄호 안에 알맞은 것을 넣으세요.

1. (If, Unless) we hurry, we will be late for the concert.
2. It's already been a year (because, since) you joined us.
3. (Unless, Because) he didn't finish the report, I was angry with him.
4. (When, As soon as) I last saw you, you were six years old.
5. (As, Though) I don't have enough money, I can't buy the car.
6. (While, Although) I buy tickets, pleas keep an eye on my bag.
7. I will forgive John (if, unless) he acknowledges his mistake.
8. The results were disappointing (in case, although) we did our best.
9. Tom works very hard (because, so that) he can study abroad.
10. (Even though, If) Mr. Lee has lived in Mexico for a long time, he still doesn't speak Spanish fluently.

VOCA finish 마치다　last 마지막으로　keep an eye on~ ~을 지켜보다　pardon 용서하다　acknowledge 인정하다
do one's best 최선을 다하다　abroad 해외로　fluently 유창하게

GRAMMAR POINT

③ 접속 부사

접속사는 문장을 연결하는 역할을 하지만, 접속 부사는 문장을 연결할 수 없습니다. 접속 부사는 하나의 문장 앞에 쓰던가, 문장 사이의 세미콜론(;)과 콤마(,) 사이에 씁니다. 접속 부사는 문법적으로 부사이고 해석상으로만 접속사입니다.

- **첨가**: besides, moreover, furthermore, in addition
- **원인, 결과**: therefore, thus, hence, consequently
- **역접**: however, nevertheless, nonetheless
- **만약 그렇지 않으면**: otherwise
- **그러면**: then
- **그동안에, 그사이에**: meantime = meanwhile

The weather was bad, **therefore** we had to cancel our picnic. (X)

The weather was bad; **therefore,** we had to cancel our picnic. (O)

The weather was bad. **Therefore,** we had to cancel our picnic. (O)
날씨가 나빴다, 그래서 소풍을 취소해야만 했다.

④ 의미가 동일한 접속사와 전치사

	접속사	전치사	접속 부사
~이기 때문에	because as since now that	because of owing to due to on account of	
~에도 불구하고	although even though	despite in spite of	however nevertheless
~일 경우에	in case that in the event that	in case of in the event of	
~하는 동안	while	during	meantime meanwhile
만약 ~ 않다면	if ~ not unless	without	otherwise

Although he was sick, he went to school.

= **Despite** his sickness, he went to school.

= He was sick. **Nevertheless**, he went to school.

= He was sick; **nevertheless**, he went to school.
그는 아팠음에도 불구하고 학교에 갔다.

GRAMMAR PRACTICE

A 보기에서 전치사, 접속사, 접속부사로 분류하세요.

> 보기 because of   during   while   otherwise   without   unless   despite
> although   because   due to   nevertheless

1. 전치사 _____

2. 접속사 _____

3. 접속부사 _____

B 다음의 한글 해석과 같은 의미의 문장이 되도록 빈칸을 채우세요.

> 보기 It will rain tomorrow, Otherwise, we will go on a picnic.
> 내일 비가 오지 않는다면, 우리는 소풍을 갈 것이다.

= Unless _____, _____.

= _____; otherwise, _____.

= Without _____, _____.

C 괄호 안에 알맞은 것을 넣으세요.

1. Our favorite baseball team's game was canceled; (however, therefore), we decided to go to a movie.

2. Hurry up; (but, otherwise), we will miss the train.

3. Linda speaks English fluently; (however, otherwise), she doesn't speak Chinese.

4. They were hungry; (although, nevertheless) they couldn't eat anything.

5. It's getting colder these days. (Therefore, However), it's still warm in the afternoon.

VOCA go on a picnic 소풍가다   favorite 좋아하는   hurry up 서두르다

GRAMMAR IN SENTENCE

▶ 의미 단위로 문장을 끊어 읽고, 해석하세요.

1. Because she is very nice, everyone likes her.

2. If you meet Tom, please give him this book.

3. It will rain tomorrow, Otherwise, we will go on a picnic.

4. Unless we hurry, we will be late for the concert.

5. It's already been a year since you joined us.

6. Because he didn't finish the report, I was angry with him.

7. When I saw you last, you were six years old.

8. As I don't have enough money, I can't buy the car.

9. While I buy tickets, please keep an eye on my bag.

10. I will forgive John if he acknowledges his mistake.

 **Outro**

접속사 II

부사절 접속사

부사절은 <부사절 접속사 + 주어 + 동사>로 이루어집니다. 부사절이란 하나의 절(주어와 동사를 갖춤)이 시간, 이유, 조건, 양보, 목적 등을 나타내는 부사로 쓰이는 것을 말합니다.

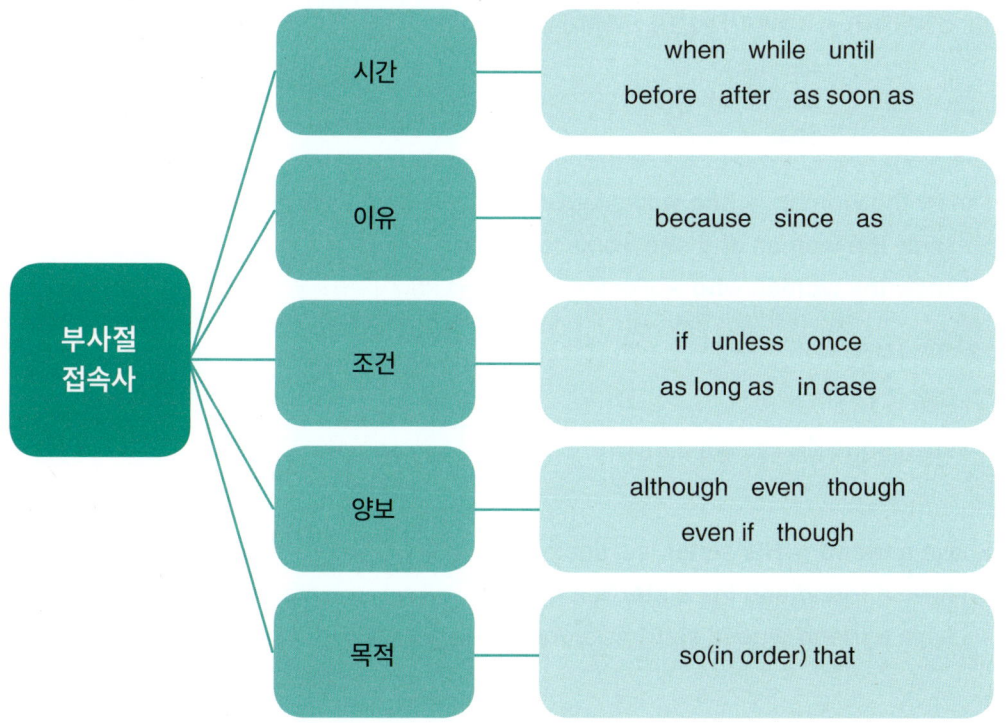

UNIT 24 관계사

GRAMMAR POINT

① 관계대명사

관계대명사는 접속사와 대명사의 역할을 하기 때문에 관계절에는 명사가 하나 빠진 불완전한 문장이 옵니다. 선행사가 사람이면 who나 whom(목적격인 경우)을, 사물이면 which를 씁니다. 관계대명사 that은 선행사가 사람인 경우나 사물인 경우 모두 쓸 수 있으며, 주격, 목적격에도 사용할 수 있지만, 전치사와 콤마(계속적 용법) 뒤에는 쓸 수 없습니다.

(1) 주격 관계대명사

선행사(명사) + 관계대명사 + 동사 ~ (주어가 없는 절)		
사람	who[that]	V ~
사물	which[that]	V ~
X	what	V ~

I know **the woman**. + **She** works for CNN.

= I know **the woman and she** works for CNN.

= I know **the woman who** works for CNN. 나는 CNN에서 근무하는 그 여자를 알고 있다.
　　　　선행사(사람)　관계대명사　동사

(2) 소유격 관계대명사

선행사(명사) + whose + 명사 + 동사 ~
(~의)

I have **a friend**. + **His sister** is a doctor.

= I have **a friend and his sister** is a doctor.

= I have **a friend whose sister** is a doctor. 나는 여동생이 의사인 친구가 있다.
　　　　선행사　관계대명사　명사　동사

(3) 목적격 관계대명사

선행사(명사) + 관계대명사 + 주어 + 동사 (목적어가 없는 절)		
사람	who[whom, that]	주어 + 타동사/자동사 + 전치사
사물	which[that]	
X	what	

Look at **the book**. + I bought **it** yesterday.

= Look at **the book and** I bought **it** yesterday.

= Look at **the book which** I bought yesterday. 내가 어제 산 저 책을 보아라.
　　　　선행사(사)물　관계대명사 주어　동사

GRAMMAR PRACTICE

A 괄호 안에 알맞은 것을 고르시오.

1. A thief is a person (who, whom) steals things.
2. I met a boy (whose, which) sister is a famous actress.
3. This is the girl (that, which) we met yesterday.
4. The concert (whom, which) I went to was exciting.
5. That's the man (whose, which) paper was published in a journal recently.

B 다음 두 문장을 한 문장으로 만들 때, 다음 빈칸을 관계대명사 **who, which, whose** 중에 하나를 써 넣으세요.

1. She is married to a man. He is rich
   She is married the man _____ is rich.
2. That's a man. His house was recently built.
   That's the man _____ house was recently built.
3. I found a key. Linda lost it yesterday.
   I found the key _____ Linda lost yesterday.
4. I know a man. He speaks English very well.
   I know the man _____ speaks English very well.
5. The park is near my school. It is beautiful.
   The park _____ is near my school is beautiful.

C 다음 두 문장을 한 문장으로 만들 때, 관계대명사 **who, whom which, whose** 를 이용하여 빈칸을 채우세요.

1. I met a man. + He was rich and kind.
   → I met the man _____.
2. This is a woman. Her husband is very diligent.
   → This is the woman _____.
3. There are girls. They are all the same age.
   → There are the girls _____.
4. I talked with a boy. The English teacher wants to meet him.
   → I talked with the boy _____.
5. A vase is on the table. I gave it to my sister.
   → The vase _____ is on the table.

GRAMMAR POINT

(4) 전치사 + 관계대명사

관계대명사가 전치사의 목적어로 쓰이는 경우로, 이때 전치사는 문장 맨 뒤로 보낼 수 있습니다. 목적격 관계대명사 whom과 which는 전치사를 수반할 수 있습니다.

This is **the house**. + I live in **the house**.
= This is **the house which** I live in.
= This is **the house in which** I live. (전치사를 관계대명사 앞으로 이동)
이곳이 내가 살고 있는 집이다.

(5) 장소를 나타내는 전치사 + 관계 대명사 = where (관계부사)

This is the house **in which** I live.
= This is the house **where** I live. (= This is the house **and** I live **there**.)
이곳이 내가 살고 있는 집이다.

② 관계부사

관계부사는 <접속사 + 부사>의 역할을 합니다. 따라서 관계부사 뒤에는 완전한 절이 옵니다.

선행사		관계부사
시간	day, year, time	when
이유	the reason	why
장소	place, building	where
방법	the way	how ★ the way와 how는 함께 쓸 수 없음

The hotel **where** we stayed was not so clean. (관계부사절)
stay는 자동사로서 빠진 성분이 없는 완전한 문장

= The hotel **which** we stayed at was not so clean. (관계대명사절)
전치사 at의 목적어가 빠진 불완전한 문장

= The hotel **at which** we stayed was not so clean.
관계부사는 '전치사+관계대명사'로 바꿔 쓸 수 있다.
우리가 투숙했던 그 호텔은 별로 깨끗하지 않았다.

I remember the day **when** I went to Paris. 나는 파리에 갔던 날을 기억한다.

I want to know the reason **why** she quits her job. 나는 그녀가 직장을 그만둔 이유를 알고 싶다.

I don't know the way how the heavy machinery works. (X)
= I don't know **how** the heavy machinery works. (O)
= I don't know **the way** the heavy machinery works. (O)
나는 중장비의 사용하는 방법을 모른다.

GRAMMAR PRACTICE

A 다음 문장의 의미가 같도록 빈칸에 알맞은 관계부사 또는 관계대명사 **which**를 넣으세요.

1. I don't know the reason <u>for which</u> my name is on the waiting list.

    = I don't know the reason _____ my name is on the waiting list.

2. The concert <u>which</u> I went to was exciting.

    = The concert _____ I went was exciting.

    = The concert _____ _____ I went was exciting.

3. Do you remember the day <u>which</u> the exhibition was held on?

    = Do you remember the day _____ _____ the exhibition was held?

    = Do you remember the day _____ the exhibition was held?

4. This is the way Tom solved the problem.

    = This is _____ Tom solved the problem.

5. I still remember the day on which we met first.

    = I still remember the day _____ we met first.

B 괄호 안에 알맞은 것을 고르세요.

1. A nurse is a person (who, which) takes care of patients.
2. I met a man (that, whose) sister is an English teacher.
3. I found the key (that, whose) Ann lost last night.
4. The party (who, which) I went to yesterday wasn't enjoyable.
5. The customer service representative (that, which) works at the company was very friendly.
6. I can't remember the time (where, when) he left the office last night.
7. This is the place (where, when) I met her the other day.
8. I can't understand (the way how, how) she was able to finish the big project by herself.
9. He didn't tell me the reason (why, that) he came here suddenly.
10. Look at the garden (where, which) is filled with flowers.

GRAMMAR IN SENTENCE

▶ 의미 단위로 문장을 끊어 읽고, 해석하세요.

1. A nurse is a person who takes care of patients.

2. I met a man whose sister is an English teacher.

3. I found the key that Ann lost last night.

4. The party which I went to yesterday wasn't enjoyable.

5. The customer service representative that works at the company was very friendly.

6. I can't remember the time when he left the office last night.

7. This is the place where I met her the other day.

8. I can't understand how she was able to finish the big project by herself.

9. He didn't tell me the reason why he came here suddenly.

10. Look at the garden which is filled with flowers.

 **Outro**

관계사

접속사와 대명사 역할을 동시에 하면 관계대명사
접속사와 부사 역할을 동시에 하면 관계부사입니다.

```
            관계사
           (절+절)
           ┌───┴───┐
    관계대명사        관계부사
  = 접속사 + 대명사   = 접속사 + 부사
```

관계대명사
who, whose, whom, that, what

- 선행사가 사람 who that
- 선행사가 사물 which/that

관계부사
where, when, why, how

- 선행사가 장소 where
- 선행사가 시간 when
- 선행사가 이유 why
- 선행사가 방법 how

ACTUAL TEST 8

A 다음 빈칸에 들어갈 수 있는 것을 고르세요.

1. Yesterday, both management ------- the labor union agreed that working hours should not exceed 9 hours a day.
   (A) but
   (B) and
   (C) or
   (D) so

2. They should --------- find a new house there or commute between Los Angeles and San Pedro every day.
   (A) both
   (B) not only
   (C) neither
   (D) either

3. The sales manager said that neither high prices -------- a lack of effort was a factor in losing customers.
   (A) or
   (B) but
   (C) nor
   (B) yet

4. The cook not only had to prepare the food ------- carry it to each room of the household.
   (A) but
   (B) also
   (C) as
   (D) and

5. All employees should know ------------ this convention is very important.
   (A) what
   (B) that
   (C) which
   (D) who

6. ------- the manager had already approved the week's work schedule, he accepted Mr. Jefferson's request for sick leave.
   (A) Nevertheless
   (B) If
   (C) Even though
   (D) Unless

7. The president ------------ donated such a large sum to our school was a billionaire.
   (A) which
   (B) whose
   (C) who
   (D) what

8. It is important to rely on valid identification rather than uniforms --------- can be replicated easily.
   (A) who
   (B) which
   (C) what
   (D) whose

9. The customer service representative ---------- works in the company was very friendly.
   (A) that
   (B) which
   (C) whose
   (D) what

10. Anyone ------- visits our company should contact the information desk for identification.
    (A) whose
    (B) what
    (C) where
    (D) who

11. Mr. Jackson's duties are not limited to recruiting, hiring, ------- evaluating employees.
    (A) that
    (B) but
    (C) and
    (D) while

12. We cannot deal with companies ------- offices are not in United States.
    (A) which
    (B) whose
    (C) what
    (D) that

B 다음 빈칸에 들어갈 수 있는 것을 고르세요.

Questions 13-15 refer to the following news report.

Are you sometimes anxious while at work? Are you often irritated during the day? Then you should listen to this informational minute. Many people drink several cups of coffee every day to help them stay alert. **13** -------, scientists have found **14** ------- the high levels of caffeine in coffee actually increase the stress experienced by most people. Researchers **15** ------- this to be especially true if the coffee is drunk on an empty stomach. The caffeine is absorbed very quickly and causes a feeling of elevation **16** ------- energy without food in the stomach. **17** ------- this serves to stimulate the mental and physical faculties of the coffee drinker, it also increases the drinker's blood pressure and heart rate. **18** ------- more caffeine is not consumed, a noticeable physical let down is experienced several hours later. As a result, to avoid this, many coffee drinkers consume it throughout the day. In order to avoid this unpleasant cycle, researchers suggest that caffeine intake be limited to two or three cups of coffee a day.

13 (A) Since
(B) Because
(C) However
(D) Moreover

14 (A) that
(B) what
(C) when
(D) whether

15 (A) has found
(B) have found
(C) has been found
(D) have been found

16 (A) or
(B) of
(C) but
(D) and

17 (A) Even though
(B) Nevertheless
(C) Additionally
(D) Otherwise

18 (A) Because
(B) Although
(C) Since
(D) If

MINI TEST 4

A 다음 빈칸에 들어갈 수 있는 것을 고르세요.

1. Individuals looking for funds for their businesses --------- to turn in two copies of their proposal.
   (A) require
   (B) requires
   (C) is requiring
   (D) are required

2. The agency was unable --------- the design specifications for the convention center
   (A) to meet
   (B) meeting
   (C) meet
   (D) met

3. Mr. Miller has decided that it is time --------- as the head of the committee.
   (A) resigning
   (B) resigned
   (C) resigns
   (D) to resign

4. This website was designed --------- your Internet searches to an absolute minimum
   (A) to keep
   (B) kept
   (C) keeping
   (D) has kept

5. Please refrain from --------- any new events on the online calendar until further notice.
   (A) to schedule
   (B) scheduled
   (C) scheduling
   (D) schedule

6. Many people, including elderly users, had difficulty --------- the devices.
   (A) handle
   (B) handles
   (C) handling
   (D) to handle

7. After carefully --------- your resume, we are glad to offer you the position.
   (A) examine
   (B) to examine
   (C) examining
   (D) examined

8. The president has announced that the company will discontinue --------- its unprofitable products
   (A) make
   (B) making
   (C) made
   (D) to make

9. There are many --------- candidates here and all of them look very well-prepared.
   (A) qualify
   (B) qualifying
   (C) qualified
   (D) qualifies

10. A cancelation must be made within five days of the ---------- departure date.
    (A) schedule
    (B) scheduling
    (C) scheduler
    (D) scheduled

11. Our company has advised most employees --------- use of the public transportation system.
    (A) to make
    (B) making
    (C) to be made
    (D) make

12. --------- been warned to be punctual by his boss, Mr. Jackson began to get up early.
    (A) Having
    (B) Had
    (C) Have
    (D) Has

13 The exhibit has included -------- historic and contemporary artifacts.
(A) that
(B) both
(C) neither
(D) but

14 New employees receive -------- health and dental insurance or health and vision insurance.
(A) either
(B) not only
(C) both
(D) whether

15 The research assistants were selected from 16 public enterprises -------- 9 government agencies.
(A) in
(B) both
(C) by
(D) and

16 We will send you some of our catalogues so that you can decide -------- you need.
(A) that
(B) what
(C) if
(D) whether

17 The staff members at the company's headquarters protested -------- they are overworked and underpaid.
(A) for
(B) what
(C) as
(D) that

18 His major concern is -------- stock prices will fluctuate again within the next quarter.
(A) whether
(B) what
(C) since
(D) and

19 -------- he had already bought a similar type of car, the man purchased a motorcycle.
(A) Though
(B) Since
(C) Until
(D) When

20 Most individuals -------- applied for the new position were tired and frustrated.
(A) whom
(B) who
(C) whoever
(D) which

21 -------- Ms. Ono does not return within a week, her assistant will lead the upcoming seminar.
(A) whether
(B) either
(C) if
(D) So that

22 The customer service representative -------- works at the company was very friendly.
(A) that
(B) which
(C) whose
(D) when

23 Mr. Robinson didn't tell me the reason -------- he came here suddenly.
(A) when
(B) why
(C) which
(D) how

24 Unless -------- instructed, take this medicine three times daily after meals.
(A) instead
(B) somewhat
(C) otherwise
(D) rather

MINI TEST 4

B 다음 빈칸에 들어갈 수 있는 것을 고르세요.

Questions 25-30 refer to the following advertisement.

Golden Planning

Now is the time for you to start **25** ------- so that you can enjoy a steady source of income after you retire. Our *Golden Retirement Planning Group* is providing just such a plan **26** ------- your current lifestyle. For example, estimating the retirement income you will need, and choose the funds **27** ------- can help make your plan work, and create a plan that will continue **28** ------- for your future. We assure you that mutual funds will be an ideal choice for your long-term retirement goals. For more **29** ------- information, call an investment representative. Also, we'll send you a free brochure **30** ------- you leave your name, address, and phone number.

Meet us with a telephone call by dialing 1-800-8080808 Now!

---

25 (A) plan
(B) planning
(C) plans
(D) planned

26 (A) maintain
(B) maintaining
(C) maintenance
(D) to maintain

27 (A) who
(B) whom
(C) what
(D) that

28 (A) work
(B) working
(C) works
(D) worked

29 (A) detail
(B) detailing
(C) details
(D) detailed

30 (A) whether
(B) unless
(C) if
(D) since

Questions 31-36 refer to the following leaflet.

To Karl Leman:

I **31** ------- a tenant in your building on Waterfront Avenue for the past 5 years. I have always paid my rent on time, and have never had any issues arise with respect to the level of service offered. **32** -------, last month my bathroom sink began leaking, and I immediately called the building manager **33** ------- told me she would contact a maintenance person. It took 2 days for a maintenance person to arrive, by which time a significant amount of water **34** ------- onto the dining room carpet. **35** ------- I did my best to dry up the water, it has left a permanent stain.

I informed the building manager of the stain, and she sent a cleaner to steam clean the carpet. The stain **36** ------- , but I arrived home today to find a bill for $75.00 for the cleaning services.
I have paid the bill, but would like to ask that I be refunded the full amount.
Thank you,

Julie Andrews, Apartment 1208

31 (A) am
   (B) was
   (C) have been
   (D) had been

32 (A) Thus
   (B) So
   (C) Additionally
   (D) However

33 (A) which
   (B) what
   (C) who
   (D) how

34 (A) has leaked
   (B) leaks
   (C) will have leaked
   (D) had leaked

35 (A) Although
   (B) If
   (C) Unless
   (D) Because

36 (A) removes
   (B) removed
   (C) is removed
   (D) was removed

FINAL TEST

A 다음 빈칸에 들어갈 수 있는 것을 고르세요.

1. Residents in this area --------- stocking up on food and water at homes after the news.
   (A) is
   (B) are
   (C) has
   (D) have

2. The main entrance to this building will automatically --------- in an emergency.
   (A) operates
   (B) operate
   (C) operated
   (D) operating

3. Next week, your --------- will notify all the employees of the assignments regarding the new project.
   (A) supervising
   (B) supervise
   (C) supervised
   (D) supervisor

4. In order to survive in today's --------- market, we should do our best.
   (A) competitive
   (B) competition
   (C) competitively
   (D) compete

5. The Accounting Department needed to conduct an --------- survey on the financial damage.
   (A) extend
   (B) extensive
   (C) extensions
   (D) extending

6. As the new air filtration system --------- last month, we can work effectively.
   (A) installed
   (B) was installed
   (C) install
   (D) is installed

7. Every candidate's application should --------- by email by the end of next month after candidates complete all the blanks.
   (A) send
   (B) be sent
   (C) sent
   (D) sending

8. This year, the gourmet restaurant --------- over 100,000 new customers.
   (A) was attracted
   (B) has attracted
   (C) attract
   (D) were attracting

9. All managers were --------- encouraged to attend the monthly meeting.
   (A) strong
   (B) strengthen
   (C) strength
   (D) strongly

10. Each manager estimates that there were --------- 2,000 people participating in the survey.
    (A) approximate
    (B) approximation
    (C) approximately
    (D) approximated

11. Kroger has been considerably more successful at --------- its new products than is widely assumed.
    (A) sell
    (B) selling
    (C) sold
    (D) sells

12. All Top Airlines passengers --------- to secure their valuables in their carry-on baggage.
    (A) advised
    (B) are advised
    (C) have advised
    (D) will advise

13 Hyper Mart is dedicated to --------- effective training programs for new employees.
(A) develop
(B) development
(C) developed
(D) developing

14 When --------- a long-distance call, please press the initial 0.
(A) make
(B) made
(C) makes
(D) making

15 Anyone --------- in the scandal is being brought to the precinct for investigation.
(A) involving
(B) involved
(C) involve
(D) involves

16 The company invited the students to see --------- new facilities.
(A) itself
(B) its
(C) it
(D) them

17 --------- of the items displayed on the floor are fully refundable.
(A) One
(B) Either
(C) Some
(D) Each

18 I tried to call you twice, but --------- times, you were out.
(A) both
(B) some
(C) one
(D) each

19 Some people love to watch movies and --------- like to go swimming.
(A) the others
(B) others
(C) other
(D) another

20 Unfortunately, time doesn't allow me to discuss it --------- detail.
(A) in
(B) on
(C) at
(D) of

21 The scene of the sunrise is impressive and --------- description.
(A) until
(B) by
(C) above
(D) beyond

22 The concert will start ------- 7:00 o'clock in the evening and be finished by 9:00 p.m.
(A) in
(B) at
(C) of
(D) on

23 Most employees have been more productive --------- the new air-filtration system was installed last month.
(A) unless
(B) since
(C) while
(D) if

24 Our favorite team's baseball game was canceled; ---------, we decided to go to a movie.
(A) however
(B) otherwise
(C) therefore
(D) while

FINAL TEST

B 다음 빈칸에 들어갈 수 있는 것을 고르세요.

Questions 25-30 refer to the following memo.

To: All employees

From: John Martin, editor of *The Opinions*

Re: Wanted

We need volunteers to assist us in **25** ------- the staff informed through our newspaper. Experience isn't absolutely necessary, **26** ------- writing and typing skills are in great demand. We need people to rewrite articles, to type and to proofread. We could also use a good photographer. **27** ------- *Opinions* comes out three days a week, we need excellent employees **28** ------- know how to budget their time efficiently.
There is some money for salaries, depending on **29** ------- involved you get with the paper. But don't expect to get rich. This isn't something you do for the money. Mostly, it's just for fun. **30** ------- who's interested in joining the staff should speak to me immediately after today's meeting. Be prepared to start right away. The first issue goes to press tomorrow.

---

25 (A) keep
(B) keeps
(C) keeping
(D) to keep

26 (A) and
(B) so
(C) or
(D) but

27 (A) Now that
(B) However
(C) While
(D) Because of

28 (A) what
(B) whose
(C) who
(D) which

29 (A) who
(B) how
(C) that
(C) where

30 (A) Someone
(B) They
(C) One
(D) Anyone

Questions 31-36 refer to the following letter.

Mr. Matt Morris
MCN Inc.
210 Grayson Ave.
NW Roanoke, VA 24016

Dear Mr. Morris:

Thank you for letting **31** ------- know the details of your itinerary for your business trip. We are **32** ------- that you will be able to visit our factory **33** ------- you are in Indonesia. Our manager, Mr. Dexter, will be available to escort you **34** ------- to answer any questions which you may have. **35** ------- you arrive on the 28th, please call me **36** ------- (202) 594-9967 and we can set a day for your visit to the factory.

Yours Truly,

Mike R. Gregory
General Manager

31 (A) we
(B) our
(C) us
(D) ours

32 (A) please
(B) pleased
(C) pleasing
(D) pleasure

33 (A) since
(B) although
(C) because
(D) while

34 (A) and
(B) but
(C) or
(D) so

35 (A) After
(B) During
(C) So as
(D) Though

36 (A) in
(B) on
(C) at
(D) of

잉글리쉬앤 그래머 START

정답 및 해설

1코스
2코스
3코스
4코스
5코스

입문편

UNIT 01 : 명사

GRAMMAR PRACTICE p.13

A
(A) salt 소금
(F) restaurant 레스토랑
(I) baseball 야구
(M) sugar 설탕
(S) water 물
(C) bread 빵
(H) soccer 축구
(K) pizza 피자
(N) air 공기

B
1. (C) rice 쌀
3. (B) chair 의자
5. (C) meal 식사
7. (C) flour 밀가루
9. (A) book 책
2. (D) letter 편지
4. (A) air 공기
6. (D) egg 달걀
8. (D) apple 사과
10. (C) information 정보

C
1. (A) a boy
3. (B) six students
5. (A) a cup of coffee
2. (C) five books
4. (D) a machine

GRAMMAR PRACTICE p.15

A
1. book → books
3. bus → buses
5. child → children
7. foot → feet
9. frog → frogs
11. tree → trees
13. roof → roofs
15. crisis → crises
17. woman → women
19. tooth → teeth
2. fox → foxes
4. bench → benches
6. man → men
8. shelf → shelves
10. house → houses
12. potato → potatoes
14. city → cities
16. fish → fish
18. person → people
20. mouse → mice

B
1. an insect
3. an apple
5. an orange
7. a book
9. an umbrella
11. a young boy
2. a window
4. a nose
6. a red apple
8. an hour
10. an old man
12. an elephant

C
1. X
2. the
3. X
4. the
5. the
6. X
7. X
8. The, the
9. X
10. The

GRAMMAR IN SENTENCE p.16

1. I have **breakfast** every **morning**.
   해석 나는 매일 아침마다 아침을 먹는다.
2. I play the **piano** in my free **time**.
   해석 나는 여가시간에 피아노를 친다.
3. We played **baseball** yesterday.
   해석 나는 어제 야구를 했다.
4. Look at the **moon**!
   해석 저 달을 보아라!
5. Let's save the **earth**!
   해석 지구를 구하자!
6. What's for **dinner** today?
   해석 오늘 저녁은 무엇입니까?
7. Let's play **tennis** this **afternoon**!
   해석 오후에 테니스를 칩시다!
8. The **sun** is shining in the **sky**.
   해석 태양이 하늘에서 빛나고 있다.
9. **Jenny** wants to talk with you by **phone**.
   해석 Jenny는 전화로 당신과 이야기하기를 원한다.
10. I know a **girl**. The **girl** is beautiful.
    해석 나는 한 소녀를 안다. 그 소녀는 아름답다.

UNIT 02 : 대명사

GRAMMAR PRACTICE p.19

A
(A) he   (C) they   (E) she   (H) we   (I) she
(K) his   (N) yours (P) her   (Q) its   (T) them
(V) hers (X) my   (Y) I

B
1. I   2. her   3. his   4. we   5. their
6. you   7. your   8. us   9. her   10. it

C
1. His hat   2. Her bag
3. Your car   4. Their ball

D
1. mine   2. yours 3. his   4. hers   5. ours
6. theirs 7. hers   8. mine   9. his   10. theirs

GRAMMAR PRACTICE   p.21

A
1. This   2. These   3. These

B
1. Those   2. That   3. that

C
1. Mike : 여보세요. 나 Mike야. Ann 이니?
2. Ann : 응, 나야. 무슨 일이야, Mike?
3. Mike : 소식 들었니? 우리 이번 주말에 소풍 갈 거래.
4. Ann : 오, 나 그 소식 못 들었는데.

D
1. myself   2. yourself
3. himself   4. herself
5. ourselves   6. themselves
7. itself   8. yourselves

E
1. myself   2. themselves
3. her   4. ourselves
5. myself

GRAMMAR IN SENTENCE   p.22

1. **You** have a nice car.
   해석 너는 좋은 차를 가지고 있다.
2. **They** have a yellow ball.
   해석 그들은 노란색 공을 가지고 있다.
3. **These** books are for me.
   해석 이 책들은 나를 위한 것이다.
4. **Did** you hear the news?
   해석 너 그 소식 들었니?
5. **We** will go on a picnic this weekend.
   해석 우리 이번 주말에 소풍 갈 거래.
6. May I introduce **myself** right now?
   해석 내 자신을 지금 소개해도 될까요?
7. **They** enjoyed **themselves** yesterday.
   해석 그들은 즐거운 시간을 보냈다.
8. Tom gave **her** a ring.
   해석 Tom은 그녀에게 반지를 주었다.
9. **We** finished the project **ourselves**.
   해석 우리는 우리자신이 스스로 프로젝트를 마쳤다.
10. **I myself** made lunch.
    해석 내가 직접 점심식사를 만들었다.

UNIT 03 : 동사

GRAMMAR PRACTICE   p.25

A
(A) go   (C) sit   (E) ride   (H) come   (I) stand
(J) is   (K) are   (M) walk   (O) learn (Q) study
(R) was   (T) call   (U) eat   (V) have   (X) were

B
1. am   2. is   3. are   4. is   5. is
6. are   7. is   8. are   9. were 10. was

C
1. do → does / did - done
2. pass → passes / passed - passed
3. watch → watches / watched - watched
4. mix → mixes / mixed - mixed
5. play → plays / played - played
6. fly → flies / flew - flown
7. enjoy → enjoys / enjoyed - enjoyed
8. cry → cries / cried - cried
9. buy → buys / bought - bought
10. dream → dreams / dreamed - dreamed
11. teach → teaches / taught - taught
12. miss → misses / missed - missed
13. fix → fixes / fixed - fixed
14. go → goes / went - gone
15. live → lives / lived - lived

D
1. goes   2. played   3. will go   4. will get   5. drinks

GRAMMAR PRACTICE   p.27

A
(A) can ~할 수 있다.   (G) will ~을 할 것이다.
(O) may 아마 ~일 것이다.   (S) should ~해야 한다.
(U) must 반드시 ~해야만 하다.

B
1. It may be perfect.
2. He can swim.
3. It will rain tomorrow.
4. You should meet Jenny.
5. You must keep your word.

C
1. I <u>am going to</u> go shopping next weekend.
2. Tom <u>is able to</u> drive a car.
3. Linda <u>has to</u> call the police.
4. I <u>should</u> go to bed now.
5. <u>Can</u> I speak to John, please?

GRAMMAR IN SENTENCE p.28

1. Ann goes to church every Sunday.
해석 Ann은 일요일마다 교회가 간다.
goes 동사

2. I played baseball last weekend.
해석 나는 지난 주말에 야구를 했다.
played 동사

3. He will go to school next year.
해석 그는 내년에 학교에 갈 것이다.
will 조동사 go 본동사

4. They will get up at 6 o'clock tomorrow.
해석 그들은 내일 6시에 일어날 것이다.
will 조동사 get 본동사

5. David drinks a glass of milk every day.
해석 David는 매일 우유 한 잔을 마신다.
drinks 동사

6. I will go shopping next weekend.
해석 나는 다음 주에 쇼핑을 갈 예정이다.
will 조동사 go 본동사

7. Tom can drive.
해석 Tom 자동차를 운전 할 수 있다.
can 조동사 drive 본동사

8. Linda must call the police.
해석 Linda는 경찰을 불러야 해야 한다.
must 조동사 call 본동사

9. I should go to bed now.
해석 나는 지금 자러 가야만 한다.
should 조동사 go 본동사

10. May I speak to John, please?
해석 John과 통화해도 될까요?
May 조동사 speak 본동사

ACTUAL TEST 1 p.30-31

A
1. (B)	2. (B)	3. (A)	4. (B)	5. (B)
6. (A)	7. (D)	8. (A)	9. (B)	10. (B)
11. (D)	12. (C)			

1. Austin is purchasing --------.
(A) book
(B) a book
(C) a books
(D) two book
해석 Austin이 책을 사고 있다.
해설 book은 가산명사이므로 관사 a 또는 the 와 함께 써야 합니다.

2. Sally and I ------ the same age.
(A) am
(B) are
(C) is
(D) be
해석 sally 와 나는 동갑이다.
해설 주어가 Sally and I로 복수이므로 복수 동사인 are를 써야 합니다.

3. The small box is filled with ------.
(A) rice
(B) rices
(C) a rice
(D) two rices
해석 작은 상자가 쌀로 가득 차 있다.
해설 rice는 불가산명사이므로 수를 나타내는 a와 함께 쓸 수 없고, 복수로 만들 수 없습니다.

4. -------- can solve this problem.
(A) my
(B) I
(C) mine
(D) me
해석 나는 이 문제를 해결할 수 있다.
해설 주어 자리이므로 주격 대명사 I를 써야 합니다.

5. -------- parents have a computer.
(A) I
(B) my
(C) me
(D) mine
해석 나의 부모님은 컴퓨터를 가지고 계신다.
해설 명사인 parents는 소유격 대명사인 my와 함께 쓸 수 있습니다.

6. Five -------- are walking toward an archway.
(A) children
(B) man
(C) woman
(D) boy
해석 다섯 명의 사람들이 아치모양의 통로를 향해서 걸어가고 있다.
해설 five는 복수 명사와 함께 써야하므로 child의 복수형인 (A) children이 정답입니다.

7. Jenny -------- to the party tomorrow.
(A) come
(B) came
(C) comes
(D) will come
해석 Jenny는 내일 파티에 갈 것이다.
해설 tomorrows는 미래시제와 함께 써야 하므로 정답은 (D) will come 입니다.

8. The ring on the table is --------.
(A) hers
(B) she
(C) herself
(D) her

해석 테이블 위에 있는 그 반지는 그녀의 것이다.
해설 be 동사 뒤에는 소유대명사가 올 수 있다. her ring = hers 이므로 정답은 (A) 이다.

9. She likes to make cake --------.
(A) she
(B) herself
(C) hers
(D) her

해석 그는 혼자 케이크 만드는 것을 좋아한다.
해설 문장에서 주어는 she 이고 동사 make의 목적어는 cake 이다. 그러므로 빈칸은 주어를 강조하는 재귀대명사가 들어가야 한다. 정답은 (B) herself이다.

10. Bob -------- on a business trip yesterday.
(A) go
(B) went
(C) gone
(D) goes

해석 밥은 어제 출장 갔다.
해설 yesterday는 과거를 나타내므로 go 과거동사인 went가 적합하다.

11. Dennis -------- baseball every Sunday.
(A) play
(B) will play
(C) played
(D) plays

해석 데니스는 일요일마다 야구를 한다.
해설 every Sunday는 매주 일요일마다 반복되는 사실을 나타낼 때 쓴다. 불변의 진리, 반복되는 사실, 습관 등은 현재시제와 함께 쓴다.

12. Your deadline is two -------- before that time.
(A) month
(B) the month
(C) months
(D) a month

해석 마감일은 두 달 전입니다.
해설 복수를 의미하는 two 와 어울리는 명사는 months 이다.

B
1. (shelfs) → (shelves)
2. (a) → (an)
3. (rices) → (rice)
4. (its) → (their)
5. (him) → (his)
6. (taste) → (tastes)
7. (wasn't) → (weren't)
8. (You) → (Your)
9. (passes) → (pass)
10. (read) → (reads)

C
(1) These → This
(4) design → designs

From : Elizabeth Linn
Received : October 10, 3:31 P.M.
To : David Manning

Good morning, Mr. Manning. (1) These is Elizabeth from Star Graphic Design. We (2) discussed the (3) designs in your office last Tuesday. The (4) design are ready. I (5) was hoping to schedule a meeting to review which ones you'd like to use in (6) your new catalog. Thank you.

발신자 : 엘리자베스 린
수신 : 10월 10일 오후 3시31분
수신자 : 데이비드 매닝

안녕하세요, 매닝 씨. 저는 스타 그래픽 디자인의 엘리자베스입니다. 지난 화요일에 당신 사무실에서 저희가 디자인에 대해 얘기를 나누었죠. 작업이 준비되었습니다. 저는 당신의 새로운 카탈로그에 사용하시고자 하는 디자인이 어떤 것인지 검토하기 위해 회의 일정을 잡고자 합니다. 감사합니다.

UNIT 04 : 형용사

GRAMMAR PRACTICE p.35

A
(A) green   (B) full   (F) pretty
(H) nice   (I) happy   (K) big
(M) small   (N) red   (O) boring
(Q) large   (R) possible   (T) fresh

B
1. This is a small car
   = The car is small.
2. He is a new teacher.
   = The teacher is new.
3. It is hot tea.
   = The tea is hot.
4. That is a beautiful rainbow.
   = The rainbow is beautiful.
5. It is a red roof.
   = The roof is red.

C
1. interesting   2. disappointed   3. surprised
4. boring   5. excited

D
1. shocking 2. bored 3. interesting

GRAMMAR PRACTICE p.37

A
(A) many (D) much (F) few (I) some (K) a little
(O) little (Q) a few (R) all

B
1. (A) 2. (C) 3. (B) 4. (D) 5. (D)

C
1. much 2. many 3. a lot of 4. a lot of 5. lots of
6. much 7. some 8. lots of 9. some 10. many

GRAMMAR IN SENTENCE p.38

1. I watched an **interesting** movie.
해석 나는 재미있는 영화를 보았다.

2. People were **disappointed** with the result.
해석 사람들은 그 결과에 실망했다.

3. Students are **surprised** by the news.
해석 학생들은 그 소식에 놀랐다.

4. I read a **boring** book yesterday.
해석 나는 지루한 책을 읽었다.

5. I saw **excited** people in the park.
해석 나는 흥분한 사람들을 보았다.

6. The children should read **a lot of** storybooks.
해석 아이들은 많은 이야기책을 읽어야만 한다.

7. Jenny collects **lots of** cans every day.
해석 Jenny는 많은 캔들을 매일 모은다.

8. There is too **much** information.
해석 너무 많은 정보가 있다.

9. I bought **some** apples at the market.
해석 나는 시장에서 몇 개의 사과를 샀다.

10. The rainbow is **beautiful**.
해석 그 무지개는 아름답다.

UNIT 05 : 부사

GRAMMAR PRACTICE p.41

A
(C) fast (D) well
(E) yet (H) high
(I) very (K) really
(L) soon (Q) seldom
(S) there

B
1. often 2. never 3. always 4. soon 5. rarely

C
1. (C) 2. (D) 3. (D)
4. (C) 5. (D)

D
1. brave 2. slowly 3. quiet
4. beautifully 5. loudly

GRAMMAR PRACTICE p.43

A
1. good, kind, quiet, angry
2. well, always, slowly, often
3. early, fast, daily, long

B
1. late 2. hard 3. highly 4. high 5. hardly
6. high 7. close 8. closely 9. close 10. hard

GRAMMAR IN SENTENCE p.44

1. He went to bed **late** last night.
해석 그는 어젯밤에 늦게 잠자리에 들었다.

2. This is a hard question for everyone.
해석 이것은 모든 사람에게 어려운 질문이다.
부사 없음

3. Beth is a **highly** respected person.
해석 Beth는 매우 존경받는 사람입니다.

4. The volume of the radio is **too** high.
해석 라디오 볼륨이 너무 크다.

5. That report is **hardly** surprising.
해석 그 보고서는 거의 놀라운 일이 아니다.

6. The birds fly **high** in the sky.
해석 새들이 하늘을 높이 난다.

7. Could you close the window?
해석 창문을 닫아주시겠어요?
부사 없음

8. I sat and read the report **closely** for a while.
해석 나는 앉아서 한동안 그 보고서를 상세히 읽었다.

9. The economy is close to recession.
해석 경제는 불황에 가깝다.
부사 없음

10. They are hard workers.
해석 그들은 열심히 일하는 사람이다.
부사 없음

UNIT 06 : 전치사

GRAMMAR PRACTICE p.47

A
(A) in   (B) at   (F) for
(I) to   (K) of   (M) on
(N) into   (P) by   (R) across
(T) with   (V) during   (W) behind

B
(A) on   (B) in   (C) on
(D) in   (E) in   (F) at
(G) on   (H) In

C
(A) during   (B) for   (C) during
(D) for   (E) for   (F) during

D
(C) above → in spring
(E) in → on Monday morning
(L) at → in April

E
1. from   2. before   3. by   4. until   5. by

GRAMMAR PRACTICE p.49

A
1. in   2. on   3. in   4. in   5. at

B
1. below   2. along   3. over   4. through   5. on
6. over   7. out of   8. to   9. across   10. on

GRAMMAR IN SENTENCE p.50

1. There are some boats **below** the bridge.
해석 다리 아래에 보트가 몇 척 있다.

2. They are walking **along** the street.
해석 그들은 길을 따라 걷고 있다.

3. The boys are jumping **over** the fence.
해석 소년들이 울타리를 뛰어넘고 있다.

4. The train passes **through** the tunnel.
해석 기차가 터널을 통과한다.

5. There is a computer **on** the desk.
해석 책상 위에 컴퓨터 한 대가 있다.

6. Lamps are hanging **over** the table.
해석 테이블 위에 램프가 걸려 있다.

7. I will be **out of** town **for** a few days.
해석 나는 며칠 동안 이곳을 떠날 것이다.

8. How far is it from here **to** your school?
해석 여기에서 당신의 학교까지 얼마나 멀어요?

9. The library is **across** the street.
해석 도서관이 길 건너편에 있다.

10. The children are playing **on** the grass.
해석 아이들이 잔디 위에서 놀고 있다.

ACTUAL TEST 2 p.52-53

A
1. (D)   2. (A)   3. (A)   4. (B)   5. (C)
6. (B)   7. (B)   8. (B)   9. (C)   10. (B)
11. (B)   12. (C)

1. I met a -------- woman on the street.
(A) beauty
(B) beautifully
(C) beautify
(D) beautiful
해석 나는 길에서 아름다운 여자를 만났다.
해설 woman 이 명사이므로 명사는 형용사가 수식한다. beautiful이 형용사이다.
어휘 **beauty** 아름다움   **beautifully** 아름답게   **beautify** 아름답게 하다

2. All of the employees are -------- thanks to the bonuses.
(A) happy
(B) happiness
(C) happily
(D) happen
해석 보너스 덕분에 모든 직원들이 행복하다.
해설 be 동사 뒤에는 형용사가 보어로 와야 한다. happiness는 명사 happily는 부사 happen은 일이 발생하다 라는 의미의 동사이다.
어휘 **employee** 직원   **thanks to** 덕분에   **bonuse** 보너스

3. Beth made -------- mistakes yesterday.
(A) several
(B) a little
(C) much
(D) little
해석 Beth는 어제 몇 가지 실수를 했다.
해설 mistakes는 가산명사의 복수형이므로 several 이 가산명사의 복수형과 함께 쓸 수 있는 수량 형용사이다. a little, much, little은 불가산명사와 함께 쓴다.
어휘 **make mistake** 실수하다

4. I saw an -------- movie last night.
(A) excited
(B) interesting

(C) bored
(D) exhausted

해석 나는 어제 재미있는 영화를 봤다.
해설 movie를 수식할 수 있는 감정동사는 현재분사 형태로 써야 한다.
어휘 **excited** 흥분된 **bored** 지겨운 **exhausted** 지친

5. Our team holds a meeting -------.
(A) week
(B) day
(C) weekly
(D) quarter

해석 우리 팀은 매주 회의를 연다.
해설 주어는 our team 동사 holds 목적어 a meeting 으로 완전한 성분을 갖춘 마지막에 올 수 있는 품사는 부사이다.
어휘 **hold** 개최하다 **meeting** 회의 **weekly** 매주 **quarter** 분기

6. Those books are -------- recommended by experts.
(A) high
(B) highly
(C) higher
(D) height

해석 전문가들이 그 책을 각별히 권합니다.
해설 '매우, 몹시, 각별히'라는 의미의 부사는 highly이다.
어휘 **recommend** 추천하다 **expert** 전문가

7. Ted will be back -------.
(A) short
(B) shortly
(C) shorten
(D) immediate

해석 Ted는 곧 돌아올 것이다.
해설 '곧, 즉시'라는 의미의 부사는 shortly이다.
어휘 **shorten** 줄이다 **immediate** 즉시의

8. Linda -------- goes to school by bus.
(A) lately
(B) sometimes
(C) well
(D) easy

해석 Linda는 때때로 학교에 버스로 간다.
해설 현재시제인 goes 와 가장 잘 어울리는 부사는 '때때로'라는 의미의 sometimes이다. lately는 '최근에'라는 의미로 과거 또는 현재완료 시제와 쓰입니다.
어휘 **lately** 최근에 **sometimes** 때때로 **well** 잘 **easy** 쉬운

9. There is a big mirror -------- the wall.
(A) at
(B) in
(C) on
(D) into

해석 벽에 거울이 있다.
해설 표면 위를 나타낼 때는 전치사 on 을 쓴다.
어휘 **mirror** 거울 **wall** 벽

10. Kathy is standing -------- the subway station exit.
(A) in
(B) at
(C) on
(D) over

해석 Kathy는 지하철역에 서 있다.
해설 정확한 지점을 나타낼 때는 전치사 at을 쓴다.
어휘 **stand** 서다 **subway** 지하철 **station** 역

11. Grace lives -------- Canada with her family.
(A) at
(B) in
(C) on
(D) for

해석 Grace는 캐나다에서 그의 가족과 함께 살고 있다.
해설 넓은 장소를 나타낼 때는 전치사 in을 쓴다.
어휘 **live** 살다 **family** 가족

12. A man is using a phone -------- the door.
(A) above
(B) beneath
(C) in front of
(D) over

해석 한 남자가 문 앞에서 전화 통화를 하고 있다.
해설 '앞에'라는 의미의 위치를 나타내는 전치사는 in front of 이다.
어휘 **use** 사용하다

B

1. (fastly) → (fast)
2. (surprising) → (surprised)
3. (Much) → (Many)
4. (safe) → (safely)
5. (Lucky) → (Luckily)
6. (highly) → (high)
7. (slow) → (slowly)
8. (at) → (in)
9. (until) → (by)
10. (at) → (along / in)

C

(1) electronic → electronics
(4) at → on

For this week only, all (1) electronic at 'Best Tech World' will be on sale. Everything will be discounted up to 50% off! Come and choose from a wide selection of (2) electronics including TVs, home stereos, and (3) refrigerators. Our store is located (4) at Washington Street. Just follow (5) the signs to "Best Tech World". Come soon before everything (6) is sold out.

금주에 한해, 베스트 테크 월드의 모든 전자제품들에 대해 세일이 실시됩니다. 모든 제품은 최대 50퍼센트까지 할인됩니다. TV, 홈 스테레오 그리고 냉장고 등이 포함된 다양한 품목에서 선택하십시오. 저희 상점은 워싱턴 거리에 위치하고 있습니다. "베스트 테크 월드"안내표지를 따라오시면 됩니다. 모든 상품이 다 팔리기 전에 서둘러 오십시오.

MINI TEST 1
p.54-55

A

1. (B)	2. (A)	3. (B)	4. (B)	5. (B)
6. (C)	7. (C)	8. (B)	9. (D)	10. (A)
11. (C)	12. (C)			

1. I saw a man and -------- is sitting beside the table.
(A) a man
(B) the man
(C) men
(D) man
해석 나는 한 남자를 보았다. 그 남자는 테이블 옆에 앉아 있다.
해설 이미 앞에서 a man 이라고 했으므로 다시 반복을 할 때는 the man 이라고 해야한다.

2. Linda loves -------- brother.
(A) her
(B) she
(C) herself
(D) herself
해석 Linda 는 그녀의 오빠를 사랑한다.
해설 명사 brother 앞에는 소유격이 와야 한다.

3. I don't know -------- name.
(A) he
(B) his
(C) him
(D) himself
해석 나는 그의 이름을 모른다.
해설 명사 name 앞에는 소유격이 와야 한다.

4. Mike and I -------- good friends.
(A) am
(B) are
(C) is
(D) be
해석 Mike와 나는 좋은 친구입니다.
해설 주어가 Mike and I로 복수이므로 동사는 are이 와야 한다.

5. The sun -------- in the east.
(A) rise
(B) rises
(C) rose
(D) risen
해석 태양은 동쪽에서 뜬다.
해설 불변의 진리이므로 현재형 동사 rises를 써야 한다.

6. Mike -------- TV last night.
(A) watch
(B) watches
(C) watched
(D) will watch.
해석 Mike는 어제 밤에 TV를 시청했다.
해설 last night 과는 과거 시제를 써야 하므로 watched가 정답이다.

7. Birds -------- in the sky.
(A) flies
(B) flied
(C) can fly
(D) is flied
해석 새들은 하늘을 날 수 있다.
해설 주어가 birds로 복수이므로 조동사 can과 함께 쓴 can fly가 가장 자연스럽다.

8. Linda bought a -------- coat in a store.
(A) run
(B) blue
(C) tall
(D) newly
해석 Linda는 상점에서 파란색 코트를 하나 샀다.
해설 coat는 명사이므로 형용사 blue와 함께 써야한다.

9. There is -------- cheese on the table.
(A) many
(B) a few
(C) several
(D) some
해석 테이블에 치즈가 있다.
해설 cheese는 셀 수 없는 명사이므로 some 과 함께 써야한다.

10. They study -------- in the library.
(A) hard
(B) hardly
(C) hardness
(D) quiet
해석 그들은 도서관에서 열심히 공부한다.
해설 '열심히'라는 의미의 부사는 hard 이다.

11. I will visit London -------- the summer vacation.
(A) on
(B) next to
(C) during
(D) for
해석 나는 여름 방학동안 런던에 갈 것이다.
해설 '~하는 동안에'라는 의미로 기간을 나타내는 명사와 함께쓰는 전치사는 during 이다.

12. We will take a mid-term -------- October 20th.
(A) in
(B) at
(C) on
(D) for

해석 우리는 10월 20일에 중간고사를 볼 것이다.
해설 특정일은 on과 함께 쓴다.

B
1. (at) → (throughout)
2. (You) → (Your)
3. (happily) → (happy)
4. (like) →(likes)
5. (shop) → (a shop)
6. (Child) → (Children)
7. (Much) → (Many)
8. (heavily) → (heavy)
9. (visit) → (will visit)
10. (have) → (has)

C
(2) constructive → construction
(4) mine → me

> To All employees
> I just want to (A) remind everyone that (B) constructive of the new (C) laboratory is going to begin on Tuesday. The Facilities Department has just informed (D) mine that the north parking area will be (E) closed for the duration of the project. You'll have to use the east, west and south parking areas, so it will take longer to enter and (F)exit company grounds. Thank you for your cooperation.

> 모든 직원들에게
> 여러분 모두에게 새로운 실험실의 공사가 화요일에 시작할 것을 알리고 싶습니다. 시설 부서가 북쪽 주차장이 그 프로젝트 기간 동안 폐쇄될 거란 사실을 방금 제게 알려왔습니다. 여러분들은 동쪽, 서쪽 또는 남쪽 주차 구역을 이용해야 할 것입니다. 그래서 회사에 들어가거나 나오기 위해 더 많은 시간이 걸릴 것입니다. 협조해 주셔서 감사합니다.

UNIT 07 : 문장의 성분, 1형식

GRAMMAR PRACTICE p.59

A
1. Birds 주어 / fly 동사
2. Linda 주어 / is 동사 / happy 보어
3. They 주어 / have 동사 / breakfast 목적어
4. Children 주어 / throw 동사 / the ball 목적어
5. The ball 주어 / is 동사 / white 보어

B
1. 주어   2. 목적어   3. 보어
4. 동사, 목적어   5. 동사, 목적어

C
1. Tom makes dinner (every day).
2. Susan studies (very hard).
3. They live (in Michigan).
4. Jenny sleeps (at ten).
5. We swim (in the river).

GRAMMAR PRACTICE p.61

A
1. Mike 주어 / works 동사. 1형식
2. She 주어 / has 동사 / a dog 목적어. 3형식
3. He 주어 / is 동사 / a doctor 보어. 2형식
4. They 주어 / sleep 동사. 1형식
5. They 주어 / walk 동사 (along the shore) 1형식

B
1. 1형식   2. 2형식   3. 3형식   4. 4형식   5. 5형식
6. 1형식   7. 1형식   8. 3형식   9. 2형식   10. 1형식

GRAMMAR IN SENTENCE p.62

1. She / sleeps (at nine).
   S   V
해석 그녀는 9시에 잔다.

2. Austin / is / (very) nice.
   S   V   C
해석 Austin은 매우 친절하다

3. Jenny / likes / apples.
   S   V   O
해석 Jenny는 사과를 좋아한다.

4. Austin / gave / Jennifer / an apple.
   S   V   IO   DO
해석 Austin은 Jennifer에게 사과를 주었다.

5. Austin / made / her / angry.
   S   V   O   C
해석 Austin은 그녀를 화나게 만들었다.

6. The leaves / are falling (on the street).
   S   V
해석 나뭇잎들이 거리에 떨어지고 있다.

7. David / works (on weekends).
   S   V
해석 David는 주말마다 일한다.

8. She / reads / a newspaper (in the morning).
   S   V   O
해석 그녀는 아침에 신문을 읽는다.

9. Eric / looks / happy.
　　 S　　V　　 C

해석 Eric은 행복해 보인다.

10. They / walk (everyday).
　　 S　　V

해석 그들은 매일 걷는다.

UNIT 08 : 2형식, 3형식

GRAMMAR PRACTICE p.65

A

1. The baby is cute.
2. The children are happy.
3. He looks sad.
4. They feel good.
5. They sing a song. 3형식 동사
6. Tommy became a doctor.
7. She made some cookies. 4형식 동사
8. She looks beautiful.
9. They discussed the problem. 3형식 동사
10. Nick resembles his brother. 3형식 동사

B

1. good
2. like a poet
3. nice.
4. like a dinosaur bone
5. like cats

C

1. The earth looks beautiful.
2. O
3. The people are happy.
4. The cake tastes good.
5. O

GRAMMAR PRACTICE p.67

A

1. The baby drinks milk.
2. They purchased a chair last weekend.
3. The movie made me sad. 4형식 동사
4. He works hard. 1형식 동사
5. This tea is great. 2형식 동사
6. Tommy read a book.
7. The girl looks like an angel. 2형식 동사
8. The man looks diligent. 2형식 동사
9. My sister took a nap.
10. She painted the wall last month.

B

(A) Justine reads a book every day.
(B) Kelly bought some bananas yesterday.
(C) Beth wrote an email last night.

C

(B) (D) (G) (H) (I) (L) (M) (P)

D

1. A letter is written every day by him.
2. A letter was written yesterday by him.
3. A letter will be written tomorrow by him.

GRAMMAR IN SENTENCE p.68

1. They / discussed / the problem.
　 S　　　V　　　　　O

해석 그들은 그 문제를 의논했다.

2. Nick / resembles / his brother.
　 S　　　V　　　　　O

해석 Nick은 그의 형을 닮았다.

3. He / will write / a letter (tomorrow).
　 S　　V　　　　　O

해석 그는 내일 편지를 쓸 것이다.

4. Justine / reads / a book (everyday).
　 S　　　V　　　　O

해석 Justine은 매일 책을 읽는다.

5. Kelly / bought / some bananas (yesterday).
　 S　　　V　　　　　O

해석 Kelly는 어제 바나나를 구매했다.

6. Beth / wrote / an email (last night).
　 S　　　V　　　　O

해석 Beth는 어젯밤에 이메일을 썼다.

7. They / purchased / a chair (last weekend).
　 S　　　V　　　　　O

해석 그들은 지난 주말에 의자 하나를 구매했다.

8. The man / looks / (very) diligent.
　 S　　　V　　　　　SC

해석 그 남자는 매우 부지런해 보인다.

9. The movie / made / me / sad.
　 S　　　V　　 O　 OC

해석 그 영화가 나를 슬프게 만들었다.

10. She / painted / the wall (last month).
　　 S　　V　　　　 O

해석 그녀는 지난달에 벽을 페인트 칠 했다.

217

UNIT 09 : 4형식, 5형식

GRAMMAR PRACTICE p.71

A
(A) (B) (F) (H) (J) (K) (M) (O)

B
1. him an email
2. Tony a gift
3. him chocolates
4. her a hat
5. me an album

C
1. to 2. for 3. to 4. for 5. for

D
1. My parents bought a pizza for me.
2. Mr. Johns sent his photo to me.
3. Can you lend the book to me?
4. Jenny will make a cake for you.
5. O

GRAMMAR PRACTICE p.73

A
(A) (D) (F) (H) (I) (K) (O)

B
1. angry 2. difficult 3. easy
4. a genius 5. the chairperson

C
1. was given 2. sent 3. made
4. was named 5. kind

D
1. → A letter was sent to his brother by Austin.
   → His brother was sent a letter by Austin.
2. → The woman was called an angel by people.
3. → I was given a weekly report by him.
   → A weekly report was given to me by him.

GRAMMAR IN SENTENCE p.74

1. My parents / bought / a pizza (for me).
   S   V   O
   해석 나의 부모님께서는 나에게 피자를 사 주셨다.

2. Mr. Johns / sent / his photo (to me).
   S   V   O
   해석 Johns씨는 그의 사진을 나에게 보내주었다.

3. Can / you / lend / me / the book?
   V(조동사) S V(본동사) IO   DO
   해석 저에게 그 책을 보내 주실 수 있나요?

4. Jenny / will make / you / a cake.
   S   V   IO   DO
   해석 Jenny가 너를 위해 케이크를 만들어 줄 것이다.

5. David / gave / me / some flowers.
   S   V   IO   DO
   해석 David가 나에게 꽃을 주었다.

6. Terry / made / me / angry.
   S   V   IO   OC
   해석 Terry는 나를 화나게 만들었다.

7. I / found / the test / difficult.
   S   V   O   OC
   해석 나는 그 시험이 어렵다는 것을 알게 되었다.

8. Students / found / the mid-term exam / easy.
   S   V   O   OC
   해석 학생들은 중간시험이 어렵다고 생각했다.

9. People / called / David / a genius.
   S   V   O   OC
   해석 사람들은 David를 천재라고 불렀다.

10. They / appointed / Mr. Tomas / the chairperson.
    S   V   O   OC
    해석 그들이 Tomas를 의장으로 임명했다.

ACTUAL TEST 3 p.76-77

A
1. (B)	2. (A)	3. (D)	4. (C)	5. (A)
6. (C)	7. (B)	8. (D)	9. (D)	10. (A)
11. (A)	12. (A)			

1. The car -------- down the hill.
(A) run
(B) ran
(C) gives
(D) gave
해석 차는 언덕을 달려 내려갔다.
해설 run은 1형식 동사로 뒤에 목적어가 오지 않는다. 주어가 the car 로 3인칭 단수이므로 (A)는 runs라고 써야한다. give는 4형식동사로 목적어를 두 개 취할 수 있다. 그러므로 정답은 (B)이다.
어휘 hill 언덕 run 달리다

2. All employees -------- Monday through Friday.
(A) work
(B) are
(C) have
(D) make
해석 모든 직원들이 월요일부터 금요일까지 일한다.
해설 Monday through Friday는 시간을 나타내는 전치사구 이므로 빈 칸에는 1형식 동사인 자동사가 적합하다.

3. Tom -------- his girlfriend a ring yesterday.
(A) was
(B) loved
(C) made
(D) gave

해석 Tom은 어제 그의 여자 친구에게 반지를 주었다.
해설 his girlfriend는 간접목적어, a ring은 직접 목적어이므로 4형식 동사인 give 가 가장 적합하다.

4. My grandmother -------- a room warm last night.
(A) were
(B) liked
(C) made
(D) gave

해석 나의 할머니께서는 어젯밤에 방을 따뜻하게 만드셨다.
해설 a room은 목적어 warm은 목적보어 이므로 5형식동사인 make 가 가장 적합하다.

5. Tommy -------- a new employee of the sales department.
(A) is
(B) runs
(C) walks
(D) drives

해석 Tommy는 영업 부서의 신입 직원이다.
해설 Tommy는 주어이고, a new employee는 주격보어이다. 그러므로 '이다'라는 의미의 be 동사인 is가 가장 적합하다.

6. The bread on the table -------- good.
(A) makes
(B) are
(C) smells
(D) smells like

해석 테이블 위에 있는 빵이 맛있는 냄새가 난다.
해설 good은 형용사로 주격 보어로 쓰였으므로 2형식 동사인 smell이 적합하다.

7. Our English teacher -------- really angry.
(A) look
(B) looks
(C) is looked
(D) look like

해석 우리 영어 선생님은 정말 화가 나 많이 난 것 같다.
해설 really는 부사이고, angry가 형용사로 주격보어로 쓰였으므로 정답은 (B) looks 이다.

8. The man in the auditorium -------- a famous singer.
(A) look
(B) looks
(C) looked
(D) looks like

해석 강당에 있는 그 남자는 유명한 가수처럼 보인다.
해설 a famous singer 이 주격 보어인데, look은 명사가 주격보어로 올 때, '~처럼'이라는 의미의 like 와 함께 써야 한다.

9. Our team will -------- the problem tomorrow.
(A) feel
(B) work
(C) look
(D) discuss

해석 우리는 다음 주에 그 문제를 논의할 것이다.
해설 목적어인 the problem 과 함께 쓸 수 있는 타동사는 discuss 이다.

10. A professor -------- his students some questions.
(A) gave
(B) found
(C) kept
(D) called

해석 교수님은 학생들에게 몇 가지 질문을 했다.
해설 his students는 간접목적어, some questions는 직접목적어로 쓰인 4형식 구조이므로 4형식 동사인 give 가 가장 적합하다.

11. Jefferson wrote a letter -------- his girlfriend.
(A) to
(B) for
(C) at
(D) in

해석 제퍼슨은 편지를 그의 여자 친구에게 썼다.
해설 4형식을 3형식으로 바꿀 때 전치사가 필요하다. 이때 write는 전치사 to를 쓴다.

12. The movie -------- Matt Damon a big star.
(A) made
(B) gave
(C) showed
(D) sent

해석 그 영화는 맷 데이먼을 대단한 스타로 만들어 주었다.
해설 Matt Damon이 목적어, a big star 이 목적보어로 쓰인 5형식 구조 문장이다.

B

1. (the sky) → (in the sky)
2. (happily) → (happy)
3. (strangely) → (strange)
4. (looks) → (looks like)
5. (strongly) → (strong)
6. (to) → (for)
7. (some paper me) → (me some paper)
8. (for) → (to)
9. (cleans) → (clean)
10. (health) → (healthy)

C

(2) uncomfortably → uncomfortable
(4) Probable → Probably

Maria 1:11 p.m.	Hi, Bob. The air conditioner isn't working here.
Bob 1:13 p.m.	OK, I'll send someone (1) to your office.
Maria 1:15 p.m.	Thanks. It's very (2) uncomfortably and (3) hot.
Bob 1:16 p.m.	(4) Probable, It is because the fan is (5) old, so we'll make it (6) clean.

Maria 1:11 p.m.	안녕하세요, 여기 에어컨이 고장 났어요.
Bob 1:13 p.m.	알았어요. 당장 봐 줄 사람을 당신의 사무실로 보낼게요.
Maria 1:15 p.m.	고마워요. 굉장히 불편하고 덥네요.
Bob 1:16 p.m.	아마 환풍기가 오래 되어서, 청소도 좀 할게요.

UNIT 10 : 구

GRAMMAR PRACTICE p.81

A

	동사	목적어
1. to go	decided	to go
2. to make	need	to make
3. to buy	wants	to buy
4. to read	plan	to read
5. to appear	wants	to appear

B
1. Going skiing is exciting.
2. Singing a song is fun.
3. Climbing a mountain is hard.
4. Jogging in the morning is good for you.

C
1. My dream is to be a millionaire.
2. We plan to go shopping.
3. Karen loves watching a movie.
4. Her hobby is reading books.
5. Playing games is fun.

GRAMMAR PRACTICE p.83

A
1. to make   2. to read   3. to see
4. to eat   5. to see

B
1. to be a doctor
2. in the room
3. to do his homework
4. Learning English
5. on the hill.

C
1. D   2. A   3. B   4. E   5. C

GRAMMAR IN SENTENCE p.84

1. Jenny wants to be a doctor. 명사구
   해석 Jenny는 의사가 되기를 원한다.
2. The bag in the room is mine. 형용사구
   해석 방 안에 있는 가방은 나의 것이다.
3. David stayed at home to do his homework. 부사구
   해석 David는 그의 숙제를 하기 위해서 집에 있다.
4. I went to bed early to get up early. 부사구
   해석 나는 일찍 일어나기 위하여 일찍 잠자리에 들었다.
5. The school is on the hill. 명사구
   해석 학교가 언덕 위에 있다.
6. Tom works hard to be rich. 부사구
   해석 Tom은 부자가 되기 위해서 열심히 일한다.
7. The ring on the table is hers. 형용사구
   해석 테이블에 있는 반지는 그녀의 것이다.
8. Swimming in this river is dangerous. 명사구
   해석 이 강에서 수영하는 것은 위험하다
9. I got up early to catch the train. 부사구
   해석 그 기차를 타기 위해서 나는 일찍 일어났다.
10. Learning English is not hard at all. 명사구
    해석 영어를 배우는 것은 전혀 어렵지 않다.

UNIT 11 : 절

GRAMMAR PRACTICE p.87

A
(B) and   (D) but   (E) although
(G) because   (J) if   (L) that
(N) so   (O) when   (P) while

B
1. that I read yesterday
2. that he is honest
3. because it snows a lot
4. who suggested the idea
5. when I was young

C
1. E 2. D 3. B 4. C 5. A

GRAMMAR PRACTICE p.89

A
1. 만약 ~하지 않으면
2. ~에도 불구하고
3. ~ 때문에
4. ~임에 반하여
5. 그래서
6. ~하는 동안, ~인 반면에
7. 그리고
8. ~한 이후로 줄곧, ~이므로
9. 또는
10. 비록 ~일 지라도

B
1. and 2. but 3. or 4. so 5. but

C
1. (시간)
주절 : Tom took a shower.
종속절 : before he went out

2. (원인)
주절 : David cannot buy the car.
종속절 : because he is poor

3. (조건)
주절 : please call me.
종속절 : if it rains tomorrow

4. (양보)
주절 : Robert is happy.
종속절 : although he is poor

5. (시간)
주절 : Tom went to school.
종속절 : after he took a shower

GRAMMAR IN SENTENCE p.90

1. That the Earth looks like a circle is true. 명사절
해석 지구가 원형처럼 보인다는 것은 사실이다.

2. People think that he is honest. 명사절
해석 사람들은 그가 정직하다고 생각한다.

3. Her problem is that she is too lazy. 명사절
해석 그녀의 문제는 너무 게으르다는 것이다.

4. Jack is the person who suggested the idea. 형용사절
해석 Jack이 그 아이디어를 제안했던 사람이다.

5. When I was young, I lived in California. 부사절
해석 내가 어렸을 때, 나는 캘리포니아에 살았다.

6. If it rains tomorrow, we won't go on a trip. 부사절
해석 만약 내일 비가 내리면, 나는 여행을 안 갈 것이다.

7. Because it snows a lot, I can't go there. 부사절
해석 눈이 너무 많이 내리기 때문에, 나는 그것에 갈 수 없다.

8. Although they are poor, they spend too much money. 부사절
해석 그들은 가난함에도 불구하고, 너무 많은 돈을 쓴다.

9. I know the man who is walking on the street. 형용사절
해석 나는 길을 걷고 그 남자를 알고 있다.

10. This is the book that I read yesterday. 형용사절
해석 이것이 내가 어제 읽었던 책이다.

UNIT 12 : 문장의 종류

GRAMMAR PRACTICE p.93

A
1. He isn't a student.
2. They aren't nice.
3. They didn't find the bag.
4. He doesn't do his homework every day.
5. Jenny doesn't have lunch at noon.
6. They won't go on a picnic this weekend.
7. Tom didn't go shopping last Saturday.
8. Tom and Jenny don't go to church every Sunday.
9. Your dog isn't sleeping now.
10. He didn't hit the ball.

B
1. I wasn't late.
2. We won't play soccer tomorrow.
3. I'm not a nurse.
4. We didn't have dinner together.
5. We didn't do our best.

GRAMMAR PRACTICE p.95

A
1. Is he a student?
2. Are they nice?
3. Did they find the bag?
4. Does he do his homework every day?
5. Does Jenny have lunch at noon?
6. Will they go on a picnic this weekend?
7. Did Tom go shopping last Saturday?
8. Do Tom and Jenny go to church every Sunday?
9. Is your dog sleeping now?
10. Did he hit the ball?

B
1. Know yourself!
2. Don't be selfish!
3. Look at yourself!
4. Don't smoke here!
5. Be careful!

GRAMMAR IN SENTENCE
p.96

1. He / is / a student.
　　S　V　　C
해석 그는 학생이다.

2. They / are / nice.
　　　S　　V　　C
해석 그들은 친절하다.

3. They / found / the bag.
　　　S　　　V　　　O
해석 그들은 가방을 찾았다.

4. He / does / his homework (every day).
　　 S　　V　　　　O
해석 그는 그의 숙제를 매일 한다.

5. Jenny / has / lunch (at noon).
　　　S　　　V　　O
해석 Jenny는 정오에 점심 식사를 한다.

6. They / will go / (on a picnic) (this weekend).
　　　S　　　V
해석 그들은 이번 주말에 소풍을 갈 것이다.

7. You / should know / yourself.
　　　S　　　V　　　　O
해석 당신은 당신 자신을 알아야 한다.

8. You / should (not) be / selfish.
　　　S　　　V　　　　C
해석 당신은 이기적으로 행동하면 안된다.

9. Your dog / is sleeping (now).
　　　S　　　　V
해석 당신의 강아지는 지금 잠을 자고 있다.

10. He / hit / the ball.
　　　S　　V　　O
해석 그는 공을 쳤다.

ACTUAL TEST 4
p.98-99

A
1. (C)	2. (D)	3. (C)	4. (A)	5. (A)
6. (D)	7. (A)	8. (B)	9. (A)	10. (B)
11. (C)	12. (B)			

1. -------- Jenny wash her face every morning?
(A) Do
(B) Did
(C) Does
(D) Has
해석 Jenny는 매일 세수를 합니까?
해설 주어가 3인칭 단수(Jenny)이고 동사가 일반 동사(wash)이면서 현재 시제(every morning)일 때 의문문은 Does를 쓴다.

2. Tom -------- a shower last night because he was too tired.
(A) doesn't take
(B) don't take
(C) didn't took
(D) didn't take
해석 Tom은 너무 피곤해서 어제 밤에 샤워를 하지 않았다.
해설 과거시제(last night)에 대한 일반 동사의 부정문은 didn't를 쓴다.
어휘 tired 피곤한

3. Jenny -------- dinner because she wants to lose weight.
(A) have
(B) don't have
(C) doesn't have
(D) didn't has
해석 Jenny는 살을 빼기를 원하기 때문에 저녁을 먹지 않는다.
해설 주어가 3인칭 단수(Jenny)이고 동사가 일반 동사(have)이면서 현재 시제(have)일 때, 부정문은 doesn't 로 만들 수 있다.
어휘 lose one's weight ~의 몸무게를 줄이다

4. Mr. Davidson -------- his new plan with his colleagues last night.
(A) discussed
(B) talked
(C) responded
(D) reacted
해석 Davidson 씨는 그의 계획을 어제 밤에 동료들과 함께 의논했다.
해설 his new plan 을 목적어로 취할 수 있는 타동사가 적합하다. 그러므로 정답은 (A)이다.

5. -------- the truth is very important.
(A) Telling
(B) Tells
(C) Told
(D) Have told
해석 진실을 말하는 것은 매우 중요하다.
해설 주어 자리에 올 수 있는 구는 동명사가 있다. 'telling the truth'는 '진실을 말하는 것'이라는 의미로 주어역할을 하는 명사구이다.
어휘 truth 진실

6. The flowers and trees in the field -------- very beautiful.
(A) is
(B) was
(C) has
(D) are
해석 들판에 있는 꽃과 나무들이 아름답다.
해설 주어가 'The flowers and trees'인 명사구이다. 이때 주어가 복수이므로 동사는 are 을 써야한다. in the field는 전치사구이다.
어휘 field 들판　beautiful 아름다운

7. My hobby is -------- a horror movies.
(A) to watch
(B) watch
(C) watched
(D) watches

해석 나의 취미는 공포 영화를 보는 것이다.
해설 be 동사 뒤에 보어로 명사구인 동명사가 to 부정사가 쓰일 수 있다. 그러므로 정답은 to watch이다.
어휘 **hobby** 취미 **watch** 보다 **horror** 공포

8. I went to a Japanese restaurant -------- lunch.
(A) have
(B) to have
(C) having
(D) has

해석 나는 점심식사를 하기 위하여 일본음식점에 갔다.
해설 '~하기 위하여'라는 의미의 부사구는 to 부정사로 표현할 수 있다. 그러므로 to have lunch는 점심식사를 하기 위하여 라는 의미이다.
어휘 **restaurant** 식당

9. Linda is nice, -------- her sister is polite.
(A) and
(B) for
(C) or
(D) so

해석 Linda는 친절하고, 그녀의 여동생은 예의바르다.
해설 대등한 의미를 연결할 때는 등위 접속사 and를 쓸 수 있다.
어휘 **nice** 친절한 **polite** 예의 바른

10. I was very busy, -------- I took a taxi.
(A) and
(B) so
(C) for
(D) but

해석 나는 너무 바빴다. 그래서 택시를 탔다.
해설 완전한 절로 연결되어, 원인과 결과를 나타낼 때는 등위접속사 so를 쓸 수 있다.
어휘 **busy** 바쁜 **take a taxi** 택시를 타다

11. Is Tomorrow Thursday -------- Friday?
(A) and
(B) but
(C) or
(D) so

해석 내일이 목요일인가요? 금요일 인가요?
해설 둘 중 하나를 선택해야 할 때는 등위 접속사 or을 쓸 수 있다.

12. -------- Beth is very nice, everybody likes her.
(A) And
(B) Because
(C) So
(D) Although

해석 Beth는 친절하기 때문에, 모든 사람들이 그녀를 좋아한다.
해설 원인과 결과를 나타내는 부사절 접속사로는 because가 있다.
어휘 **nice** 친절한 **although** 그럼에도 불구하고

B

1. (but) → (and)
2. (and) → (but)
3. (and) → (or)
4. (go) → (goes)
5. (Does) → (Do)
6. (don't) → (doesn't)
7. (ordered) → (order)
8. (going) → (to go)
9. (Although) → (Because)
10. (goes) → (go)

C

(2) did → do
(5) because → and

Tina 10:09 a.m.	Donna! How (1) was your trip?
Donna 10:11 a.m.	Wonderful, thanks. I stayed at a small hotel with my family.
Tina 10:12 a.m.	Did you (2) did a lot of sightseeing?
Robin 10:14 a.m.	Only a bit. We (3) were (4) interested in lying on the beach in front of the hotel every day. I also went shopping (5) because bought something (6) for you.

Tina 10:09 a.m.	돌아오셨군요. 도나! 여행은 어땠어요?
Donna 10:11 a.m.	아주 좋았어요, 감사합니다. 가족들과 작은 호텔에서 머물렀어요.
Tina 10:12 a.m.	관광 많이 했어요?
Robin 10:14 a.m.	조금 했어요. 우리는 매일 호텔 앞 해안에서 누워있는 것을 더 즐겼어요. 쇼핑을 가서 당신을 위해서 뭔가 샀어요.

MINI TEST 2

p.100-101

A

1. (A)	2. (C)	3. (C)	4. (B)	5. (D)
6. (A)	7. (A)	8. (B)	9. (A)	10. (D)
11. (B)	12. (A)			

1. I have -------- every morning.
(A) breakfast
(B) the breakfast
(C) a breakfast
(D) breakfasts
해석 나는 매일 아침 식사를 한다.

2. -------- are Tom's book.
(A) This
(B) That
(C) These
(D) It
해석 이것은 Tom 의 책이다.

3. Mr. Johns -------- a nice doctor.
(A) am
(B) are
(C) is
(D) be
해석 Johns 씨는 친절한 의사입니다.

4. I need something -------- to wear.
(A) newly
(B) new
(C) cloth
(D) clothing
해석 나는 입을 새 것이 필요하다.

5. The contracts are -------- kept in the safe.
(A) securing
(B) security
(C) secure
(D) securely
해석 그 계약서는 금고 안에 안전하게 보관되어 있다.

6. We passed -------- a long and huge tunnel.
(A) through
(B) at
(C) on
(D) during
해석 우리는 길고 큰 터널을 통과했다.

7. Tom will finish his assignment -------- tomorrow.
(A) by
(B) for
(C) during
(D) at
해석 Tom은 내일까지 과제를 마칠 것이다.

8. Her voice is too -------.
(A) loudly
(B) loud
(C) highly
(D) noisily
해석 그녀의 목소리가 너무 크다.

9. He will -------- come today.
(A) hardly
(B) hard
(C) hardness
(D) harder
해석 그는 오늘 올 것 같지 않다.

10. Ann -------- that she was late because of the bus strike.
(A) talked
(B) spoke
(C) complied
(D) explained
해석 앤은 버스의 파업 때문에 지각했다고 변명했다
해설 빈칸은 that 절을 목적어로 취할 수 있는 타동사가 와야 한다. 그러므로 정답은 (D) explained 가 적합하다.

11. I will -------- in the workshop in an hour.
(A) attend
(B) participate
(C) join
(D) contact
해석 저는 한 시간 후에 워크숍에 참석할 겁니다.
해설 빈칸 뒤에 전치사 in 과 함께 쓸 수 있는 자동사가 와야 한다. attend, join, contact은 모두 타동사이다.

12. -------- you going to the laboratory this afternoon?
(A) Are
(B) Do
(C) Is
(D) Did
해석 오늘 오후에 실험실 가실 건가요?
해설 ~할 예정이다, 라고 할 때는 be going to 를 쓰고 빈칸에는 의문문의 형태로 주어가 you 이므로 are 을 써야 한다.

B
1. (surprising) → (surprised)
2. (Does) → (Do)
3. (take) → (took)
4. (Him) → (His)
5. (lately) → (late)
6. (has) → (have)
7. (send) → (sent)
8. (to) → (to go)
9. (impressing) → (impressed)
10. (forgetting) → (forget)

C
(2) strangely → strange
(4) by → until

> M: Good afternoon, Can I help you?
> W: Yes, I'm having some (1) problems with my car. The engine is making some very (2) strangely noises. I think something is (3) wrong with the engine. Could you check it out for me?
> M: Sure. It's already Friday afternoon and we are closed on Saturday. You might have to wait (4) by next Monday or Tuesday to get your car back.
> W: Oh, that's fine. I'll leave it here and (5) take the subway. Thanks a lot.

> M : 안녕하세요? 도와드릴까요?
> W : 네. 제 자동차에 문제가 있어요. 이 엔진에서는 이상한 소리가 나요. 엔진에 이상이 있는 것 같아요. 확인해 주시겠어요?
> M : 물론입니다. 이미 금요일 오후고, 토요일에는 문을 닫아요. 자동차를 다시 찾으려면 월요일이나 화요일까지 기다리셔야 할 것 같습니다.
> W : 괜찮아요. 여기에 자동차를 두고 지하철 타고 가야겠습니다. 감사합니다.

어휘 headlight 헤드라이트 dim 희미한 engine 엔진
strange 이상한 noise 소음 wrong 잘못된

입문 FINAL TEST
p.102-103

A
1. (B)	2. (B)	3. (A)	4. (D)	5. (C)
6. (C)	7. (B)	8. (B)	9. (A)	10. (C)
11. (B)	12. (B)			

1. -------- was canceled last Friday.
(A) Train
(B) The train
(C) The trains
(D) Trains
해석 기차는 지난 금요일에 취소되었다.
해설 동사는 was 이므로 주어는 가산명사의 단수인 The train이 와야 한다. 이 때 train은 한정사 the 또는 A 와 함께 써야 한다.

2. Jenny isn't -------- with her pay.
(A) satisfy
(B) satisfied
(C) satisfying
(D) satisfies
해석 Jenny는 월급에 만족을 못한다.
해설 satisfy는 감정 동사이므로, 주어가 Jenny 이므로 과거분사와 함께 써야 한다.

3. I think -------- Mr. Dupont has a good chance.
(A) that
(B) and
(C) because
(D) but
해석 저는 Dupont 씨가 좋은 기회를 가지리라 생각합니다.
해설 I는 주어 think는 동사 Mr. Dupont has a good chance는 목적어 이므로 명사절을 이끄는 접속사 that이 와야 할 자리이다.

4. -------- you know who is working extra hours tonight?
(A) Are
(B) Is
(C) Does
(D) Do
해석 누가 오늘밤에 추가 근무하는지 아세요?
해설 주어가 you이고 일반 동사 know 가 왔으므로 의문문을 만들 때, 조동사 Do가 쓰여야 한다.

5. I need to get a quick bite before we go to the workshop.
(A) or
(B) for
(C) before
(D) until
해석 워크숍에 가기 전에 잠깐 뭐 좀 먹어야겠다.
해설 워크숍에 가기 전에 잠깐 뭐 좀 먹어야겠다는 표현이 자연스럽다. 그러므로 before이 와야 한다.

6. I worked -------- four in the morning due to the project.
(A) on
(B) to
(C) until
(D) in
해석 그 프로젝트 때문에 새벽 4시까지 일했다.
해설 하던 일을 계속 한다는 의미로 ~까지는 until 이 적합하다.

7. My sister made me -------- yesterday.
(A) anger
(B) angry
(C) angered
(D) to anger
해석 나의 여동생이 어제 나를 화나게 만들었다.
해설 make + 목적어 + 목적격보어의 형태로 쓰이는 5형식 구문이다. 형용사 angry 가 적합하다.

8. The manager -------- about going on a business trip.
(A) talks
(B) talked
(C) were talking
(D) talk

해석 매니저는 회의에서 출장 가는 것에 대해 이야기했다.
해설 주어가 manger 이므로 (B) talked 가 적합하다.

9. The president will -------- his new plan with his employees next week
(A) discuss
(B) talk
(C) reply
(D) speak

해석 데이빗슨 씨는 그의 계획을 어제 밤에 동료들과 함께 의논했다.
해설 his new plan 을 목적어로 취할 수 있는 타동사가 적합하다. 그러므로 정답은 (A)이다.

10. For help with your mortgage loan plans, -------- our professional financial experts.
(A) contacted
(B) contacting
(C) contact
(D) contacts

해석 당신 주택 담보 대출 계획에 도움을 받기 위해 우리의 전문 재정 전문가들에게 연락하세요.
해설 명령문은 동사원형으로 시작하므로 contact 이 적합하다.

11. All the employees -------- the annual conference next month.
(A) enrolled
(B) will attend
(C) have participated
(D) will comply

해석 모든 직원들은 다음 달에 열리는 연례 컨퍼런스에 참석할 것이다.
해설 빈칸 뒤에 전치사 없이 목적어인 the annual conference가 나왔으므로 타동사인 attend를 써야한다.
어휘 **annual** 연례의 **enroll in~** ~에 등록하다 **attend** 참석하다 **participate in** 참석하다 **comply with~** ~에 따르다

12. All the employees in the Marketing Department should -------- in group activities.
(A) attend
(B) participate
(C) join
(D) contact

해석 마케팅 직원들은 그룹 활동에 참여해야 한다.
해설 조동사 should 뒤에는 본동사가 와야 하며, 빈칸 뒤에 전치사 in 과 함께 쓸 수 있는 자동사가 와야 한다. attend, join, contact은 모두 타동사이다.
어휘 **participate in** ~에 참가하다 **group activity** 그룹 활동

B

1. (looks) → (looks like)
2. (interesting) → (interested)
3. (Do) → (Are)
4. (how solve) → (how to solve)
5. (if) → (while)
6. (broad) → (broaden)
7. (as well) → (as well as)
8. (through) → (throughly)
9. (disposing) → (dispose)
10. (consist) → (consists)

C

(3) cost → costs
(5) if → before

M: Hello. I'd like to mail (1) this package to California.
W: Okay. Would you (2) like delivery confirmation on the package? It only (3) cost extra 3 dollars.
M: Yes, that would be wonderful. And could you mark the package fragile?
W: Of course. Your total is 20 dollars. Also, you (4) need to fill out a form for the delivery confirmation service (5) if you leave.

M : 안녕하세요? 저는 캘리포니아로 이 소포를 배송하고 싶습니다.
W : 좋습니다. 소포에 배송확인을 해 드릴까요? 추가 3달러면 됩니다.
M : 좋아요. 그리고 이 소포에 깨지기 쉽다는 표시를 해 주시겠어요?
W : 물론이죠. 총 20달러입니다. 또한 배송확인서비스를 위해서 가시기 전에 이 서류를 작성해 주세요.

어휘 **delivery** 배송 **confirmation** 확인 **package** 소포 **notice** 통보 **extra** 추가의 **mark** 표시하다 **fragile** 깨지기 쉬운

기본편

UNIT 13 : 명사와 대명사

GRAMMAR PRACTICE p.107

A
1. invitation
2. conclusion
3. development
4. attendance
5. approval
6. department
7. analysis
8. impression
9. agreement
10. production

B
1. manager
2. president
3. property
4. construction
5. argument

C
1. All the residents filed a complaint due to the noise.
2. Our company needs knowledgeable applicants.
3. The first impression is very important to everyone.
4. The price seldom directly reflects the cost of delivery.
5. O

GRAMMAR PRACTICE p.109

A
1. he
2. himself
3. that
4. mine
5. Those

B
1. We
2. her
3. it
4. Its
5. them

C
1. His hat is blue, and hers is orange.
2. Their ball is yellow. Look at it!
3. O
4. O
5. Jenny just finished the project on her own.

GRAMMAR IN SENTENCE p.110

1. All the residents / filed a complaint / due to the noise.
   ▶ 대부분의 주민들이 / 민원을 신고했다 / 소음 때문에
   해석 대부분의 주민들이 민원을 신고했다.

2. Our company / needs / knowledgeable applicants.
   ▶ 우리 회사는 / 필요하다 / 지식이 풍부한 지원자들을
   해석 우리 회사는 지식이 풍부한 지원자들을 원한다.

3. The first impression is very important / to everyone.
   ▶ 첫인상이 / 매우 중요하다 / 모든 사람들에게
   해석 첫인상이 모든 사람들에게 매우 중요하다.

4. The price / seldom directly reflects / the cost of delivery.
   ▶ 가격은 / 거의 직접 하지 않는 반영하다 / 배달 비용을
   해석 가격은 배달 비용을 직접 반영하지는 않는다.

5. Despite his denial / that he robbed the bank, / he was found guilty.
   ▶ 부인했음에도 불구하고 / 그가 은행을 털었다는 것 / 그는 유죄가 되었다.
   해석 그가 은행을 털었다는 것을 부인했음에도 불구하고, 그는 유죄가 되었다.

6. Richard / told / me / that he can help us.
   ▶ Richard는 / 말했다 / 나에게 / 그는 우리를 도와 줄 수 있다고
   해석 Richard는 나에게 그는 우리를 도와 줄 수 있다고 말했다.

7. Austin / started / learning Korean / by himself.
   ▶ Austin은 / 시작했다 / 한국어를 배우는 것을 / 혼자서
   해석 Austin은 혼자서 한국어 공부를 시작했다.

8. The new policy / is more efficient / than that of the previous year.
   ▶ 이 새로운 정책은 / 더 효율적이다 / 지난해 것보다
   해석 이 새로운 정책은 지난해 것보다 더 효율적이다.

9. Jenny just finished the project on her own.
   ▶ Jenny는 / 마쳤다 / 그 프로젝트를 / 혼자서
   해석 Jenny는 혼자서 그 프로젝트를 마쳤다.

10. Those who apply for the position / should fill out / this form.
    ▶ 사람들은 / 그 직책에 지원하는 / 작성해야 한다 / 이 양식을
    해석 그 직책에 지원하는 사람들은 이 양식을 작성해야 한다.

UNIT 14 : 형용사와 부사

GRAMMAR PRACTICE p.113

A
1. considerable
2. payable
3. accessible
4. impressive
5. protective
6. environmental
7. economic
8. historical
9. costly
10. friendly

B
1. friendly
2. happy
3. colorful
4. angry
5. sweet

C
1. The driver of the bus had serious injuries.
2. Mr. Smith is responsible for hiring staff.
3. Mr. Glee is interested in environmental issues.
4. Everything possible should be done to help you.
5. O

GRAMMAR PRACTICE p.115

A
1. secret   2. happy   3. significantly
4. absolutely   5. approximately

B
1. absolutely   2. Apparently   3. considerably
4. impressive   5. finally

C
1. Personally, I agree completely with the author.
2. Everything seems to be conveniently set up for people.
3. O
4. All the staff members have been trained extensively by professional instructors.
5. Recently, there have been many car thefts in the area.

GRAMMAR PRACTICE p.117

A
strong - stronger - strongest
nice - nicer - nicest
hot - hotter - hottest
pretty - prettier - prettiest
confident - more confident - most confident

B
good - better - best
much - more - most
badly - worse - worst
little - less - least
late (순서) - latter - last

C
1. as tall as   2. as nice as
3. just as thick as   4. as soon as possible

D
1. happier   2. smartest
3. more difficult   4. most expensive

GRAMMAR IN SENTENCE p.118

1. You / should keep / it / a secret.
▶ 너는 / 유지해야 한다 / 그것을 / 비밀로
해석 너는 그것을 비밀로 해야 해.

2. The restaurant / makes / its customers / happy.
▶ 그 레스토랑은 / 해 준다 / 손님들을 / 즐겁게
해석 그 레스토랑은 손님들을 즐겁게 해 준다.

3. Since last year, the net profit / has significantly increased.
▶ 작년 이후로 / 순수익이 / 상당히 오르고 있다.
해석 작년 이후로 순수익이 상당히 오르고 있다.

4. Everything possible / should be done / to help you.
▶ 가능한 모든 일은 / 되도록 해야 한다 / 당신을 돕기 위하여
해석 당신을 도울 수 있는 모든 가능한 일을 할 것이다.

5. The policeman / made a timely appearance / on the scene.
▶ 경찰관이 / 때맞춰 나타났다 / 현장에
해석 때맞춰 경찰관이 현장에 나타났다.

6. Personally, / I agree completely / with the author.
▶ 개인적으로 / 나는 / 동의한다 / 전적으로 / 그 작가에게
해석 개인적으로 나는 그 작가에게 전적으로 동의한다.

7. Everything / seems to be conveniently set up / for people.
▶ 모든 것이 / 있는 것 같다 / 편리하게 설치되어 / 사람들을 위해
해석 모든 것이 사람들을 위해 편리하게 설치되어 있는 것 같다.

8. Managers / are asked to regularly check / the attendance rates of their employees.
▶ 관리자들은 / 요구 받습니다 정기적으로 점검하도록 / 직원들의 출근율을
해석 관리자들은 직원들의 출근율을 정기적으로 점검하도록 요구받습니다.

9. All the staff members / have been trained extensively / by professional instructors.
▶ 모든 직원은 / 교육을 받고 있다 광범위하게 / 전문 강사에 의해
해석 모든 직원은 전문 강사에 의해 광범위하게 교육을 받고 있다.

10. Mathematics / is more difficult / than English for me.
▶ 수학은 / 더 어렵다 / 영어보다 / 나에게
해석 수학은 나에게 영어보다 더 어렵다.

UNIT 15 : 동사와 전치사

GRAMMAR PRACTICE p.121

A
1. access   2. comply with   3. deal with
4. speak to   5. deal   6. join
7. answer   8. explained   9. oppose
10. contact

B
1. O
2. Don't interfere with our conversation.
3. O
4. The manager is talking on the phone now.
5. If you accept the position, we would appreciate it.

GRAMMAR PRACTICE   p.123

A
1. because of
2. despite
3. for
4. until
5. for
6. throughout
7. during
8. for
9. by
10. during

B
1. You need to submit this report by Wednesday.
2. O
3. O
4. I stay in bed until late afternoon on Saturday.
5. O

GRAMMAR IN SENTENCE   p.124

1. Mike / contacted / his supervisor immediately.
▶ Mike는 / 연락했다 / 그의 상관에게 즉시
해석 Mike는 즉시 그의 상관에게 연락했다.

2. Don't interfere with our conversation.
▶ 끼어들지 마세요 우리 대화에
해석 우리 대화에 끼어들지 마세요.

3. Do not exceed / the daily dose.
▶ 초과하지 마세요 / 하루 복용량을
해석 하루 복용량을 초과하지 마세요.

4. You / can't access / the building without a permit.
▶ 당신은 / 들어갈 수 없다 / 건물에 허가증 없이
해석 당신은 허가증 없이 건물에 들어갈 수 없다.

5. We / must comply with the terms of the contract.
▶ 우리는 / 반드시 지켜야 한다 계약서 조항을
해석 우리는 반드시 계약서 조항을 지켜야 한다.

6. The plane / was delayed because of the weather.
▶ 비행기는 / 지연되었다 날씨 때문에
해석 비행기는 날씨 때문에 지연되었다.

7. They / love / him despite his faults.
▶ 그들은 / 사랑한다 / 그를 그의 결점에도 불구하고
해석 그의 결점에도 불구하고, 그들은 그를 사랑한다.

8. Managers / should contact / their local business office.
▶ 매니저들은 / 연락을 해야만 한다 / 그들의 지역 사업 사무소를.
해석 매니저들은 그들의 지역 사업 사무소에 연락을 해야만 한다.

9. An epidemic / spread throughout the country.
▶ 전염병이 퍼졌다 나라 전역에
해석 나라 전역에 전염병이 퍼졌다.

10. You / need to submit / this report by Wednesday.
▶ 너는 / 제출해야 한다 / 이 보고서를 수요일까지
해석 너는 이 보고서를 수요일까지 제출해야 한다.

ACTUAL TEST 5   p.126-127

A
1. (D)	2. (C)	3. (A)	4. (C)	5. (C)	6. (D)
7. (C)	8. (C)	9. (C)	10. (A)	11. (D)	12. (D)

B
13. (C)	14. (D)	15. (A)	16. (C)	17. (A)	18. (A)

1. For your --------, we have these two large tables in the center of the room.
(A) convenient
(B) convenient
(C) convene
(D) convenience
해석 여러분의 편의를 위해서, 여기 큰 책상 두 개가 방 중앙에 마련되어 있습니다.
해설 소유격 your 뒤에는 명사가 와야 하므로 정답은 (D)이다.

2. Three -------- proposed by the board of directors are highlighted in blue.
(A) changing
(B) change
(C) changes
(D) changed
해석 이사회에 의해 제안된 세 가지 변화들은 파란색으로 강조되어 있다.
해설 과거분사 proposed의 수식을 받고 있는 명사(The --------)를 찾는 문제이다. 보기 중에서 명사로 쓰일 수 있는 것은 동명사 (A)와 (B), (C)인데 동명사는 관사가 올 수 없으므로 먼저 제거한다. 위 문장에서 동사가 are highlighted in blue로 나와 있으므로 답은 복수형 changes '변화들'이다.
어휘 propose 제안하다   board of directors 이사회   highlight 강조하다, 눈에 띄게 하다

3. Dr. Hatley will speak in -------- about how this building came to be.
(A) depth
(B) deep
(C) deepen
(D) deeply
해석 헤이틀리 박사님이 이 건물이 어떻게 탄생되었는지 깊이 있게 말씀해 주실 겁니다.
해설 전치사 뒤에는 명사가 와야 하므로 정답은 (A) depth이다.

4. The -------- for this summer festival was made a year in advance.
(A) reserve
(B) reserved

(C) reservation
(D) reserves

해석 올해 여름 페스티벌 예약은1년 전에 이루어졌다.
해설 정관사 the 와 전치사 for 사이는 명사자리이다.
어휘 **festival** 축제, 페스티벌 **in advance** 미리, 이전에

5. All passengers are advised to secure all -------- valuables in their carry-on baggage.
(A) they
(B) them
(C) their
(D) theirs

해석 모든 승객들은 모든 귀중품을 기내 휴대가방에 보관하도록 권고 받는다.
해설 명사 valuables를 수식할 수 있는 것은 한정사인 소유격 인칭대명사이다. 보기 중 소유격 인칭 대명사는 (C) their이다.
어휘 **secure** 확보하다, 보장하다   **valuables** 귀중품
carry-on baggage 기내 휴대가방   **ABC Inc**.

6. -------- who want to continue their contracts will have their fringe benefits renewed each year.
(A) They
(B) One
(C) Anyone
(D) Those

해석 계약을 연장하기를 원하는 직원들의 급부금이 매년 갱신될 것이다.
해설 주격관계대명사 who 의 선행사로 쓰일 수 있는 대명사는 those 이다. anyone은 단수취급을 하므로 anyone who wants to~~가 되어야 한다.
어휘 **contract** 계약   **fringe benefit** (보험, 사회 보장 제도의) 급부금
renew 갱신하다

7. ABC, Inc. provides -------- products that revolutionize business operations for our customers.
(A) innovator
(B) innovate
(C) innovative
(D) innovation

해석 ABC 주식회사는 고객들에게 사업 운영을 급격히 변하게 하는 혁신적인 제품을 제공한다.
해설 품사문제로, 명사 products를 수식하는 형용사가 필요하다.

8. Employees are -------- for making LED monitors that have the highest quality possible.
(A) responsibility
(B) responsibly
(C) responsible
(D) responsive

해석 직원들은 최대한으로 높은 질의 LED 모니터를 만드는 데 책임이 있다.
해설 '~의 책임이 있다'라는 뜻을 가진 숙어 be responsible for~가 정답이다.

9. -------- the tight deadline for the project, the staff needs to work overtime this week.
(A) Therefore
(B) Moreover
(C) Because of
(D) Nevertheless

해석 빠듯한 프로젝트 마감일 때문에, 그 직원들은 다음 주에 사무실에서 늦게까지 근무 해야만 한다.
해설 '빠듯한 마감일__ 직원들이 주말에 사무실에 나와야만 한다'라는 문장으로 보아, 빈칸에는 이유를 나타내는 전치사 (C) Because of (~때문에)가 와야 한다.
어휘 **therefore** 그러므로   **moreover** 게다가   **nevertheless** 그럼에도 불구하고   **tight** 빠듯한   **deadline** 마감시간

10. -------- the one-year contract period, replacement parts will be provided free of charge.
(A) during
(B) before
(C) between
(D) beyond

해석 1년의 계약 기간 동안 대체 부품이 무료로 제공될 것이다.
해설 '1년 계약 기간 __ 부품 교체가 무료로 제공 될 것이다.'라는 문장에서 빈칸에 적절한 전치사는 (A) during (~동안) 이다.
어휘 **contract** 계약   **replacement** 대체   **free of charge** 무료로

11. A number of middle school students in the city -------- in the special event held by Dell this weekend.
(A) participates
(B) are participated
(C) is participating
(D) are participating

해석 도시의 많은 중학생들이 이번 주말에 Dell에 의하여 개최되는 특별행사에 참석할 것이다.
해설 주어가 middle school students 로 복수이므로 복수 동사인 **are participating**을 써야합니다. a number of는 '많은'의 의미이며, participate in은 자동사이므로 수동태로 쓸 수 없습니다.
어휘 **middle school students** 중학생   **special** 특별한
hold 개최하다

12. You can find the books on analysts who are -------- recommended by Adam Smith, an economist.
(A) height
(B) higher
(C) highest
(D) highly

해석 여러분은 경제학자인 아담 스미스 에 의해 높게 추천된 분석가들에 관한 책을 보실 수 있습니다.
해설 부사자리 문제이며, highly는 매우, 몹시의 추상적인 의미를 가지고 있다.
어휘 **analyst** 분석가   **height** 높이   **highly** 높이, 세게
recommend 추천하다

Seattle Times

Next week, almost 5,000 students are expected to **13.** -------- the Winter Career Fair.
More than 100 companies in Washington **14.** -------- to set up booths at the fair, and expect to fill over 1,000 intern positions **15.** -------- the winter vacation. This is the first year that the Winter Career Fair is being held. However, if it is a success, the fair is expected to be a **16.** -------- occurrence in Seattle every December, and it will expand to other university cities **17.** -------- the United States.
Doors open at 9:00 A.M., and the fair will **18.** -------- at 5:00 P.M.

Entrance is free for all students, but a valid student card must be presented at the door.

Seattle Times

내일 5,000명이 넘는 학생들이 동계 구직박람회에 참석할 예정입니다. 워싱턴 주의 100여개 업체가 박람회장에 장소를 마련하기 위해 등록했으며 1000개가 넘는 동계 수습사원 자리를 내놓을 것으로 예상됩니다. 동계 구직 박람회는 처음으로 개최되는 것입니다. 그러나 성공한다면 박람회는 Seattle에서 매년 12월에 정기적으로 개최되는 행사가 될 것으로 기대되며 미국 전역의 다른 대학 도시들로 확대될 것입니다.

박람회는 오전 9시에 시작하여 오후 5시에 끝납니다.
학생들은 모두 무료로 입장할 수 있습니다. 그러나 입구에서 유효한 학생증을 제시해야 합니다.

어휘 more than ~이상 set up ~을 세우다 booth 칸 막은 좌석
fair 박람회 intern 인턴 regular 정기적인 occurrence 일어나는 일 expand 넓히다, 확장하다 entrance 입구, 출입구
free 무료인 valid 유효한 present 제출하다

13.
(A) enroll
(B) take part
(C) attend
(D) go

해설 are expected to --------the Winter Career Fair.는 구직박람회에 참석할 예정이라는 의미이다. 참석하다의 의미로 목적어인 the Winter Career Fair를 취할 수 있는 타동사로 쓰일 수 있는 것은 attend 뿐이다.

어휘 enroll in ~ ~에 등록하다 take part in ~에 참석하다
go to ~ ~로 가다

14.
(A) register
(B) registration
(C) has registered
(D) have registered

해설 More than 100 companies in Washington state -------- to set up booths at the fair 에서 주어는 복수인 100 companies 이므로 복수 동사인 have registered 를 넣어야 한다.

어휘 register 등록하다

15.
(A) during
(B) for
(C) to
(D) on

해설 '겨울 방학 동안'이라는 의미로 특정 명사 앞에는 during 이 온다.

16.
(A) regulate
(B) regulation
(C) regular
(D) regularly

해설 명사는 형용사의 수식을 받는다. 그러므로 명사인 occurrence (발생)를 꾸며주는 것은 형용사 regular (정기적인) 이다

어휘 regulate 동사 : 규정하다 regulation 명사 : 규정
regularly 부사 : 정기적으로

17.
(A) throughout
(B) by
(C) at
(D) over

해설 미국 전역에 걸쳐서라는 의미로 전치사 throughout을 써야 한다.

18.
(A) close
(B) closed
(C) closing
(D) closure

해설 Doors open at 9:00 A.M., and the fair will -------- at 5:00 P.M.
해석 조동사 will 뒤에는 동사원형을 써야 한다.

어휘 close 닫다

UNIT 16 : 시제

GRAMMAR PRACTICE   p.131

A
1. goes   2. attending   3. boils
4. is boiling   5. will be attending 6. open
7. keeps   8. will attend   9. played
10. have

B
1. O
2. The water is boiling now, so can you turn it off?
3. I saw Lisa downtown last weekend.
4. Ann was listening to music when the phone rang.
5. Sally will be working in her office at 3 o'clock tomorrow.

GRAMMAR PRACTICE p.133

A
1. have known
2. lived
3. have lived
4. had played
5. will have attended
6. haven't seen
7. has been waiting
8. lost
9. will have left
10. will meet

B
1. Have you ever been to Paris?
2. O
3. It has been cold since yesterday, so I bought a coat.
4. O
5. As long as you love me, I can do everything for you.
(조건 부사절)

GRAMMAR IN SENTENCE p.134

1. Nurses / take care / of patients in hospitals.
▶ 간호사들은 / 돌본다 / 환자들을 병원에서
해석 간호사들은 병원에서 환자들을 돌본다.

2. The water / is boiling now / , so can you turn it off?
▶ 물이 끓고 있다 / 지금 / 그러니까 지금 꺼 줄 수 있어요?
해석 물이 지금 끓고 있으니까, 지금 꺼 줄 수 있어요?

3. I / saw / Lisa downtown last weekend.
▶ 나는 / 보았다 / Lisa를 시내에서 지난 주말에
해석 나는 지난 주말에 시내에서 Lisa를 보았다.

4. Ann / was listening to music when the phone rang.
▶ 앤은 / 듣던 중 이었다 음악을 전화벨이 울렸을 때.
해석 전화벨이 울렸을 때 앤은 음악을 듣던 중이었다.

5. Sally / will be working in her office at 3 o'clock tomorrow.
▶ Sally는 / 일하는 중일 것이다 그녀의 사무실에서 3시에 내일.
해석 내일 3시에 Sally는 자기 사무실에서 일하는 중일 것이다.

6. I / have known / Sandra since she / was / a child.
▶ 나는 / 알고 지낸다 / Sandra를 그녀가 어린아이였을 때부터
해석 나는 Sandra가 어린 아이였을 때부터 알고 지낸다.

7. Tony / had played / the game when I visited him.
▶ 그는 / 하고 있었다 / 게임을 내가 그를 만나러 갔을 때
해석 내가 그를 만나러 갔을 때 그는 게임을 하고 있었다.

8. I / will have attended / the seminar / 10 times / by next year.
▶ 내년이면 내가 그 워크숍에 10번을 참석하는 것이 된다.
해석 나는 Sandra가 어린 아이였을 때부터 알고 지낸다.

9. They / will have left / home by the time we / arrive.
▶ 그들은 / 나섰을 것이다 / 집을 / 때면 우리가 / 도착할
해석 우리가 도착할 때면 그들은 집을 나섰을 것이다.

10. As long as you / love / me, / I can do / everything for you.
▶ ~한 당신이 사랑한다 나를 나는 / 할 수 있다. / 무엇이든지 당신의 위해서
해석 당신이 나를 사랑하는 한 나는 당신의 위해서 무엇이든지 할 수 있다.

UNIT 17 : 수일치

GRAMMAR PRACTICE p.137

A
1. goes   2. are   3. was   4. are   5. attends
6. was   7. is   8. is   9. are   10. helps

B
1. There are a lot of people in the square.
2. The clerks in this store work overtime every Monday.
3. What the president said was true.
4. Eating breakfast every day is good for your health.
5. O

GRAMMAR PRACTICE p.139

A
1. is   2. are   3. All   4. is   5. lives
6. is   7. are   8. is   9. were   10. are

B
1. much   2. a lot of   3. some   4. a little   5. several

GRAMMAR IN SENTENCE p.140

1. What / the teacher said / was absolutely true.
▶ 것은 / 선생님이 말했던 / 확실히 진실이었다.
해석 선생님이 말했던 것은 확실히 진실이었다.

2. When / you / meet / people, being polite / is important.
▶ 때 / 당신이 / 만나다 / 예의바른 것이 / 중요하다.
해석 사람을 만날 때 예의바른 것이 중요하다.

3. The president, together with / his employees, is dining here / tonight.
▶ 사장님은, 함께 / 그의 직원들과, 식사한다 여기서 / 오늘밤에
해석 사장님은 그의 직원들과 함께 오늘 밤 여기서 식사한다.

4. There are / many books on the shelves.
▶ 있다 / 많은 책들이 선반에.
해석 선반에 많은 책들이 있다.

5. Running every day / helps / you / keep / healthy.
▶ 달리는 것은 매일 / 도움이 된다 / 당신을 / 유지시켜주는 데 / 건강하게.
해석 매일 달리는 것은 당신을 건강하게 유지시켜주는 데 도움이 된다.

6. Each of the designers / is planning / to attend / the seminar.
▶ 디자이너들이 / 계획이다 / 참석할 / 그 세미나에
해석 디자이너들이 그 세미나에 참석할 계획이다.

7. There is a little juice left / in the glass.
▶ 있다 / 약간의 쥬스가 / 남겨진 / 유리잔에
해석 유리잔에 남겨진 약간의 주스가 있다.
해석 유리잔에 주스가 조금 있다.

8. Twenty years / is / such a long time.
▶ 20년은 / 이다 / 너무나도 긴 세월
해석 20년은 너무나도 긴 세월이다.

9. Some of the books / were written in the 1900s.
▶ 몇 권의 책들은 / 쓰여졌다 1900년대에
해석 몇 권의 책들은 1900년대에 쓰여 졌다.

10. All the supervisors / are required / to submit / reports every day.
▶ 모든 감독관들은 / 요구 받는다 / 제출하도록 / 보고서를 매일
해석 모든 감독관들은 매일 보고서를 제출해야 한다.

UNIT 18 : 태

GRAMMAR PRACTICE p.143

A

1. 현재
A picture is taken everyday (by him).

2. 미래
A picture will be taken tomorrow (by him).

3. 과거
A picture was taken yesterday (by him).

4. 현재완료
These pictures have been taken since yesterday (by her).

5. 미래완료
These pictures will have been taken by tomorrow (by her).

6. 과거완료
hese pictures had been taken (by her)when I called her.

7. 현재진행
Some pictures are being taken now (by him).

8. 과거진행
Some pictures were being taken (by her) when I arrived there.

B
1. The wall is being painted.
2. The room will be cleaned tomorrow.
3. The old house was built in 1960.
4. The movie is loved by many people.
5. Computers were given to all the employees by the company. All the employees were given computers by the company.

GRAMMAR PRACTICE p.145

A
1. These houses are called igloos (by people).
2. Mr. Lee will be appointed the president tomorrow (by them)
3. The woman was made angry by his attitude.
4. The actor was made popular by the movie.
5. Your passwords should be kept secret (by you).

B
1. was elected   2. amazing   3. satisfied
4. surprised   5. interested

C
1. O
2. Pets are not allowed in this restaurant.
3. The bottles are filled with water.
4. The conference is held every month.
5. The town is crowded with many tourists.

GRAMMAR IN SENTENCE p.146

1. The old house / was built in 1960.
▶ 그 오래된 집은 / 지어졌다 1960년도에
해석 그 오래된 집은 1960년도에 지어졌다.

2. The movie is loved by many people.
▶ 그 영화는 / 사랑 받는다 / 많은 사람들에 의해
해석 그 영화는 많은 사람들에 의해 사랑받는다.

3. The company / gave / all the employees / computers.
▶ 그 회사는 / 주었다 / 모든 직원들에게 / 컴퓨터를.
해석 그 회사는 모든 직원들에게 컴퓨터를 주었다.

4. All the employees / were given / computers by the company.
▶ 모든 직원들은 / 주어졌다 / 컴퓨터를 / 회사에 의하여
해석 모든 직원들은 회사에 의해 컴퓨터를 받았다.

5. Computers / were given to all the employees by the company.
▶ 컴퓨터들이 / 주어졌다 모든 직원들에게 회사에 의하여
해석 컴퓨터들이 회사에 의하여 모든 직원들에게 주어졌다.

6. His attitude / made / the woman / angry.
▶ 그의 행동은 / 만들었다 / 그 여자를 / 화나게
해석 그의 행동은 그 여자를 화나게 만들었다.

7. The woman / was made / angry by his attitude.
▶ 그 여자는 / 되었다 / 화나게 그의 행동에 의하여
해석 그 여자는 그의 행동에 의하여 화가 나게 되었다.

8. You / should keep / your passwords / secret.
▶ 당신은 / 지켜야한다 / 당신의 암호를 / 비밀로
해석 당신은 당신의 암호를 비밀로 지켜야한다.

9. Your passwords / should be kept / secret.
▶ 당신의 암호는 / 유지되어야 한다 / 비밀로
해석 당신의 암호는 비밀로 유지되어야 한다.

10. Pets / are not allowed in this restaurant.
▶ 애완동물들은 / 허락되지 않는다 이 레스토랑에
해석 애완동물들은 이 레스토랑에 들어올 수 없다.

ACTUAL TEST 6
p.148-149

A
| 1. (C) | 2. (A) | 3. (B) | 4. (B) | 5. (A) | 6. (D) |
| 7. (D) | 8. (A) | 9. (B) | 10. (A) | 11. (B) | 12. (B) |

B
| 13. (B) | 14. (D) | 15. (A) | 16. (C) | 17. (C) | 18. (D) |

1. All application forms should -------- by email by the end of this month.
(A) send
(B) are sending
(C) be sent
(D) have sent

해석 모든 지원서들은 이번 달 말까지 이메일로 보내야만 한다.
해설 빈칸에 들어가야 할 품사는 동사이며, 조동사 should 다음에는 동사원형을 써야한다. 또한 send는 타동사인데 목적어가 없으므로 수동형인 (C) be sent 가 정답이다.

2. The Maintenance Department -------- with new computers last month.
(A) was equipped
(B) equipped
(C) equips
(D) was equipping

해석 관리부서는 지난달에 새로운 컴퓨터로 장비를 갖추었다.
해설 A be equipped with B(A는 B라는 장비를 갖추다)는 관용어구로 외워두자.
어휘 **maintenance department** 시설의 유지 및 보수를 전담하는 부서

3. Because the new system -------- last month, we can work effectively.
(A) installed
(B) was installed
(C) is installed
(D) has been installed

해석 새로운 시스템이 지난 달 설치되었기 때문에 우리는 효율적으로 일할 수 있다.
해설 install은 타동사인데 뒤에 목적어가 없으므로 수동태를 써야 합니다. 또한 last month 와 적합한 시제는 과거형이다. 그러므로 정답은 (B) 이다.

4. The floor plan -------- a gorgeous fireplace as the focal point of the living room.
(A) featuring
(B) features
(C) is featured
(D) feature

해석 그 평면 도면은 호화스러운 벽난로를 거실의 중점으로 부각시켰다.
해설 문장에서 동사가 없다, 그러므로 본동사가 들어가야 하고, 주어가 floor plan으로 3인칭 단수이므로 features가 알맞다.
어휘 **floor plan** 평면도 **feature** 특징을 이루다
gorgeous 호화스러운 **focal** 초점

5. The design specifications for the convention center -------- very strict.
(A) were
(B) was
(C) is
(D) has been

해석 컨벤션 센터에 대한 디자인 주문서가 아주 엄격하다.
해설 주어가 The design specifications로 복수 명사이므로 동사는 (A) were 이 와야 한다.
어휘 **specifications** (복수로 사용되어) 설계서, 설명서
strict 엄격한, 정밀한

6. The number of freelance writers -------- remarkably in recent years.
(A) have increased
(B) increasing
(C) are increased
(D) has increased

해석 자유 계약한 작가들의 수가 최근 몇 년간 두드러지게 증가하였다.
해설 the number이 주어이므로 동사는 단수 동사로 받아야 하며, in recent years는 현재 완료시제와 함께 써야 한다.
어휘 **freelance** 자유 계약의 **remarkably** 상당히, 두드러지게

7. Almost all of the people in this area -------- their electricity from hydroelectric power plants.
(A) is gotten
(B) has gotten
(C) gets
(D) get

해석 이 지역의 거의 대부분의 사람들이 수력발전소로부터 전기를 얻고 있다.
해설 주어가 people 이므로 복수이다. 그러므로 동사는 (D) get이 적합하다.
어휘 **electrical** 전기에 관한 **electric** 전기의 **electronic** 전자의
electricity 전기 **hydro-power plants** 수력발전소

8. Royal, Inc. -------- a wide range of environmentally friendly products in Iowa.
(A) offers
(B) offer
(C) is offered
(D) offering

해석 Royal 주식회사는 Iowa에서 다양한 환경 친화적 제품을 제공하고 있다.

해설 주어가 Royal Inc.로 고유명사이다. 고유명사는 언제나 단수 취급을 하며, 목적어인 a wide range of environmentally-friendly products 가 있으므로 능동형으로 써야 한다.

어휘 **a wide range of** 광범위한 ~
environmentally-friendly 환경 친화적인

9. The freshness of the bread served at this restaurant -------- a great deal depending upon the time.
(A) vary
(B) varies
(C) varying
(D) to vary

해석 이 음식점에서 제공되는 빵의 신선함은 시간에 따라 매우 다양하다.

해설 문장 상에 주어는 있으나 동사가 없으므로 동사가 필요한데 주어 freshness가 3인칭 단수이고 시제가 현재이므로 varies가 정답이다.

어휘 **freshness** 신선함   **depend on** ~에 달려있다, 의지하다

10. All employees -------- a coffee break between 3:30 and 4:00 p.m. every working day.
(A) take
(B) took
(C) takes
(C) was taken

해석 모든 직원들은 근무일에는 항상 오후 3시30분에서 4시 사이에 휴식 시간을 갖는다.

해설 every working day는 매일 반복되는 사실이므로 현재시제인 take 를 써야 합니다.

어휘 **take a break** 휴식을 취하다   **every working day** 근무일

11. According to the news, the rate of inflation -------- by 7.5 percent last quarter.
(A) rises
(B) rose
(C) has risen
(D) rise

해석 뉴스에 따르면 지난분기에 물가 상승률은 7.5 퍼센트 올랐다.

해설 last quarter은 과거의 사실이므로 과거시제로 써야 합니다.

어휘 **the rate of inflation** 물가상승률

12. This year, the gourmet restaurant -------- over 100,000 new customers, which is the highest number record in its history.
(A) was attracted
(B) has attracted
(C) had attracted
(D) has been attracted

해석 올해 Gourmet 레스토랑은 10만 명의 새 고객을 유치했는데, 이는 최고의 기록이다.

해설 this year은 현재완료와 함께 쓰는 시간의 부사입니다.

어휘 **attract** 끌다, 유치하다

Questions 13-18 refer to the following guarantee.

GUARANTEE

Magic Cooker 13. -------- against defective material or workmanship. The two-year guarantee entitles owners to receive replacements. Damage due to accidents or abuse by the user 14. --------. It doesn't cover normal wear over the years. If Magic Cooker 15. -------- commercially, the warranty 16. -------- to six months. After examination, if parts are considered 17. -------- , delivery 18. -------- .

보증서

Magic Cooker는 재질상의 결함이나 제작상의 기술 결함에 대해 보증해 드립니다. 2년 보증 기간 동안 구매하신 고객께서는 부품을 교환받으실 수 있습니다. 사고나 고객의 부주의로 인한 손상은 포함되지 않습니다. 사용에 따른 일반적인 손실도 포함되지 않습니다. Magic Cooker가 상업적으로 사용되는 경우, 보증기간은 6개월로 제한됩니다. 검사 후 부품이 손상된 것으로 여겨지는 경우에는 배송료는 환불됩니다.

어휘 **defective** 결함이 있는   **workmanship** 제작기술
entitle 목적어 to ~가 뭐하도록 도와주다   **wear** 마모
warranty 보증

13.
(A) guarantee
(B) is guaranteed
(C) guaranteed
(D) has guaranteed

해설 Magic Cooker -------- against에서 guarantee는 타동사이므로 수동태를 써야합니다. 그러므로 정답은 (B) is guaranteed이다

14.
(A) are not covered
(B) did not cover
(C) does not cover
(D) is not covered

해설 문맥상 사고나 고객의 부주의로 인한 손상은 포함되지 않습니다.라는 의미이므로 수동형으로 써야하며 주어가 damage로 단수 동사를 써야이므로 정답은 (D) is not covered 이다.

15.
(A) is used
(B) are used
(C) uses
(D) use

해설 If Magic Cooker 15 -------- commercially에서 'Magic Cooker 가 상업적으로 사용되는 경우'라는 의미로 빈칸 뒤에 목적어가 없으므로 수동형으로 써야 한다.

16.
(A) limits
(B) are limited
(C) is limited
(D) had been limited

해설 warranty -------- to six months에서 limit는 타동사인데 뒤에 목적어가 없으므로 수동태가 적합하며, 시제는 if 절과 보증서의 특징에 맞추어 변함없는 사실이므로 현재시제를 써야 한다. 그러므로 정답은 (C) is limited 이다.

17.
(A) defect
(B) defected
(C) defective
(D) defection

해설 consider는 5형식 동사이다. 5형식 동사는 '주어 + consider + 목적어 + 목적보어(형용사)' 구조로 쓰며 수동형으로 바뀔 경우, '주어(목적어) be considered + 목적보어(형용사)'가 된다. 위의 'if parts are considered --------'를 능동형으로 전환하면, 'if you consider parts --------'이다. 빈칸은 목적어인 parts를 보충해주는 목적보어 자리이므로 형용사가 적합하다. 그러므로 정답은 (C) defective 이다.

어휘 **defect** 결점, 결함 **defection** 의무 불이행, 태만

18.
(A) will repay
(B) repaid
(C) was repaid
(D) will be repaid

해설 배송료는 환불되어 질 것이라는 의미로 미래 시제이면서 수동형으로 써야 한다.

MINI TEST 3
p.150-153

A
1. (C)	2. (B)	3. (A)	4. (C)	5. (B)
6. (C)	7. (A)	8. (C)	9. (D)	10. (A)
11. (C)	12. (A)	13. (D)	14. (A)	15. (A)
16. (A)	17. (B)	18. (A)	19. (A)	20. (B)
21. (B)	22. (B)	23. (A)	24. (B)	25. (D)

B
26. (B)	27. (D)	28. (A)	29. (B)	30. (D)
31. (C)	32. (C)	33. (B)	34. (D)	35. (A)
36. (D)	37. (C)			

1. The company have spent -------- time and money developing new products.
(A) consider
(B) considered
(C) considerable
(D) consideration

해석 그 회사는 신제품을 개발하는데 상당한 시간과 돈을 쓰고 있다.

해설 time and money가 명사이므로 명사를 수식하는 것은 형용사인 (C) considerable이다.

어휘 **develop** 개발하다 **consider** 고려하다 **considerable** 상당한, 중요한 **consideration** 고려, 숙려

2. The directors -------- arguing among themselves about the new proposal yesterday.
(A) was
(B) were
(C) is
(C) are

해석 이사들은 어제 새로운 제안에 대해 서로 논쟁하고 있었다.

해설 주어가 복수인 directors 이므로 복수 동사인 were이 정답이다.

어휘 **director** 이사 **argue** 논쟁하다 **among** ~ 중에서 **proposal** 제안

3. No -------- would be made without a proper assessment of the return.
(A) investment
(B) invest
(C) investing
(D) invested

해석 수익의 적절한 평가가 없다면 투자는 이루어지지 않을 것이다.

해설 동사인 would be 앞에는 주어인 명사 investment가 필요하다..

어휘 **investment** 투자 **invest** 투자하다 **proper** 적절한 **assessment** 평가 **return** 수익

4. You should submit -------- about the sales figures by tomorrow morning.
(A) reporting
(B) reported
(C) the report
(D) report

해석 판매 수치에 대한 보고서를 내일 오전까지 보내야 한다.

해설 특정 보고서라는 의미이며, report는 가산 명사이므로 앞에 정관사와 함께 써야 합니다.

어휘 **sales figures** 판매 수치

5. The flight was delayed by the late arrival of some -------- and was finally cleared for takeoff at 5:15 p.m.
(A) luggages
(B) luggage
(C) bag
(D) baggages

해설 그 비행기는 승객들의 짐이 늦게 도착해서 출발이 지연되었고, 오후 5시 15분에 드디어 이륙 허가가 났다.

해설 luggage는 불가산 명사이므로 복수형이 없다. 그러므로 정답은 (B) luggage 이다.

어휘 delay 지연하다 arrival 도착 finally 마침내
be cleared for take off 이륙 허가가 내리다

6. Real estate agencies have more information about available housing than you could have --------.
(A) itself
(B) himself
(C) yourself
(D) myself

해설 부동산 사무실들은 빈 집에 대한 정보를 당신이 가진 것보다 더 많이 가지고 있다.

해설 재귀대명사의 강조용법으로 you could have 문장의 주어인 you에 일치시켜서 yourself가 와야 한다.

7. FTD will conduct an -------- search in order to find a manager to be in charge of the Accounting Department.
(A) extensive
(B) extension
(C) extend
(D) extensively

해설 FTD는 회계 부서를 책임질 매니저를 찾기 위해 광대한 조사를 실행할 것이다.

해설 명사 search를 수식하는 형용사의 자리이다.

어휘 extensive 광범위한 in order to 동사원형 ~하기 위하여
in charge of ~ ~ 책임이 있는

8. The Department of Health has a -------- website providing a good deal of information.
(A) use
(B) usably
(C) useful
(D) using

해설 보건부는 많은 정보를 제공하는 유익한 웹사이트를 운영하고 있다.

해설 부정관사 a 와 명사 web-site 사이에는 형용사가 적합하다.

어휘 provide 제공하다 a good deal of 많은

9. -------- international pressure, the government decided not to follow the agreements.
(A) According
(B) Whenever
(C) Unless
(D) In spite of

해설 국제적인 압력에도 불구하고, 정부는 협약을 따르지 않기로 결정했다.

해설 '~에도 불구하고'의 뜻을 가진 전치사는 despite, unless와 whenever는 절이 와야 하며 according은 to가 함께 와야 한다.

어휘 pressure 압력 government 정부

10. -------- new employees are encouraged to get a complete physical examination.
(A) All
(B) Little
(C) Less
(D) Much

해설 모든 새로운 직원들이 완전한 신체검사를 받도록 한다.

해설 가산명사의 복수인 employees를 수식할 수 있는 수를 나타내는 대명사이자 형용사는 all 이다.

11. World Architecture decided to build the most -------- responsible office building in the country.
(A) environmental
(B) environment
(C) environmentally
(D) environmentalist

해설 World Architectural은 국내에서 가장 환경을 생각하는 빌딩을 만들 계획을 세웠다.

해설 형용사 responsible을 꾸며주는 부사가 필요하므로 정답은 (C) environmentally이다.

12. Openings are available for -------- all of the courses offered on the company webpage.
(A) nearly
(B) nearer
(C) nearest
(D) nearing

해설 회사 웹페이지에서 제공되는 거의 모든 강좌에 대해서 수강할 수 있다.

해설 형용사 all을 수식하는 품사로 가장 적절한 것은 부사인 nearly이다.

13. Sales of luxury goods have risen recently -------- the recession.
(A) According
(B) Whenever
(C) Unless
(D) In spite of

해설 국제적인 압력에도 불구하고, 정부는 협약을 따르지 않기로 결정했다.

해설 '~에도 불구하고'의 뜻을 가진 전치사는 despite, unless와 whenever는 절이 와야 하며 according은 to가 함께 와야 한다.

어휘 pressure 압력 government 정부

14. The offices are closed -------- the inclement weather and a corporation-wide strike.
(A) due to
(B) while
(C) since
(D) as if

해설 악천후와 회사 전반에 걸친 파업으로 인해 사무실들의 절반이 휴업 중이다.

해설 빈칸 뒤에 명사 어구인 the inclement weather and a corporation-wide strike 가 왔으므로 빈칸에는 전치사가 들어 가야한다. 그러므로 전치사인 (A)의 'due to ~때문에'가 정답이다.

어휘 **due to** ~ 때문에　**inclement** 나쁜　**corporation-wide** 회사 전반에 걸친　**strike** 파업

15. Everyone in the office -------- overtime to meet the deadline today.

(A) has worked
(B) have worked
(C) has been worked
(D) have been worked

해석 사무실의 모든 사람들이 오늘 마감일을 맞추기 위하여 추가근무를 하고 있다.

해설 주어인 everyone은 단수 취급을 한다. 그러므로 정답은 has worked이다.

어휘 **overtime** 규정 시간 외에　**deadline**

16. Every applicant will -------- a written notification with the results of their applications.

(A) receive
(B) receives
(C) be received
(D) received

해석 모든 신청자들은 그들의 신청 결과에 대한 서면 통지를 받을 것입니다.

해설 주어의 단수, 복수에 상관없이 조동사 다음에는 항상 동사원형을 쓴다. 그러므로 답은 receive이다.

어휘 **applicant** 지원자　**application** 지원, 신청　**written** 서면상의　**notification** 통지, 통보

17. The entiire staff in the marketing division needs to -------- the annual conference next month.

(A) enroll
(B) attend
(C) participate
(D) comply

해석 마케팅 부서의 모든 직원들은 다음 달에 열리는 연례 컨퍼런스에 참석해야 한다.

해설 빈칸 뒤에 전치사 없이 목적어인 the annual conference가 나왔으므로 타동사인 attend를 써야한다.

어휘 **annual** 연례의　**enroll in** ~ ~에 등록하다　**attend** 참석하다　**participate in** 참석하다　**comply with** ~ ~에 따르다

18. The number of Koreans traveling overseas -------- twenty percent over last year.

(A) has increased
(B) have increased
(C) increase
(D) are increased

해석 해외를 여행하는 한국인의 숫자가 작년에 20% 증가했다.

해설 주어가 the number 로 단수이므로 단수 동인 has increased를 써야 한다.

어휘 **overseas** 해외에서

19. Flight attendants should confirm and announce the estimated time of -------- in Chicago.

(A) arrival
(B) arriving
(C) arrive
(D) arrived

해석 기내 승무원들은 시카고 도착예정시간을 확인하고 방송을 해야 한다.

해설 전치사 of 와 in 사이에는 반드시 명사가 와야 한다. 그러므로 답은 (A) arrival 이다.

어휘 **confirm** 확인하다　**announce** 방송하다　**estimated time** 예상시간

20. Effective next year, a subway pass -------- you a 30% discount off the regular city subway fare.

(A) give
(B) will give
(C) gives
(D) gave

해석 내년부터 이 승차권은 정규 시내 지하철 요금의 30 퍼센트가 할인됩니다.

해설 effective next year는 미래시제와 함께 써야 한다. 그러므로, 정답은 (C)이다.

21. As the new air filtration system -------- last month, we can work effectively.

(A) installed
(B) was installed
(C) has installed
(D) installs

해석 새로운 공기 정화 시스템을 지난 달 설치되었기 때문에 우리는 효율적으로 일할 수 있다.

해설 install은 타동사인데 뒤에 목적어가 없으므로 수동태를 써야 한다. 또한 last month 와 적합한 시제는 과거형이다. 그러므로 정답은 (B)이다.

어휘 **air filtration system** 공기 정화 시스템　**effectively** 효율적으로

22. Every candidate's application should -------- by email by the end of next month after the candidates fill in all the blanks.

(A) send
(B) be sent
(C) sent
(D) be sending

해설 응시자들은 모든 빈칸을 써 넣은 뒤, 지원서를 다음 달 말까지 이메일로 보내야만 한다.

해설 빈칸에 들어가야 할 품사는 동사이며, 조동사 should 다음에는 동사원형을 써야한다. 또한 send는 타동사인데 목적어가 없으므로 수동형인 (C) be sent 가 답이다.

어휘 **candidate** 응시자　**complete** 완성하다　**blank** 빈칸

23. All of the employees -------- a coffee break between 3:30 p.m. and 4:00 p.m. every working day.
(A) take
(B) took
(C) taken
(D) had taken

해석 모든 직원들은 근무일에는 항상 오후 3시30분에서 4시 사이에 휴식 시간을 갖는다.

해설 every working day는 매일 반복되는 사실이므로 현재시제인 take를 써야 한다.

어휘 **take a break** 휴식을 취하다 **every working day** 근무일

24. According to the news, the rate of inflation -------- by 7.5 percent last quarter.
(A) rises
(B) rose
(C) risen
(D) wil rise

해석 뉴스에 따르면 지난분기에 물가 상승률은 7.5 퍼센트 올랐다.

해설 last quarter은 과거의 사실이므로 과거시제와 써야 한다.

어휘 **the rate of inflation** 물가상승률

25. The company -------- bonuses to its employees at the end of each year.
(A) gave
(B) is given
(C) give
(D) will give

해석 그 회사는 매년 연말에 직원들에게 상여금을 제공하고 있다.

해설 주어가 the company 로 단수이고, at the end of each year은 매년이라는 의미이므로 정답은 현재 시제인 (C)이다.

B

Questions 26-32 refer to the following advertisement.

Are you looking for the perfect place to live?

Are you interested in a **25.** -------- and quiet house? This apartment is a must-see. It **26.** -------- in a suburban area of Kingston Mountain and features three large bedrooms, each with its own full bathroom. The **27.** -------- kitchen includes all essential appliances. Included in the unit **28.** -------- a washing machine and a dryer for your laundry needs. The combined **29.** -------- living room and dining room is a must-see. This condo has a beautiful view of Kingston Mountain. If you **30.** -------- a perfect and quiet living space, this is what you should get

---

완벽한 주택을 찾으시나요?

사적이며 조용한 집에 관심이 있으신가요? 이 아파트는 꼭 보셔야 합니다. Kingston 산의 외곽에 위치해 있으며 개인 욕실을 갖춘 세 개의 큰 침실을 구비하고 있습니다. 편리한 주방은 모든 필수 가전제품을 갖추고 있습니다. 유닛에 포함되는 것은 세탁하는데 필요한 세탁기와 건조기입니다. 넓은 거실 겸 식사 공간은 꼭 보셔야 할 부분입니다. 이 콘도는 Kingston 산의 아름다운 경관을 가지고 있습니다. 만약 당신이 사적이고 완벽하고 조용한 삶의 공간을 원하신다면, 이곳이 바로 당신이 원하는 그 곳입니다.

어휘 **suburban** 외각의 **feature** 특징 **private** 개인적인 **convenient** 편리한 **include** 포함하다 **appliance** 가전 기구 **laundry** 세탁물 **spacious** 넓은 **view** 경관

26.
(A) privacy
(B) private
(C) privately
(D) privates

해설 a -------- and quiet house에서 등위접속사 and 로 연결된 형용사 quiet 와 대등한 위치로 형용사 private가 적합하다. private 이 명사로 쓰이면 병사라는 뜻이 있다.

27.
(A) locates
(B) located
(C) will locate
(D) is located

해설 ~에 위치되어 있다. 라는 의미이므로 is located 로 수동형으로 써야 한다.

28.
(A) convenient
(B) convenience
(C) convene
(D) conveniently

해설 The -------- kitchen에서 명사 kitchen을 수식하는 형용사 자리이다. 그러므로 정답은 convenient(편리한)이다. convene 소집하다 모으다(동사)

29.
(A) is
(B) are
(C) has
(D) have

해설 Included in the unit -------- a washing machine and a dryer for your laundry needs.은 도치 구문으로 주어는 a washing machine and a dryer for your laundry needs 이고 ~을 포함하고 있다는 의미이므로 be 동사인 are을 써야한다.

30.
(A) probable
(B) potential
(C) foreseeable
(D) spacious

해설 The combined -------- living room and dining room에서 명사구인 living room and dining room을 수식하는 형용사 자리이며 해석상 spacious 공간이 넓은 이라는 의미가 가장 적합하다.

어휘 **probable** 유망한, 있음직한　**potential** 잠재적인
foreseeable 미리 알 수 있는

31.
(A) needs
(B) are needed
(C) need
(D) will need

해설 시간과 조건의 부사절에서는 미래시제 대신 현재시제를 쓰며, 주어가 you 이므로 동사는 need가 적합하다.

Questions 32-37 refer to the following email.

To : Sandra Stones
From : Mary Johns
Subject : The job offer

I'm writing **32.** -------- you email regarding the job offer you got from Sigma Inc. It seems that they want you to work as their new accounting **33.** -------- as soon as possible. However, you are having a hard time **34.** -------- on this matter, so you'd like some **35.** -------- from me. I suggest that you move to the new company since Sigma Inc. is offering you a great **36.** -------- . Also, I think you should tell this to your boss as soon as possible, so that he will have **37.** -------- time to find some to replace you. This would be a good chance for your future. Good luck!

수신 : Sandra Stones
발신 : Mary Johns
제목 : 일자리 제안

저는 Sigma 사로부터 제의 받은 일자리와 관련하여 답장을 드립니다. 그들이 가능한 빨리 당신이 새로운 회계 매니저로 일하기를 원하는 것 같군요. 하지만, 당신은 이 이일을 결정하기가 어려워 제게 조언을 받고 싶다고 했습니다. Sigma 사에게 당신에게 아주 좋은 조건을 제시했기 때문에 저는 당신에게 새로운 회사로 옮길 것을 권합니다. 또한 저는 당신이 가능한 빨리 이 일을 상사에게 이야기해서, 당신을 대체할 사람을 그가 찾는데 충분한 시간을 주어야 한다고 생각합니다. 당신의 장래를 위해 아주 좋은 기회가 될 것입니다. 행운을 빕니다.

어휘 **regrading** ~에 대하여　**accounting** 회계
have a hard time ~ing ~하느라 어려움을 겪다
replace 제자리에 놓다, 대신하다

32.
(A) return
(B) returning
(C) to return
(D) returned

해설 '~하기 위해서 편지를 쓴다'고 할 때는 write to 부정사를 사용한다.

33.
(A) manage
(B) manager
(C) managing
(D) managed

해설 as 다음에는 사람의 신분이나 직책을 나타내는 명사가 온다. 그러므로 단수인 manager를 써야 편지를 쓴 당신(you)과 수일치가 된다.

34.
(A) decide
(B) to decide
(C) decided
(D) deciding

해설 ~하느라 어려운 시간을 보내다는 have a hard time ~ing 이다. 그러므로 deciding 이 적합하다.

35.
(A) advice
(B) advise
(C) advisor
(D) advices

해설 빈칸은 한정사 some 뒤의 명사자리이며, advice 가 명사이며 불가산 명사이다.

36.
(A) dealer
(B) dealing
(C) deals
(D) deal

해설 부정관사 a 와 형용사 great 뒤에는 가산명사의 단수가 와야 한다. 그러므로 답은 deal이다.

37.
(A) so
(B) too
(C) enough
(D) very

해설 충분한 시간이라는 의미로 enough time 이 가장 적합하다.

UNIT 19 : 부정사

GRAMMAR PRACTICE   p.157

A
1. hard to fix
2. difficult to learn
3. fun to make
4. dangerous to ski
5. hard to understand

B
1. B decide to stay
2. C plan to study
3. E hope to see
4. A want to buy
5. D plan to save

C
1. E   2. D   3. C   4. B   5. A

GRAMMAR PRACTICE   p.159

A
1. to talk
2. to help
3. to drink
4. to eat
5. to go

B
1. Olivia went to the store to buy new pants.
2. Tom practices all day to win at the Olympics.
3. My family went to the restaurant to eat some delicious food.
4. I go to the library to read books.
5. I ran to catch the bus.

C
1. I asked him where to go.
2. I don't know what to do.
3. Please tell me where to put these things.
4. I can't decide what to wear for my birthday party.
5. I want to learn how to use this machine.

GRAMMAR IN SENTENCE   p.160

1. It is hard to fix / the broken machine.
▶ 어렵다 / 고치는 것은 / 고장이 난 기계를
해석 고장이 난 기계를 고치는 것은 어렵다.

2. It's not easy / to understand / my sister.
▶ 쉽지 않다 / 이해하기가 / 나의언니를
해석 나의 언니를 이해하기가 쉽지 않다.

3. The children / hope / to see their parents / soon.
▶ 그 아이들은 / 원한다 / 만나기를 / 그들의 부모님을 / 곧.
해석 그 아이들은 그들의 부모님을 곧 만나기를 원한다.

4. My mom / advised / me / to clean / the room.
▶ 엄마는 / 충고하셨다 / 나에게 / 청소하라고 / 방을.
해석 엄마는 나에게 방을 청소하라고 충고하셨다.

5. I / asked / my sister / to close / the window.
▶ 나는 / 요청했다 / 나의 여동생에게 / 닫으라고 / 창문을.
해석 나는 나의 여동생에게 창문을 닫으라고 요청했다.

6. My parents / allowed / me / to go there.
▶ 부모님께서는 / 허락하셨다 / 내가 / 가도록 거기에
해석 부모님께서는 내가 거기에 가도 좋다고 허락하셨다.

7. I've just finished / my work. I / have / time to talk / with you.
▶ 나는 방금 막 끝냈어 / 내 일을 / 나는 / 있다 / 시간이 / 얘기할 / 너랑
해석 나는 방금 막 내 일을 끝냈어. 너랑 얘기할 시간 있어.

8. Tom / practices / all day / to win / at the Olympics.
▶ Tom은 / 연습한다 / 하루 종일 / 우승하기 위하여 / 올림픽에서.
해석 Tom은 올림픽에서 우승하기 위하여 하루 종일 연습한다.

9. I can't decide / what to wear for my birthday party.
▶ 나는 / 결정을 못했다 / 무엇을 입어야 할지 / 내 생일 파티에.
해석 나는 내 생일 파티에 무엇을 입어야 할지 결정을 못했다.

10. I / want / to learn / how to use / this machine.
▶ 나는 / 원한다 / 배우기를 / 방법을 / 사용하는 / 이 기계를
해석 나는 이 기계를 사용하는 방법을 배우기를 원한다.

UNIT 20 : 동명사

GRAMMAR PRACTICE   p.163

A
1. Fixing
2. Learning
3. Making, fun
4. Skiing, dangerous
5. Understanding, hard

B
1. avoided
2. to go
3. reading
4. refused
5. jogging
6. mastering
7. to visit
8. smoking
9. to join
10. listening

GRAMMAR PRACTICE   p.165

A
1. studying
2. watching
3. speaking
4. playing
5. creating

B
1. washing
2. reading
3. to get
4. seeing
5. using

C
1. O
2. Do you mind opening the window?
3. They are dedicated to preserving natural resources.
4. He is accustomed to working in dangerous environments.
5. O

GRAMMAR IN SENTENCE   p.166

1. Learning / English / is not / difficult.
▶ 영어를 배우는 것은 / 않다 / 어렵지
해석 영어를 배우는 것은 어렵지 않다.

2. Skiing / here / is dangerous.
▶ 스키를 타는 것은 / 여기서 / 위험하다
해석 여기서 스키를 타는 것은 위험하다.

3. Mike avoided talking about it.
▶ Mike는 / 피했다 / 이야기하는 것을 / 그것에 대해서
해석 Mike 는 그것에 대해서 이야기하는 것을 피했다.

4. I / always use / this brush / for washing the dishes.
▶ 나는 / 항상 이용한다 / 이 브러시를 / 설거지하기 위하여
해석 나는 (설거지하기 위하여) 항상 이 브러시를 이용한다.

5. Tom / is skilled at / using all the equipment.
▶ Tom 은 / 능숙하다 / 사용하는 것에 / 모든 장비를
해석 Tom 은 모든 장비를 능숙하게 사용한다.

6. I / am used / to jogging / every morning.
▶ 나는 / 익숙하다 / 조깅하는 것에 / 매일 아침
해석 나는 매일 아침 조깅하는 것에 익숙하다.

7. Do you / mind / opening the window?
▶ 당신은 / 싫으십니까? / 여기는 것이 / 창문을
해석 창문 열어도 될까요?

8. They / are dedicated / to preserving natural resources.
▶ 그들은 / 전념하고 있다 / 보존하는데 / 천연 자원을
해석 그들은 천연 자원을 보존하는데 전념하고 있다.

9. He / is accustomed / to working in dangerous environments.
▶ 그는 / 익숙하다 / 일하는 것에 / 위험한 환경에서
해석 그는 위험한 환경에서 일하는 것에 익숙하다.

10. They / are committed / to preventing the accident.
▶ 그들은 / 전념하고 있다 / 예방하는데 / 그 사고를
해석 그들은 그 사고를 예방하는데 전념하고 있다.

UNIT 21 : 분사

GRAMMAR PRACTICE   p.169

A
1. Let's listen to the singing birds.
노래하는 새들의 소리를 들어 보자.

2. Look at the falling leaves.
떨어지고 있는 낙엽들을 보세요.

3. I saw her smiling face.
나는 그녀의 웃는 얼굴을 보았다.

4. History is an interesting subject.
역사는 흥미로운 과목이다.

5. The eggs are boiling now. I like to eat boiled eggs.
달걀이 끓고 있다. 나는 삶은 달걀을 좋아한다.

B
1. Kathy found her stolen purse.
Kathy는 도난당한 지갑을 찾았다.

2. Look at the fallen leaves.
떨어진 낙엽들을 보세요.

3. I bought some painted chairs.
나는 페인트 칠 해진 책상들을 몇 개를 샀다.

4. These are broken dishes.
이것들이 깨진 그릇이다.

5. I'm not interested in science.
나는 역사에 과학에 관심이 없다.

C
1. disappointing, disappointed
2. boring, bored
3. exciting, tired
4. surprising, shocked
5. annoyed, annoying

GRAMMAR PRACTICE   p.171

A
1. Being sick,
2. Left alone,
3. Having eaten lunch,
4. Having been advised not to be late,
5. interested in history,

B
1. After we had finished the project,
2. Because I am interested in the game,
3. When you apply for the position,

4. Because he is unemployed,
5. Because I live in the city,

C
1. used
2. surprising
3. sleeping
4. Fallen
5. satisfied

GRAMMAR IN SENTENCE p.172

1. Having finished / the project, we / had / a party.
▶ 끝낸 후에 / 그 프로젝트를 / 우리는 / 했다 / 파티를.
해석 그 프로젝트를 끝낸 후에, 우리는 파티를 했다.

2. Interested / in the game, I / bought / some tickets.
▶ 관심이 있어서 / 그 게임에 , 나는 / 샀다 / 티켓을
해석 그 게임에 관심이 있어서, 나는 티켓을 샀다.

3. Applying / for the position, you / must submit / a letter of recommendation.
▶ 지원을 할 때 / 그 직책에 / 당신은 제출 해야만 한다 / 추천서를
해석 그 직책에 지원할 때, 추천서를 제출 해야만 한다.

4. Unemployed, Mike / doesn't have / much money.
▶ 직업이 없어서, / Mike은 / 가지고 있지 않다 / 충분한 돈을
해석 직업이 없어서, Mike은 돈을 충분히 가지고 있지 않다.

5. Living / in the city, I / don't know / about country life.
▶ 살고 있어서 / 도시에, 나는 / 모른다 / 시골 생활에 대하여
해석 나는 도시에 살기 때문에, 시골의 생활을 잘 모른다.

6. He / bought / a used car / last month.
▶ 그는 / 샀다 / 중고차를 / 지난달에
해석 그는 지난달에 중고차를 샀다.

7. I / heard / surprising news from my cousin / yesterday.
▶ 나는 / 들었다 / 놀라운 소식을 / 나의 사촌으로부터 / 어제
해석 나는 나의 사촌으로부터 어제 놀라운 소식을 들었다.

8. The baby / sleeping / in the bed / is / my daughter.
▶ 아기는 / 잠을 자고 있는 / 침대에서 / 이다 / 나의 딸
해석 침대에서 자고 있는 아기는 나의 딸이다.

9. Fallen leaves / on the ground / make / me / sad / all the time.
▶ 떨어진 잎들은 / 땅에 / 만든다 / 나를 / 슬프게 / 항상
해석 땅에 떨어진 잎들은 나를 항상 슬프게 만든다.

10. Sprint.com / tries / to make / the customers / satisfied
▶ Sprint.com은 / 노력한다 / 만들기 위해서 / 고객들을 / 만족스럽게 /
해석 Sprint.com은 고객을 만족스럽게 해 주기 위해서 노력한다.

ACTUAL TEST 7 p.174-175

A
1. (B) 2. (B) 3. (B) 4. (C) 5. (D) 6. (B)
7. (C) 8. (B) 9. (B) 10. (A) 11. (C) 12. (A)

B
13. (C) 14. (A) 15. (B) 16. (D) 17. (B) 18. (A)

1. The government plans -------- the environmental policies.
(A) following
(B) to follow
(C) followed
(D) to following
해석 국가는 환경 협약을 따를 계획이다.
해설 빈칸은 plan의 목적어 자리이다. 목적어 자리에 올 수 있는 명사구로는 to 부정사가 있는데, plan는 to 부정사를 목적어로 취하는 타동사이다.
어휘 environmental 환경의 policy 정책, 협약

2. All the residents in this area are opposed -------- the building.
(A) to construct
(B) to constructing
(C) constructing
(D) constructed
해석 이 지역의 모든 주민들은 건물을 건설하는 것을 반대하고 있다.
해설 <be opposed to + (동)명사>는 '~하는 데 반대하다'란 의미이다.
어휘 resident 주민

3. The supervisor offered -------- some schedules for the team members.
(A) rearranging
(B) to rearrange
(C) to rearranging
(D) rearranges
해석 감독관은 팀원들을 위해서 일부 일정을 재조정할 것을 제안했다.
해설 offer은 to 부정사를 목적어로 취하는 타동사이다. 그러므로 정답은 (B)이다.
어휘 environmental 환경의 policy 정책, 협약

4. Staff members are allowed -------- in the lot downstairs starting next week.
(A) to parking
(B) park
(C) to park
(D) parking
해석 직원들은 다음 주부터 지하주차장에서 주차를 하도록 허용 받는다.
해설 문맥상 '직원들이 ~한 것을 허용 받았다'의 의미가 되어야 하므로 be allowed to 부정사를 써야한다.

5. The education grant will be used in order -------- the school with new computer equipment.
(A) to providing
(B) provide
(C) providing
(D) to provide

해석 교육 기금은 학교에 새로운 컴퓨터 장비를 들이는 데 사용될 것이다.
해설 in order to 동사원형은 ~하기 위하여 라는 의미로 to 부정사인 (D) to provide 가 정답이다.
어휘 **provide A with B** A에게 B를 제공하다

6. David Russel, the president of the company, has announced that it is going to discontinue -------- its unprofitable pagers.
(A) make
(B) making
(C) to make
(D) to making

해석 회사의 사장인 David Russel씨는 회사의 수익성이 없는 호출기를 만드는 것을 그만둘 것이라고 발표했다.
해설 discontinue는 동명사를 목적어로 받는 동사이다. 그러므로 정답은 (B) making이다.
어휘 **discontinue** 그만두다, 중지하다
unprofitable 이익 없는, 수지가 안 맞는

7. According to the booklet, this furniture is on sale for a -------- period of time.
(A) limiting
(B) limits
(C) limited
(D) limit

해석 안내책자에 따르면, 이 가구들은 한정기간 동안만 할인 판매된다.
해설 period (기간) 과 limit (제한하다)는 수동관계이다. 그러므로 과거분사인 limited 가 적합하다.

8. Most participants were -------- that the workshop had been canceled without any explanation.
(A) disappointing
(B) disappointed
(C) to disappoint
(C) to disappointing

해석 어떠한 설명도 없이 워크숍이 취소 되서 대부분의 참석자들은 실망했다.
해설 disappoint는 감정동사로 사람이 주어로 오면 수동형을 써야한다. 그러므로 정답은 (B) disappointed이다..

9. -------- a walk in the park yesterday, Mr. Conner met a colleague of his.
(A) Taken
(B) Taking
(C) To be taken
(D) To taking

해석 Tom은 어제 공원을 산책하다가 동료를 만났다.
해설 분사 구문을 사용하지 않으면, While he was taking a walk in the park yesterday, Tom met a colleague of his.가 된다. a walk라는 목적어가 있으므로 능동의 의미인 현재 분사가 적합하다.
어휘 **take a walk** 산책을 하다   **colleague** 동료

10. Nowadays, most people prefer small cars because of the -------- cost of gasoline.
(A) rising
(B) risen
(C) rose
(D) rise

해석 요즘, 증가하는 유류비 때문에 대부분의 사람들이 작은 차를 선호한다.
해설 정관사 (the) 뒤에 명사 (cost)를 수식하는 분사는 능동과 진행의 의미를 가지고 있는 현재분사인 rising이 적합하다. 또한 rise는 자동사이므로 수동의 의미인 과거분사로 명사를 수식할 수 없다.
어휘 **nowadays** 요즘   **prefer** 더 좋아하다 선호하다
gasoline 가솔린, 휘발유

11. People -------- in joining the baseball club should contact Mr. Clarkson.
(A) interesting
(B) interest
(C) interested
(D) interests

해석 야구 클럽에 가입을 원하는 분들은 Clarkson씨에게 연락을 해야 한다.
해설 문장의 주어는 people 이고 동사는 should contact 이므로 주어를 수식하는 분사가 필요하다. 원래 people who are interested in~ 인데 who are이 생략되어 있는 구조이며, interest는 감정 동사이므로 사람을 수식할 때는 수동형을 쓴다.
어휘 **join** ~에 가입하다   **contact** 연락을 취하다

12. Applications -------- after September 10 will not be considered for the program.
(A) arriving
(B) arrived
(C) arrive
(D) to be arrived

해석 9월 10일 이후에 도착하는 신청서들은 그 프로그램의 심사에서 제외된다.
해설 문장의 주어는 applications 이고 동사는 will not be considered 이므로 주어를 수식하는 분사가 필요하다. 원래 applications which are arriving~인데 which are이 생략되어 있는 구조이며, arrive는 자동사이므로 능동형인 현재분사만을 쓸 수 있다.
어휘 **application** 신청서, 원서

Questions 13-18 refer to the following letter.

Dear Phillip Greg

Hello, My name is Jim Bright. I am one of the people participating in the upcoming job expo **13.** -------- in Chicago. Susan Williams and I were supposed **14.** -------- the job fair together. We **15.** -------- many things for this event starting two months ago. As you had determined, I was going to give an introduction of our company and conduct interviews and with individuals **16.** -------- in our company for potential employment, However,

However, Susan cannot come and **17.** -------- me because of the flu. Without her, I cannot do anything. I need your help in **18.** -------- a solution to this matter. Thank you.

Phillip Greg씨에게

안녕하세요? 저는 Jim Bright입니다. 저는 시카고에서 열리는 직업 박람회에 참석할 사람 중 한명입니다. Susan Williams와 저는 직업 박람회에 참여하기로 되어있었습니다. 저희는 두 달 전부터 이번 행사를 위해 많은 것을 준비해왔습니다. 당신이 지시했던 대로, 저희 회사에 대한 소개를 해주고, 개인적으로 우리 회사에 관심이 있는 구직자들과 인터뷰를 하기로 했습니다. 하지만, 독감 때문에 Susan 이 올 수도 없고 저를 도와줄 수도 없습니다. 그녀 없이는 저는 아무것도 할 수가 없습니다. 이 문제에 대한 해결책을 알아보는 것을 도와주시기 바랍니다. 감사합니다.

어휘 upcoming 곧 있을   be supposed to ~하기로 되어있다
take part in ~ ~에 참여하다   assign 일을 맡기다
conduct ~을 하다   potential 잠재적인

13.
(A) hold
(B) holding
(C) held
(D) was held

해설 upcoming job expo -------- in Chicago에서 upcoming job expo (which is) held in Chicago에서 which is가 생략된 형태이며, hold는 '개최하다'라는 의미 일때 타동사로 쓰이므로 수동형으로 써야한다. 그러므로 정답은 held이다.

14.
(A) to take part in
(B) taking par in
(C) to be taken part in
(D) take part in

해설 'be supposed to 동사원형'으로 ~하기로 되어 있다라는 의미이다. take part in은 항상 능동형으로 써야 한다.

15.
(A) have been prepared
(B) have been preparing
(C) are prepared
(D) prepared

해설 since two months ago가 있으므로 현재완료형을 본동사로 써야 한다.

16.
(A) interesting
(B) interest
(C) interests
(D) interested

해설 individuals -------- in our company에서 individuals(who are) interested in에서 who are이 생략된 형태이며, interest는 감정 동사이므로 사람이 individuals 를 수식할 때는 수동형을 써야 한다

17.
(A) assists
(B) assist
(C) assisted
(D) assisting

해설 Susan cannot come and 17 -------- me 에서 등위 접속사 and 로 연결되어 come 과 같은 위치에 와야 하므로 정답은 assist 이다

18.
(A) finding
(B) find
(C) found
(D) to find

해설 on -------- a solution 에서 전치사 on 과 명사구인 a solution 사이에는 동명사가 와야 한다.

UNIT 22 : 접속사 1

GRAMMAR PRACTICE   p.179

A
1. The baseball game was interesting and exciting.
2. I bought a book yesterday but haven't read it yet.
3. Will you hang out with me or stay at home?
4. It was very hot, so I opened the window.
5. He should stay at home, for he is sick.

B
1. and   2. but   3. or   4. so   5. for

C
1. or   2. and   3. nor   4. but also   5. but

GRAMMAR PRACTICE   p.181

A
1. (2)   2. (1)   3. (3)   4. (2)   5. (3)

B
1. that   2. What   3. whether   4. that   5. whether

C

1. What I need right now is your report.
2. O
3. What I want to know is what you like.
4. Whether I can finish this project is another matter.
5. O

GRAMMAR IN SENTENCE p.182

1. I / didn't know / that Linda was a teacher.
▶ 나는 몰랐다 / 것을 Linda가 선생님이라는
해석 나는 Linda가 선생님인지 몰랐다.

2. What / I want / now / is / your help.
▶ 것은 / 내가 / 원하는 / 지금 이다 너의 도움
해석 내가 지금 원하는 것은 너의 도움이다.

3. I / cannot be sure whether he / will attend / the meeting / or not.
▶ 나는 / 확실히 모른다 것을 그가 회의에 참석할지 아닐 지를
해석 나는 그가 회의에 올지 안 올지 확실히 모른다.

4 It / is certain that / he / is innocent.
▶ 명백하다 / 것은 / 그가 / 결백하다는
해석 그가 결백하다는 것은 명백하다.

5. I / wonder whether / he is / at home / or / at the office.
▶ 나는 궁금하다 그가 집에 있을지 회사에 있을지
해석 그가 집에 있을지 회사에 있을지 궁금하다.

6. What / I need right now is your report.
▶ 내가 필요한 것은 지금 / 이다 / 당신의 보고서
해석 내가 지금 필요한 것은 당신의 보고서이다.

7. I'm / not sure whether / he / is Korean or not.
▶ 나는 잘 모르겠다 / ~를 / 그가 / 한국인인지 아닌지
해석 나는 그가 한국인인지 아닌지를 잘 모르겠다.

8. What / I / want / to know is what / you / like.
▶ 것은 / 내가 / 원하는 / 알기를 이다 것 / 네가 / 좋아하는
해석 내가 알고 싶은 것이 네가 무엇을 좋아하느냐이다.

9. Whether / I / can finish / this project / is / another matter.
▶ ~인지 아닌지를 / 나는 / 마칠 수 있다 / 그 프로젝트를 이다 / 또 다른 문제
해석 내가 이 프로젝트를 다 마칠 수 있는 지는 또 다른 문제이다. /

10. It / is not clear whether / he / will accept / the offer / or not.
▶ 분명하지 않다 / 그가 / 수락할 지 / 그 제안을 / 말지는
해석 그가 그 제안을 수락할 지 말지는 분명하지 않다.

UNIT 23 : 접속사 2

GRAMMAR PRACTICE p.185

A
1. (B) 2. (A) 3. (E) 4. (C) 5. (D)

B
1. unless   2. since   3. Because
4. When   5. As   6. While
7. if   8. although 9. so that
10. Even though

GRAMMAR PRACTICE p.187

A
1. during, due to, because of, without, despite, in spite of
2. while, unless, although
3. otherwise, nevertheless

B
Unless it rains tomorrow, we will go on a picnic.
= It will rain tomorrow; otherwise, we will go on a picnic.
= Without rain, we will go on a picnic.

C
1. therefore   2. otherwise   3. however
4. nevertheless 5. However

GRAMMAR IN SENTENCE p.188

1. Because / she / is / very nice, everyone / likes / her.
▶ 때문에 / 그녀는 / 매우 / 친절하다 모든 사람들이 / 좋아한다 / 그녀를
해석 그녀는 친절하기 때문에 모든 사람들이 그녀를 좋아한다.

2. If you meet Tom, please give him this book.
▶ 만약에 / 당신이 / 만난다 / Tom을 주어라 / 그에게 / 이 책을
해석 만약에 Tom을 만나면, 그에게 이 책을 주세요.

3. It will rain tomorrow, Otherwise, we will go on a picnic.
▶ 비가 / 내릴 것이다 / 내일 / 그렇지만 않으면, 우리는 갈 것이다 / 소풍을 /
해석 내일 비가 내릴 것이다. 그렇지만 않으면, 우리는 소풍을 갈 것이다.

4. Unless we hurry, we / will be late / for the concert.
▶ 않으면 / 우리가 / 서두른다 우리는 / 늦을 것이다 / 콘서트에
해석 서두르지 않으면 우리는 콘서트에 늦을 것이다.

5. It's already been / a year since you joined us.
▶ 이미 / 일 년이 / 되었다 이래로 / 당신이 / 합류했다 / 우리와.
해석 당신이 우리와 합류한 지 벌써 일 년이 되었네요.

6. Because / he / didn't finish / the report, I was angry with him.
▶ 때문에 / 그가 / 끝내지 않았다 / 보고서를, 나는 / 화를 냈다 / 그에게.
해석 그가 보고서를 끝내지 않았기 때문에 나는 그에게 화를 냈다.

7. When / I / saw / you / last, you / were / six years old.
▶ 때 / 내가 / 보았다 / 너를 / 마지막으로 / 너는 / 6살이었다.
해석 내가 너를 마지막으로 봤을 때, 너는 6살이었다.

8. As / I / don't have / enough money, I can't buy the car.
▶ 때문에 / 나는 / 없다 / 충분한 돈이, 나는 / 살 수 없다 / 그 차를.
해석 나는 충분한 돈이 없어서 그 차를 살 수가 없다.

9. While / I / buy / tickets. keep / an eye / on my bag.
▶ 동안에 / 내가 / 산다 / 티켓을, 지켜봐 주세요 / 내 가방을 /
해석 내가 티켓을 사는 동안, 내 가방을 지켜봐 주세요.

10. I / will pardon / John if / he / acknowledges / his mistake.
▶ 나는 / 용서할 것이다 / John을 만약 / 그가 / 인정하다 / 그의 실수를
해석 만약 그가 그의 실수를 인정하면 나는 John을 용서해 줄 것이다.

UNIT 24 : 관계사

GRAMMAR PRACTICE p.191

A
1. who 2. whose 3. that 4. which 5. whose

B
1. who 2. whose 3. which 4. who 5. which

C
1. who was rich and kind.
2. whose husband is very diligent.
3. who are all the same age.
4. who(m) the English teacher wanted to meet.
5. which I gave to my sister

GRAMMAR PRACTICE p.193

A
1. why 2. where, to which 3. on which, when
4. how 5. when

B
1. who 2. whose 3. that
4. which 5. that 6. when
7. where 8. how 9. why
10. which

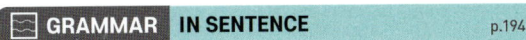

GRAMMAR IN SENTENCE p.194

1. A nurse / is a person who / takes care / of patients.
▶ 간호사는 / 사람이다 돌봐주는 / 환자들을
해석 간호사는 환자들을 돌봐주는 사람이다.

2. I / met / a man whose sister / is / an English teacher.
▶ 나는 / 만났다 / 한 남자를 / 여동생이 이다 영어 교사
해석 나는 그의 여동생이 영어 교사인 남자를 만났다.

3. I / found / the key that Ann / lost / last night.
▶ 나는 / 찾았다 / 열쇠를 / Ann 이 / 잃어버렸다 / 어제
해석 나는 Ann 이 어제 잃어버렸던 열쇠를 찾았다.

4. The party which I went to yesterday / wasn't enjoyable.
▶ 파티는 / 내가 / 갔던 / 어제 갔던 / 즐겁지 않았다.
해석 내가 어제 갔던 파티는 즐겁지 않았다.

5. The customer service representative that works / in the company was very friendly.
▶ 고객 서비스 직원은 일하다 / 그 회사에서 매우 친절했다.
해석 그 회사의 고객 서비스 직원은 매우 친절했다.

6. I / can't remember / the time when / he / left / the office / last night.
▶ 나는 기억이 나지 않는다 / 시간이 / 그가 / 떠난 / 사무실을 / 어젯밤에
해석 나는 그가 어젯밤에 퇴근한 시간이 기억이 나지 않는다.

7. This / is / the place where / I / met / her / the other day.
▶ 이곳이 / 그 장소다 / 내가 만났던 그녀를 요전 날에
해석 이곳이 요전 날 그녀를 만났던 곳이다.

8. I / can't understand / how she / was able to finish / the big project / by herself.
▶ 나는 이해가 안된다 / 어떻게 / 그녀가 / 마쳤는지 / 대규모의 프로젝트를 / 혼자서
해석 나는 그녀가 어떻게 혼자서 대규모의 프로젝트를 마쳤는지 이해가 안 된다.

9. He / didn't tell / me / the reason why / he / came / here / suddenly.
▶ 그는 / 말하지 않았다 / 나에게 / 이유를 / 그가 / 온 / 이곳에 / 갑자기
해석 그는 나에게 그가 이곳에 갑자기 온 이유를 말하지 않았다.

10. Look / at the garden which / is filled with / flowers.
▶ 보세요 / 정원을 / 가득 찬 / 꽃들로
해석 꽃들로 가득 찬 정원을 보세요.

ACTUAL TEST 8

p.196-197

A
1. (B) 2. (D) 3. (C) 4. (A) 5. (B) 6. (C)
7. (C) 8. (B) 9. (A) 10. (D) 11. (C) 12. (B)

B
13. (C) 14. (A) 15. (B) 16. (D) 17. (A) 18. (D)

---

1. Yesterday, both management -------- the labor union agreed that working hours should not exceed 9 hours a day.
(A) but
(B) and
(C) or
(D) so

해석 어제 경영진과 노동조합 양측이 근무시간이 하루에 9시간을 초과해서는 안 된다는 것에 동의했다.

해설 등위 상관 접속사 both A and B 의 구문이므로 빈칸에는 and가 적합하다.

어휘 **management** 경영진   **labor union** 노동조합   **deal with** ~을 다루다   **object to** 반대하다

2. They should -------- find a new house there or commute between Los Angeles and San Pedro every day.
(A) both
(B) not only
(C) neither
(D) either

해석 이들은 이곳에 새 집을 구하거나, 아니면 Los Angles와 San Pedro 사이를 매일 출퇴근해야 한다.

해설 등위상관접속사 either A or B 구문이다.

어휘 **commute** 출퇴근하다

3. The sales manager said that neither high prices -------- a lack of effort was a factor in losing customers.
(A) or
(B) but
(C) nor
(B) yet

해석 판매담당자는 높은 가격뿐만 아니라 노력의 부족이 고객을 잃는 요소라고 말했다.

해설 상관접속사 neither A nor B의 형태가 되어야 하므로 정답은 (A) nor이다.

4. The cook not only had to prepare the food -------- carry it to each room of the household.
(A) but
(B) also
(C) as
(D) and

해석 그 요리사는 음식을 장만할 뿐만 아니라 가족의 방까지 가져다주어야만 했다.

해설 등위 상관접속사인 not only A but also B(A뿐만 아니라 B도)에서 also를 생략하고 not only A but B라고 할 수도 있다.

어휘 **cook** 요리사   **prepare** 준비하다   **household** 가족, 온 집안 식구

5. All employees should know -------- this convention is very important.
(A) what
(B) that
(C) which
(D) who

해석 모든 직원들은 그 집회가 매우 중요하다는 것을 알고 있어야만 한다.

해설 접속사 that이 이끄는 명사절은 <주어 + 동사 + 보어> 또는 <주어 + 동사 + 목적어>의 완전한 문장 구조를 갖고 있으며, 타동사 know의 목적어로 쓰여 명사절이 된다.

어휘 **convention** 집회

6. -------- the manager had already approved the week's work schedule, he accepted Mr. Jefferson's request for sick leave.
(A) Nevertheless
(B) If
(C) Even though
(D) Unless

해석 부장은 주간 근무 스케줄을 이미 승인했음에도 불구하고, Jefferson 씨의 병가 요청을 받아들였다.

해설 문맥상 양보의 접속사가 필요하다. '~에도 불구하고'라는 의미의 양보를 타나내는 부사절 접속사는 even though 또는 although이다. 따라서 정답은 (D).

어휘 **approve** 승인하다   **sick leave** 병가

7. The president -------- donated such a large sum to our school was a billionaire.
(A) which
(B) whose
(C) who
(D) what

해석 사람을 나타내는 선행사인 president와 동사 donated 사이에는 주격 관계대명사 who 또는 that이 적합하다.

해설 우리 학교를 위해서 그렇게도 많은 돈을 기부했던 그 사장은 억만장자였다.

8. It is important to rely on valid identification rather than uniforms -------- can be replicated easily.
(A) who
(B) which
(C) what
(D) whose

해석 그것은 쉽게 복제될 수 있는 유니폼보다 유효한 신분 증명에 의존하는 것이 중요하다.

해설 선행사는 사물인 uniforms입니다. 그러므로 정답은 사물을 선행사로 취하는 주격 관계대명사 which이다.

어휘 **rely on** 의존하다   **valid** 유효한   **identification** 신분증   **replicate** 복제하다

9. The customer service representative -------- works in the company was very friendly.
(A) that
(B) which
(C) whose
(D) what

해석 그 회사의 고객 서비스 직원은 매우 친절했다.
해설 사람을 나타내는 선행사인 customer service representative와 동사 works 사이에는 주격 관계대명사 who 또는 that이 적합하다.

10. Anyone -------- visits our company should contact the information desk for identification.
(A) whose
(B) what
(C) where
(D) who

해석 저의 회사를 방문하는 모든 분들은 신원 확인을 위해 안내 데스크에 연락하여야 합니다.
해설 'Anyone -------- visits~'에서는 선행사가 anyone 이고 동사 visit을 연결해야 하므로 주격관계대명사 who 가 적합하다.
어휘 **information desk** 안내데스크

11. Mr. Jackson's duties are not limited to recruiting, hiring, -------- evaluating employees.
(A) that
(B) but
(C) and
(D) while

해석 Jackson씨의 임무는 직원을 모집하고, 고용하고, 평가하는 것에 그치지 않는다.
해설 문맥에 알맞는 접속사 넣기 - 문장들 사이의 관계를 파악하는 문제로 recruiting, hiring과 evaluating는 같은 구조이자 의미이므로 등위 접속사 and가 필요한 자리이다.
어휘 **evaluate** 평가하다 **hire** 고용하다 **recruit** (사람을) 모집하다, 보충하다 **be limited to** 명사 -에 국한되다

12. We cannot deal with the companies -------- offices are not in United States.
(A) which
(B) whose
(C) what
(D) that

해석 우리는 미국에 사무실이 없는 회사와는 거래할 수 없다.
해설 '회사의 사무실'이라는 소유의 의미가 되어야 하므로 소유격 관계대명사 whose 가 적합하다.
어휘 **deal with** 거래하다

Questions 13-15 refer to the following news report.

Sometime, are you anxious while at work? Are you often irritated during the day? Then you should listen to this informational minute. Many people drink several cups of coffee every day to help them stay alert. **13.** --------, scientists have found **14.** -------- the high levels of caffeine in coffee actually increase the stress experienced by most people. Researchers **15.** -------- this to be especially true if the coffee is drunk on an empty stomach. The caffeine is absorbed very quickly and causes a feeling of elevation **16.** -------- energy without food in the stomach. **17.** -------- this serves to stimulate the mental and physical faculties of the coffee drinker, it also increases the drinker's blood pressure and heart rate. **18.** -------- more caffeine is not consumed, a noticeable physical let down is experienced several hours later. As a result, to avoid this, many coffee drinkers consume it throughout the day. In order to avoid this unpleasant cycle, researchers suggest that caffeine intake be limited to two or three cups of coffee a day.

때때로 일하는 도중에 불안해 지십니까? 일과 중 종종 짜증이 나기도 하시나요? 그렇다면 본 정보 시간에 귀를 기울이셔야만 합니다. 많은 사람들이 정신을 깨기 위해 매일 여러 잔의 커피를 마십니다. 그러나 커피에 들어 있는 높은 카페인 수치가 대부분의 사람들이 느끼는 스트레스를 실제로 가중시킨다는 사실을 연구학자들이 밝혀냈습니다. 연구학자들은 커피를 음식을 섭취하지 않은 상태에서 마실 경우, 이러한 현상이 두드러진다는 것을 밝혀냈습니다. 공복인 상태에서는 빠르게 흡수되어 상승감과 에너지를 느끼게 합니다. 이로 인해 커피를 마신 사람의 정신적 신체적 기능은 자극되지만, 동시에 혈압과 심장 박동수도 높아집니다. 만약 카페인을 더 이상 섭취하지 않으면 몇 시간 후에는 신체 기능이 눈에 띄게 저하되는 것을 느낄 것입니다. 그 결과로, 커피를 마시는 많은 삶들은 이것을 방지하기 위해 하루 종일 커피를 마시게 되는 것입니다. 이러한 악순환을 방지하기 위해서 연구학자들은 카페인 섭취를 하루 두 세잔의 커피로 줄일 것을 제안합니다.

어휘 **anxious** 불안한 **irritated** 신경질이 난 **informational minute** (방송에서) 정보를 제공해 주는 시간 **stay alert** 정신을 차리고 있다 **key up** 긴장시키다 **on empty stomach** 공복에 **let down** 감퇴, 이완 **unpleasant** 불쾌한, 싫은 **intake** 섭취량

13.
(A) Since
(B) Because
(C) However
(D) Moreover

해설 빈칸은 부사 또는 접속 부사자리이며, 앞뒤 문맥상, '많은 사람들이 정신을 깨기 위해 매일 여러 잔의 커피를 마십니다. 그러나 커피에 들어 있는 높은 카페인 수치가 대부분의 사람들이 느끼는 스트레스를 실제로 가중시킨다는 사실을 연구학자들이 밝혀냈습니다.'의 의미이므로 빈칸에는 접속부사 however이 적합하다.

14.
(A) that
(B) what

(C) when
(D) whether

해설 과학자(scientists) ~을 발견하다(have found)라는 의미로 타동사의 find 의 목적어로 쓰일 수 있는 명사절 that 이 적합한 자리이다.

15.
(A) has found
(B) have found
(C) has been found
(D) have been found

해설 주어가 Researchers 로 복수명사이고 빈칸 뒤에 목적어인 this 가 있으므로 능동형인 have found 가 정답이다.

16.
(A) or
(B) of
(C) but
(D) and

해설 elevation -------- energy에서 상승감과 에너지를 느끼게 된다는 의미로 등위접속사 and 가 적합한 자리이다.

17.
(A) Even though
(B) Nevertheless
(C) Additionally
(D) Otherwise

해설 빈칸은 접속사 자리이다. 보기 중 접속사는 Even though이며, Nevertheless(그럼에도 불구하고), Additionally(게다가), Otherwise(만약 그렇지 않다면)의 의미의 접속부사이다.

18.
(A) Because
(B) Although
(C) Since
(D) If

해설 '만약 카페인을 더 이상 섭취하지 않으면 몇 시간 후에는 신체 기능이 눈에 띄게 저하되는 것을 느낄 것입니다.'라는 뜻이므로 접속사 if가 적합하다.

MINI TEST 4
p.198-201

A

1. (D)	2. (A)	3. (D)	4. (A)	5. (C)
6. (C)	7. (C)	8. (B)	9. (C)	10. (D)
11. (A)	12. (A)	13. (B)	14. (A)	15. (D)
16. (B)	17. (D)	18. (A)	19. (B)	20. (B)
21. (C)	22. (A)	23. (B)	24. (C)	

B

25. (B)	26. (D)	27. (D)	28. (B)	29. (D)
30. (C)	31. (C)	32. (D)	33. (C)	34. (D)
35. (A)	36. (D)			

1. Individuals looking for funds for their business -------- to turn in two copies of their proposal.
(A) require
(B) requires
(C) is requiring
(D) are required

해석 그들의 사업을 위한 자금을 구하는 사람들은 계획안 사본 2부를 제출해야 한다.

해설 '기금을 구하는 사람들은 ~을 제출해야 한다(제출할 것이 요구된다)'라는 의미로 보아, 복수 주어(Fund seekers)와 동사(require)는 수동 관계에 있다. 따라서 빈칸에는 '~해야 한다, ~할 것이 요구되다'라는 의미의 수동태 동사 (D) are required가 와야 한다.

어휘 **fund** 자금 **turn in** 제출하다 **sponsorship guarantee** 후원 보증서 **in the running** 승산이 있는

2. The agency was unable -------- the design specifications for the convention center.
(A) to meet
(B) meeting
(C) meet
(D) met

해석 그 회사는 컨벤션 센터에 대한 디자인 주문서를 충족시킬 수 없었다.

해설 '~할 수 없다.'라는 의미의 'be (un)able to 부정사'구문이다.

어휘 **agency** 서비스 제공 기관(회사) **be unable to** ~할 수 없다 **meet** 충족시키다

3. Mr. Miller has decided that it is time -------- as the head of the committee.
(A) resigning
(B) resigned
(C) resigns
(D) to resign

해석 밀러 씨는 위원회의 회장 자리를 사임할 시기라고 결심했다.

해설 time 뒤에서 to 부정사의 수식을 받는 명사이다. 그러므로 정답은 (D)이다.

어휘 **decide** 결정하다 **head** 회장, 총재 **committee** 위원회 **resign** 사임하다

4. This website was designed -------- your Internet searches to an absolute minimum.
(A) to keep
(B) kept
(C) keeping
(D) has kept

해석 이 웹 사이트는 당신의 인터넷 검색을 최소로 줄이도록 고안되었습니다.

해설 '~라기 위하여 유지시킨다.'라는 의미로 빈칸은 to 부정사의 부사적 용법이 필요한 자리이다.

어휘 **keep / reduce sth to a minimum** ~을 최소로 유지하다 / 줄이다

250 잉글리쉬앤 그래머 START

5. Please refrain from -------- any new events on the online calendar until further notice.
(A) to schedule
(B) scheduled
(C) scheduling
(D) schedule

해석 추가 공지가 있을 때까지 온라인 일정표에 새로운 행사를 기입하는 것을 삼가주십시오.

해설 빈 칸이 전치사 from 뒤에 오고 있으므로 빈칸에는 전치사의 목적어로 사용될 수 있는 명사 (C)scheduling과 명사 (D) schedule이 정답이 될 가능성이 있는데 빈 칸 뒤에 목적어에 해당하는 명사구가 오고 있으므로 목적어를 취할 수 있는 동명사 (C)scheduling이 정답이다.

어휘 **error** 오류 **refrain from** 자제하다, 삼가다 **calendar** 행사예정표, 일정표 **notice** 공지 **schedule** …을 표에 써넣다, 기입하다

6. Many people, including elderly users, had difficulty -------- the devices.
(A) handle
(B) handles
(C) handling
(D) to handle

해석 고령자를 포함하여 많은 사람들이 기기 조작을 어려워하고 있다.

해설 have difficulty (in)~ing 구문이다.

어휘 **have difficulty ~ing** 구문이다.

7. After carefully -------- your resume, we are glad to offer you the position.
(A) examine
(B) to examine
(C) examining
(D) examined

해석 신중하게 귀하의 이력서를 검토하고 나서, 저희가 귀하에게 그 직책을 제안하게 되어 기쁩니다.

해설 전치사 다음에는 명사가 와야 하는데 목적어로 your resume가 와 있으므로 타동사 역할도 동시에 하는 동명사가 필요한 자리이다.

어휘 **carefully** 신중히, 조심스럽게 **examine** 검토하다 **be glad to do** ~하게 되어 기쁘다 **offer sbd sth** ~에게 …을 제공하다

8. The president has announced that the company will discontinue -------- its unprofitable products.
(A) make
(B) making
(C) made
(D) to make

해석 사장님은 회사의 수익성이 없는 제품들을 만드는 것을 그만둘 것이라고 발표했다.

해설 avoid / give up / enjoy / mind / discontinue 등은 동명사를 받는 동사이다. 여기에서는 동명사가 동사의 목적어의 역할을 한다.

어휘 **discontinue** 그만두다, 중지하다 **unprofitable** 이익 없는, 수지가 안 맞는

9. There are many -------- candidates here and all of them look very well-prepared.
(A) qualify
(B) qualifying
(C) qualified
(D) qualifies

해석 이 자리에는 자질을 갖춘 많은 지원자들이 있고 그들 모두가 준비가 잘 되어 있는 것 같습니다.

해설 명사 candidates를 수식하는 분사형 형용사 자리이다. (C) qualified 이다.

어휘 **candidate** 후보자 **well-prepared** 준비가 잘된

10. A cancellation must be made within five days of the -------- departure date.
(A) schedule
(B) scheduling
(C) scheduler
(D) scheduled

해석 예정 출발일로부터 5일 이전에 취소를 해야 한다.

해설 '예정된'의 의미로 과거분사인 scheduled를 써야 한다.

어휘 **cancellation** 취소 **departure date** 출발일

11. Our company has advised most employees -------- use of the public transportation system.
(A) to make
(B) making
(C) to be made
(D) make

해석 회사에서는 대부분의 직원들이 대중 교통수단을 이용하기를 권장하고 있다.

해설 advise A to do B A 에게 B를 하게 하다 에 관한 문제로서 보기에서 to 부정사를 찾아야 한다. 이러한 동사로는 enable persuade advice 등이 있다, 그러므로 정답은 (A)이다.

어휘 **advise A to do B** A 에게 B를 하게 하다

12. -------- been warned to be punctual by his boss, Mr. Jackson began to get up early.
(A) Having
(B) Had
(C) Have
(C) Has

해석 잭슨 씨는 그의 상사로부터 시간을 지키라는 경고를 받고 난 후에 일찍 일어나기 시작했다.

해설 완료 분사구문은 항상 Having 으로 시작된다. After he had been warned to be punctual by his boss, Tom **began** to get up early.를 완료분사구문으로 바꾼 형태이다.

어휘 **warn** 경고하다 **punctual** 시간을 엄수하는

13. The exhibit has included -------- historic and contemporary artifacts.
(A) that
(B) both
(C) neither
(D) but

해설 그 전시회는 역사적이고 동시대적인 문화 유물을 둘 다 포함하고 있었다.

해설 both A and B 구문 이다. historic and contemporary 의 관계가 순접 관계 이므로 공통적으로 artifacts를 수식하는 형용사 이고 앞에 both 가 필요하다.

어휘 **exhibit** 전시회 **historic** 역사상 **contemporary** 동시대의 **artifact** 문화유물, 인공물, 가공물

14. New employees receive -------- health and dental insurance or health and vision insurance.
(A) either
(B) not only
(C) both
(D) whether

해설 신규 직원들은 건강과 치과보험 또는 건강과 안과보험을 받는다.

해설 health and dental insurance와 health and vision insurance을 or이 연결하고 있으므로 or 과 함께 사용될 수 있는 상관접속사는 (A) either이다. not only~but also~, both~and~로 함께 쓰인다.

어휘 **dental insurance** 치과보험 **vision insurance** 안과보험

15. The research assistants were selected from 16 public enterprises -------- 9 government agencies.
(A) in
(B) both
(C) by
(D) and

해설 연구 보조원은 16개의 공기업과 9개의 정부기관으로부터 선발되어 있다.

해설 앞 뒤 구를 연결해주는 대등하게 연결해주는 등위 접속사 and가 정답이다.

어휘 **research assistant** 연구원 **enterprise** 기업

16. We will send you some of our catalogues so that you can decide -------- you need.
(A) that
(B) what
(C) if
(D) whether

해설 귀하께서 필요한 것을 결정하실 수 있도록 저희가 안내 책자 몇 부를 보내겠습니다.

해설 decide의 목적어로 쓰이는 명사절이 필요하다 you need에서 타동사 need 의 목적어가 없으므로 what 이 적합하다.

17. The staff member at the company's headquarters protested -------- they are overworked and underpaid.
(A) for
(B) what
(C) as
(D) that

해설 본사의 직원들은 그들이 초과근무를 하고 수당이 덜 지급 됐음을 항의했다.

해설 they are overworked and underpaid절이 타동사 protest의 목적어 역할을 하고 있다. 그러므로 명사절 접속사 that이 적합하다.

18. His major concern is -------- stock prices will fluctuate again within the next quarter.
(A) whether
(B) what
(C) since
(D) and

해설 그의 주요한 관심사는 주식 가격이 다음 분기에 등락할 것인가이다.

해설 be 동사 보어로 쓰일 수 있는 명사절 접속사 필요한 자리이다. 주식 가격이 다음 분기에 등락할 것인가이다. 라는 의미이므로 whether 이 가장 적합하다.

어휘 **major** 주요한 **concern** 관심, 걱정 **stock** 주식 **fluctuate** 등락하다

19. -------- he had already bought a similar type of car, the man purchased a motorcycle.
(A) Though
(B) Since
(C) Until
(D) When

해설 그는 비슷한 차종을 이미 샀었기 때문에 오토바이를 구입하기로 결정했다.

해설 알맞은 부사절 접속사를 고르는 문제이다. '비슷한 차종을 샀다' '오토바이를 구입하기로 결정했다'는 인과관계를 이루므로 빈칸에는 ~때문에'라는 뜻의 접속사 (B) Since가 들어가야 한다. since에는 '~이래로라는 뜻 외에도 '~때문에'라는 뜻이 있다는 것을 꼭 기억해 두자.

어휘 **similar** 비슷한 **motorcycle** 오토바이 **instead** 대신에

20. Most individuals -------- applied for the new position were tired and frustrated.
(A) whom
(B) who
(C) whoever
(D) which

해설 새로운 직책에 지원한 지원자들 대부분은 지치고 좌절했다.

해설 알맞은 관계 대명사를 고르는 문제이다. 선행사가 사람 (applicant)이고, 관계 대명사절의 주어 자리가 비어있으므로 사람 주격 대명사인 (B) who가 정답이다.

어휘 **applicant** 지원자 **apply for** ~에 지원하다 **position** 직책 **frustrated** 좌절한

21. -------- Ms. Ono does not return within a week, her assistant will lead the upcoming seminar.
(A) whether
(B) either
(C) if
(D) So that

해설 Ono 씨는 일주일 안에 돌아오지 않는다면 비서가 다가올 세미나를 이끌 것이다.

해설 문맥상 적절한 의미의 접속사를 고르는 문제이다. 문맥상 만약 그녀가 일주일 안에 돌아오지 않는다면'이 되는 것이 적절하므로 (C) if가 정답이다. whether은 부사절의 접속사로 쓰일 때는 '~이든지 아니든지'라는 뜻이므로 문맥상 적절하지 않다. either은 상관접속사로 either A or B의 형태로만 쓰이므로 빈칸에는 적절하지 않다.

어휘 **assistant** 비서, 조수 **lead** 이끌다 **upcoming** 다가오는 곧

22. The customer service representative -------- works at the company was very friendly.
(A) that
(B) which
(C) whose
(D) when

해석 그 회사의 고객 서비스 직원은 매우 친절했다.

해설 사람을 나타내는 선행사인 customer service representative와 동사 works 사이에는 주격 관계대명사 who 또는 that이 적합하다.

23. Mr. Robinson didn't tell me the reason -------- he came here suddenly.
(A) when
(B) why
(C) which
(D) how

해석 로빈슨 씨는 나에게 그가 이곳에 갑자기 온 이유를 말하지 않았다.

해설 선행사가 이유를 나타내는 the reason이고, he came here suddenly가 완전한 절이므로 관계부사 why가 적합하다.

24. Unless -------- instructed, take this medicine three times daily after meals.
(A) instead
(B) somewhat
(C) otherwise
(D) rather

해석 다른 식으로 지시되지 않는다면, 이 약을 매일 식후 하루에 세 번 복용하세요.

해설 관용적으로 '다른 식으로 ~되지 않는다면'을 의미하는 unless otherwise p.p.를 숙지 해두면 쉬운 문제이다. unless otherwise specified, unless other stated, unless otherwise noted '다른 식으로 명시 되지 않는다면'도 기억해 두자.

어휘 **instruct** 지시하다 **somewhat** 다소 **rather** 다소

Questions 25-30 refer to the following advertisement.

Golden Planning

Now is the time for you to start **25.** -------- so that you can enjoy a steady source of income after you retire. Our Golden Retirement Planning Group is providing just such a plan **26.** -------- your current lifestyle. For example, estimating the retirement income you will need, and choose the funds **27.** -------- can help make your plan work, and create a plan that will continue **28.** -------- for your future. We assure you that mutual funds will be an ideal choice for your long-term retirement goals. For more **29.** -------- information, call your investment representative. Also, we'll send you a free brochure **30.** -------- you leave your name, address, and phone number.
Meet us with a telephone call by dialing 1-800-8080808 Now!

Golden Planning

바야흐로 정년퇴직 후의 안전한 수입을 보장 받기 위해 계획을 세워야 할 때가 되었습니다. 'Golden Retirement Planning Group' 은 바로 여러분이 현재의 생활수준을 유지하기 위해 필요한 계획, 예를 들어 퇴직 후의 수입에 대한 예상 또는 당신의 계획을 구체화 할 수 있는 재원의 선택 그리고 퇴직 후에도 활동 할 수 있는 계획 등을 제공합니다. 퇴직 후에 장기간의 활동 목적을 위해서는 개방형 투자신탁회사가 최상의 선택임을 확신합니다. 보다 상세한 점은 여러분의 투자 대리인에게 전화를 하십시오. 또한 당신의 이름, 주소 그리고 전화번호를 남겨 주시면, 무료 안내 책자도 보내드리겠습니다.
지금 무료 전화 1-800- 8080808 으로 전화하십시오!

어휘 **steady** 안정된 **source** 원천, 근원 **retire** 은퇴하다 **maintain** 유지하다 **estimate** 견적하다 **retirement** 은퇴 **assure** 보증하다 **mutual fund** 뮤추얼 펀드, 개방형 투자 신탁 **long-term** 장기간의 **brochure** 안내 책자, 소책자

25.
(A) plan
(B) planning
(C) plans
(D) planned

해설 start --------에서 start는 to 부정사 또는 동명사를 모두 목적어로 취할 수 있으므로 정답은 (B) planning이다.

26.
(A) maintain
(B) maintaining
(C) maintenance
(D) to maintain

해설 a plan -------- your current lifestyle에서 현재의 생활수준을 유지하는데 필요한 계획이라는 의미이므로 to 부정사의 형용사적 용법이 적합하다.

27.
(A) who
(B) whom
(C) what
(D) that

해설 choosing the funds ____ can help make your plan work에서 선행사를 the funds로 하는 주격관계대명사 that 또는 which 자리이다.

28.
(A) work
(B) working
(C) works
(D) worked

해설 continue는 to 부정사 또는 동명사를 모두 목적어로 취할 수 있으므로 정답은 (B) working이다.

29.
(A) detail
(B) detailing
(C) details
(D) detailed

해설 For more -------- information, 에서 상세한 정보라는 의미로 detailed가 들어가야 한다.

30.
(A) whether
(B) unless
(C) if
(D) since

해설 '당신의 이름, 주소 그리고 전화번호를 남겨 주시면, 무료 안내 책자도 보내드리겠습니다.'라는 의미로 접속사 if 가 적합하다.

Questions 31-36 refer to the following leaflet.

To Karl Leman:

I **31.** -------- a tenant in your building on Waterfront Avenue for the past 5 years. I have always paid my rent on time, and have never had any issues arise with respect to the level of service offered. **32.** --------, last month my bathroom sink began leaking, and I immediately called the building manager **33.** -------- told me she would contact a maintenance person. It took 2 days for a maintenance person to arrive, by which time a significant amount of water **34.** -------- onto the dining room carpet. **35.** -------- I did my best to dry up the water, it has left a permanent stain.

1. informed the building manager of the stain, and she sent a cleaner to steam clean the carpet. The stain **36.** --------, but I arrived home today to find a bill for $75.00 for the cleaning services.
1. have paid the bill, but would like to ask that I be refunded the full amount.
Thank you,

Julie Andrews, Apartment 1208

Karl Leman 씨에게,

저는 Waterfront 가에 위치한 귀하의 건물에 세입자로서 5년간 살았습니다. 저는 집세를 항상 제때 냈으며 제공되는 서비스에 관해 발생되는 문제도 없었습니다. 그러나 지난달 제 화장실 세면대에서 물이 새기 시작해서, 저는 즉시 건물 관리인에게 전화했고 그녀는 수리공에게 연락하겠다고 제게 말했습니다. 수리공이 도착하는 데는 이틀이 걸렸는데 그동안 상당한 양의 물이 식당 카펫까지 흘렀습니다. 물을 제거하느라 최선을 다 했지만 지워지지 않는 얼룩이 생기고 말았습니다.

저는 건물 관리인에게 얼룩에 대해 통지했고 그녀는 세탁업자를 보내 카펫을 증기로 세탁했습니다. 얼룩은 제거되었지만 오늘 집에 와보니 세탁 비용으로 75달러가 청구되었다는 것을 알게 되었습니다.

저는 청구 대금을 지불했으나 전액을 돌려받을 수 있도록 부탁드립니다.

감사합니다,
1208호 Julie Andrews 드림

어휘 tenant 세입자 with respect to ~에 관하여 leak 새다 maintenance 보수 관리, 정비 permanent 영구적인, 불변의 stain 얼룩 deduct 빼다, 공제하다

31.
(A) am
(B) was
(C) have been
(D) had been

해설 for the past 5years는 지난 5년 동안을 나타내므로 동사는 현재완료를 써야 한다. 그러므로 정답은 (C) have been 이다.

32.
(A) Thus
(B) So
(C) Additionally
(D) However

해설 저는 집세를 항상 제때 냈으며 제공되는 서비스에 관해 발생되는 문제도 없었습니다. 그러나 지난달 제 화장실 세면대에서 물이 새기 시작해서~ 라는 의미가 되어야 하므로 역접관계를 나타내는 접속부사, (D) however 이 적합하다.

33.
(A) which
(B) what
(C) who
(D) how

해설 선행사가 사람인 the building manager 이므로 주격 관계대명사 (C) who 가 정답이다.

34.
(A) has leaked
(B) leaks
(C) will have leaked
(D) had leaked

해설 It took 2 days for a maintenance person to arrive, by which time a significant amount of water -------- onto the dining room carpet, 문장에서 해석을 해 보면, 수리공이 도착하는 데는 이틀이 걸렸는데 그동안 상당한 양의 물이 식당 카펫까지 흘렀다는 건 대과거의사건이므로 과거완료를 써야한다. 그러므로 정답은 (D) had leaked 이다.

35.
(A) Although
(B) If
(C) Unless
(D) Because

해설 '물을 제거하느라 최선을 다 했지만 지워지지 않는 얼룩이 생기고 말았습니다.'라는 의미이므로 '~이지만', '그럼에도 불구하고'라는 의미의 (A) Although 가 정답이다.

36.
(A) removes
(B) removed
(C) is removed
(D) was removed

해설 The stain --------,에서 얼룩이 제거되었다는 의미로 수동형이면서 과거시제를 써야한다. 그러므로 정답은 (D) was removed 이다.

기본 FINAL TEST
p.202-205

A
1. (B)	2. (B)	3. (D)	4. (A)	5. (B)
6. (B)	7. (B)	8. (B)	9. (D)	10. (C)
11. (B)	12. (B)	13. (D)	14. (D)	15. (B)
16. (B)	17. (C)	18. (A)	19. (B)	20. (A)
21. (D)	22. (B)	23. (B)	24. (C)	

B
25. (C)	26. (B)	27. (A)	28. (C)	29. (B)
30. (D)	31. (C)	32. (B)	33. (D)	34. (A)
35. (A)	36. (C)			

1. Residents in this area -------- stocking up on food and water at homes after the news.
(A) is
(B) are
(C) has
(D) have

해석 그 뉴스 이후로 이 지역의 주민들은 집에 음식과 물을 비축하고 있다.

해설 in this area는 (전치사+명사) 형태의 수식어구이며, 주어는 resident 입니다. 그러므로 동사는 복수 동사인 are 을 써야 합니다.

어휘 resident 주민 stock up 비축하다

2. The main entrance to this building will automatically -------- in an emergency.
(A) operates
(B) operate
(C) operated
(D) operating

해석 이 건물의 정문은 비상시에는 자동으로 작동 할 겁니다.

해설 조동사 뒤에는 부사가 있다고 하더라도 반드시 동사원형이 와야 한다.

어휘 main entrance 정문 automatically 자동으로 emergency 비상 operate 작동하다

3. Next week, your -------- will notify all the employees of the assignments regarding the new project.
(A) supervising
(B) supervise
(C) supervised
(D) supervisor

해석 다음 주에 새로 프로젝트에 대한 업무들을 당신의 감독이 알려 줄 것입니다.

해설 빈칸은 주어 자리이며, 소유격(your) 뒤에는 명사가 와야 한다. 그러므로 답은 (C) supervisor이다.

어휘 notify 알려주다 assignment 임무, 과제 regarding ~에 대하여

4. In order to survive in today's -------- market, we should do our best.
(A) competitive
(B) competition
(C) competitively
(D) compete

해석 오늘날 경쟁적인 시장에서 살아남기 위하여, 우리는 최선을 다해야만 합니다.

해설 명사 market 을 수식하기 위해서는 형용사인 competitive를 써야 한다.

어휘 in order to 동사원형 ~하기 위하여 do one's best 최선을 다하다

5. The Accounting Department needed to conduct an -------- survey on the financial damage.
(A) extend
(B) extensive
(C) extensions
(D) extending

해석 회계 부서는 재정 피해에 대한 전반적인 조사가 필요했다.

해설 '관사+형용사+명사' 형태의 문제이다. 따라서 빈칸은 뒤의 명사 survey를 수식하는 형용사 자리입니다.

어휘 accounting department 회계 부서 conduct a survey 조사를 실시하다 extensive 광범위한 financial 재정의 damage 손실

6. As the new air filtration system -------- last month, we can work effectively.
(A) installed
(B) was installed
(C) install
(D) is installed

해석 새로운 공기 정화 시스템을 지난 달 설치되었기 때문에 우리는 효율적으로 일할 수 있다.

해설 install은 타동사인데 뒤에 목적어가 없으므로 수동태를 써야 한다. 또한 last month 와 적합한 시제는 과거형이다. 그러므로 정답은 (B) 이다.

어휘 air filtration system 공기 정화 시스템 effectively 효율적으로

7. Every candidate's application should -------- by email by the end of next month after candidates complete all the blanks.
(A) send
(B) be sent
(C) sent
(D) sending

해석 응시자들은 모든 빈칸을 써 넣은 뒤, 지원서를 다음 달 말까지 이메일로 보내야만 한다.

해설 빈칸에 들어가야 할 품사는 동사이며, 조동사 should 다음에는 동사원형을 써야한다. 또한 send는 타동사인데 목적어가 없으므로 수동형인 (C) be sent 가 답이다.

어휘 **candidate** 응시자　**complete** 완성하다　**blank** 빈칸

8. This year, the gourmet restaurant -------- over 100,000 new customers.
(A) was attracted
(B) has attracted
(C) attract
(D) were attracting

해석 올해 Gourmet 레스토랑은 10만 명의 새 고객을 유치했다.

해설 this year은 현재완료와 함께 쓰는 시간의 부사이다.

어휘 **attract** 끌다, 유치하다

9. All managers were -------- encouraged to attend the monthly meeting.
(A) strong
(B) strengthen
(C) strength
(D) strongly

해석 모든 매니저들은 월례 회의에 참석 하도록 강력히 요구 받았다.

해설 'were -------- encouraged '에서 be동사 + p.p 사이에는 부사가 적합하다. 그러므로 정답은 (D) strongly이다.

10. Each manager estimates that there were -------- 2,000 people participating in the survey.
(A) approximate
(B) approximation
(C) approximately
(D) approximated

해석 관리들은 약 2,000 명이 이 조사에 참여했다고 추정하고 있다.

해설 숫자(2,000)를 앞에서 꾸며줄 수 있는 품사는 (C) approximately (대략)입니다.

어휘 **approximate** (수량 등이) ~에 가깝다　**approximation** 접근, 유사한 것　**approximately** 대략　**estimate** 추정하다　**participate in** ~에 참여하다

11. Kroger has been considerably more successful at -------- its new products than is widely assumed.
(A) sell
(B) selling
(C) sold
(D) sells

해석 Kroger는 일반적으로 생각되는 것 보다 상당히 성공적으로 새로운 상품을 판매하였다.

해설 전치사 in 다음에는 목적어가 필요한데 목적어인 its new products 가 있으므로, 목적어인 its new products에 대해서는 동사역할을 하고 전치사 뒤에는 명사역할을 동시에 하는 동명사가 적합합니다. 그러므로 정답은 (B) selling입니다.

어휘 **considerably** 상당히, 꽤　**successful** 성공적인　**product** 상품　**widely** 널리, 일반적으로　**assume** 사실이라고 생각하다, 추측하다　**assumption** 사실이라고 생각함, 가정

12. All Top Airlines passengers -------- to secure their valuables in their carry-on baggage.
(A) advised
(B) are advised
(C) have advised
(D) will advise

해석 Top 항공의 모든 승객들은 모든 귀중품을 기내 휴대가방에 보관하도록 권고 받는다.

해설 타동사인 advise는 주어 + advise + 목적어 + to 부정사의 형태를 취하며, 목적어 없이 to 부정사가 나올 때는 반드시 수동태로 써야합니다. 그러므로 정답은 (B) advised입니다.

어휘 **secure** 확보하다, 보장하다　**valuables** 귀중품　**carry-on baggage** 기내 휴대가방　**avoid** 피하다　**inconvenience** 불편　**theirs** 그들의 것

13. Hyper Mart is dedicated to -------- effective training programs for new employees.
(A) develop
(B) development
(C) developed
(D) developing

해석 Hyper 마트는 신입직원들에 대한 효율적인 교육 프로그램을 개발하는 데 전념하고 있다.

해설 <be dedicated to + -ing>는 '~에 헌신하다, ~에 전념하다'라는 의미의 관용어구입니다.

어휘 **effective** 효과적인, 효율적인

14. When -------- a long-distance call , please press the initial 0.
(A) make
(B) made
(C) makes
(D) making

해석 장거리 전화를 걸 때, 이전의 절차가 그러하듯이 지역 전화번호에서 처음 "0"을 누르세요.

해설 분사 구문을 사용하지 않으면, When you make a long-distance call , do not drop the initial 0~가 됩니다. a long-distance call 라는 목적어가 있으므로 능동의 의미인 현재 분사가 적합합니다.

어휘 **long-distance** 장거리　**initial** 최초의, 처음의　**formerly** 이전에　**procedure** 절차

15. Anyone -------- in the scandal is being brought to the precinct for investigation.
(A) involving
(B) involved
(C) involve
(D) involves

해설 누구든 부정행위에 연루된 사람은 조사 관할 구역으로 오게 되어있다.
해설 문장에 주어(Anyone)와 동사(is being brought)가 있으므로 __ in the scandal 의 빈칸에는 또 다른 동사 (C) involve 나 (D) involves는 올 수 없다. 빈칸에는 주어를 꾸며주는 역할의 분사가 와야 합니다. 꾸밈을 받는 주어(Anyone)와 분사가 '누구나가 부정행위에 연루되다'라는 의미에서처럼 "수동"의 관계에 있으므로, 과거분사 (B) involved 를 써야 합니다.
어휘 **precinct** (행정상의) 구역, 관할

16. The company invited the students to see -------- new facilities.
(A) itself
(B) its
(C) it
(D) them

해설 회사에서는 학생들을 초대하여 새 시설들을 견학시켰다.
해설 단수주어 the company를 지칭하면서, new facilities를 수식할 수 있는 소유격 대명사 its가 적합합니다.
어휘 **invite** 초대하다 **facility** 시설

17. -------- of the items displayed on the floor are fully refundable.
(A) One
(B) Either
(C) Some
(D) Each

해설 1층에 진열되어 있는 상품들 중 일부는 전액 환불이 가능하다.
해설 items가 가산 명사의 복수이므로 some과 함께 쓸 수 있다.
어휘 **refundable** 환불할 수 있는

18. I tried to call you twice, but -------- times you were out.
(A) both
(B) some
(C) one
(D) each

해설 내가 너에게 두 번이나 연락을 했는데 너는 두 번 다 외출 중이었다.
해설 앞에 twice 가 있으므로 둘이라는 의미를 가진 both를 써야 합니다.

19. Some people love to watch movies and -------- like to go swimming.
(A) the others
(B) others
(C) other
(D) another

해설 어떤 사람들은 영화를 보는 것을 좋아하고, 다른 사람들은 수영을 하는 것을 좋아한다.
해설 막연한 수를 표현할 때는 정관사 the가 없는 others 를 써야 합니다.

20. Unfortunately, time doesn't allow me to discuss it -------- detail.
(A) in
(B) on
(C) at
(D) of

해설 유감스럽게도 시간제약 때문에 자세히 말씀드리지 못하겠습니다.
해설 '상세히'라는 의미의 관용구는 in detail입니다.
어휘 **unfortunately** 유감스럽게도

21. The scene of the sunrise is impressive and -------- description.
(A) until
(B) by
(C) above
(D) beyond

해설 해가 떠오르는 풍경은 감동적이고, 말로 표현할 수 없다.
해설 '말로 표현할 수 없는'이란 의미의 전치사 관용어 구는 beyond description입니다.
어휘 **impressive** 감동적인 **beyond description** 형용할 수 없을 정도로

22. The concert will start -------- 7:00 o'clock in the evening and be finished by 9:00 p.m.
(A) in
(B) at
(C) of
(D) on

해설 콘서트는 저녁 7시에 시작해서 9시까지는 끝날 것이다.
해설 시간을 나타내는 7:00 o'clock 앞에는 전치사 at 이 적합합니다.
어휘 **concert** 콘서트 **finish** 끝나다, 마치다

23. Most employees have been more productive -------- the new air-filtration system was installed last month.
(A) unless
(B) since
(C) while
(D) if

해설 대부분의 직원들은 새로운 공기 정화 시스템을 지난 달 설치하고 난 후 생산성이 더 높아 졌다.
해설 '~이래로'의 뜻을 가지고, 완료 시제와 쓸 수 있는 접속사 since가 정답으로 알맞습니다.
어휘 **productive** 생산적인 **air filtration system** 공기 정화 시스템

24. Our favorite team's baseball game was canceled; --------, we decided to go to a movie.
(A) however
(B) otherwise
(C) therefore
(D) while

해설 우리가 좋아하는 야구 경기가 취소되었다. 그래서 우리는 영화를 보러 가기로 결정했다.

해설 접속부사는 문장에서 세미콜론(;)과 콤마(,) 사이에 넣습니다. 문맥상 '그러므로'라는 의미의 접속부사가 필요하므로 therefore가 정답입니다.

어휘 **favorite** 좋아하는 **cancel** 취소하다 **however** 그러나 **otherwise** 달리 그렇지 않으면

Questions 25-30 refer to the following memo.

To: All employees
From: John Martin, editor of *The Opinions*
Re: Wanted

We need volunteers to assist us in **25.** -------- the staff informed through our newspaper. Experience isn't absolutely necessary, **26.** -------- writing and typing skills are in great demand. We need people to rewrite articles, to type and to proofread. We could also use a good photographer. **27.** -------- *The Opinions* comes out three days a week, we need excellent employees **28.** -------- know how to budget their time efficiently.
There is some money for salaries, depending on **29.** -------- involved you get with the paper. But don't expect to get rich. This isn't something you do for the money. Mostly, it's just for fun. **30.** -------- who's interested in joining the staff should speak to me immediately after today's meeting. Be prepared to start right away. The first issue goes to press tomorrow.

수신: 전 직원
발신: *The Opinions* 편집장
주제: 편집진 모집

*The Opinions*의 편집장으로서, 우리는 회보를 통해 직원들에게 소식을 전하는 일을 도와줄 자원봉사자가 필요합니다. 경험이 절대적으로 필요한 것은 아닙니다만, 집필과 타자 실력은 아주 필요합니다. 우리는 원고를 고쳐 쓰고, 타자치고, 또 교정을 볼 사람이 필요합니다. 또한 우리는 사진을 잘 찍는 사람이 필요합니다. *The Opinions*는 일주일에 세 번 발행되기 때문에 자기 시간을 효과적으로 짤 줄 아는 유능한 직원이 필요합니다. 여러분이 신문에 얼마나 관여하느냐에 따라 약간의 보수가 지급됩니다만, 그것으로 부자가 되리라고는 기대하지 마십시오. 이 일은 돈을 벌기 위해 하는 것이 아니라, 주로 재미로 하는 것입니다. 편집진으로 일하는 것에 관심이 있는 분은 누구나 이 모임이 끝나는 즉시 저에게 이야기해 주세요. 곧장 일할 준비를 해야 합니다. 첫 신문이 내일 인쇄에 들어갑니다.

어휘 **wanted** 구인 **employee body** 전 직원 **in great demand** 매우 필요한[요구되는] **proofread** 교정보다 **budget one's time** 시간을 안배하다 **efficiently** 효율적으로 **for fun** 재미삼아 **be interested in** ~에 관심이 있다 **issue** (잡지 등의) 호 **go to press** 인쇄에 들어가다

25.
(A) keep
(B) keeps
(C) keeping
(D) to keep

해설 in -------- the employees에서 전치사 + 동명사 + 명사(구) 구조이므로 동명사 keeping이 가장 적합하다.

26.
(A) and
(B) so
(C) or
(D) but

해설 경험이 절대적으로 필요한 것은 아닙니다만, 집필과 타자 실력은 아주 필요합니다. 라는 의미이므로 but이 적합하다.

27.
(A) Now that
(B) However
(C) While
(D) Because of

해설 접속사 문제로서 'The Opinions는 일주일에 세 번 발행되기 때문에 자기 시간을 효과적으로 짤 줄 아는 유능한 직원이 필요합니다.'라는 뜻이므로 because, as, since, now that 등이 빈칸에 들어갈 수 있다. 그러므로 (A) Now that이 정답이다.

28.
(A) what
(B) whose
(C) who
(D) which

해설 관계대명사 문제이다. 선행사가 employees로 사람을 나타내고 빈칸 뒤에 주어 없이 바로 동사가 나오므로 주격 관계대명사 who가 빈칸에 적합하다.

29.
(A) who
(B) how
(C) that
(C) where

해설 '여러분이 신문에 얼마나 관여하느냐에 따라 약간의 보수가 지급됩니다'라는 의미이므로 how가 적합하다.

30.
(A) Someone
(B) They
(C) One
(D) Anyone

해설 관계대명사 who의 선행사로 올 수 있는 대명사는 those와 anyone이다. those는 복수로, anyone은 단수로 취급된다. 그런데 who 뒤에 나오는 동사가 is이므로 빈칸에는 anyone이 적합하다.

Questions 31-36 refer to the following letter.

Mr. Matt Morris
MCN Inc.
210 Grayson Ave.
NW Roanoke, VA 24016

Dear Mr. Morris:

Thank you for letting **31.** -------- know the details of your itinerary for youur business trip. We are **32.** -------- that you will be able to visit our factory **33.** -------- you are in Indonesia. Our manager, Mr. Dexter, will be available to escort you **34.** -------- to answer any questions which you may have. **35.** -------- you arrive on the 28th, please call me **36.** -------- (202) 594-9967 and we can set a day for your visit to the factory.

Yours Truly,
Mike R. Gregory
General Manager

우편번호 24016
Virginia 주 NW Roanoke 시
Grayson 가 210 번지
MCN 사
Mr. Matt Morris

Mr. Morris 씨에게

귀하의 이번 출장에 대한 일정을 자세히 알려주셔서 감사드립니다. 귀하가 인도네시아에 계시는 동안 저희 공장을 방문하실 수 있다니 반갑습니다. 저희 회사에서는 Dexter 부장이 귀하를 안내할 것이며 귀하께서 알고 싶으신 사항에 대해서 설명할 것입니다. 28일 도착하시고 난 후 전화 (202) 594-9967번으로 연락해 주시면 저희 공장 방문 일자를 정하도록 하겠습니다.

부장 Mike R. Gregory 드림

어휘 Inc. 주식회사(Incorporated의 약자) Ave. 가(Avenue의 약자)
set a day 날짜를 정하다

31.
(A) we
(B) our
(C) us
(D) ours

해설 let 사람목적어 동사원형의 구조이므로 정답 (C) us이다.

32.
(A) please
(B) pleased
(C) pleasing
(D) pleasure

해설 '우리가 기쁘다'라는 의미로 사람 we가 주어이므로 감정동사인 please는 과거분사 형태로 pleased라고 써야 한다.

33.
(A) since
(B) although
(C) because
(D) while

해설 부사절 접속사 문제이다. -------- you are in Indonesia는 '당신이 인도네시아에 있는 동안'이라는 의미가 되어야 하므로 접속사 while이 적합하다.

34.
(A) and
(B) but
(C) or
(D) so

해설 to escort you와 to answer any questions는 대등한 관계이므로 등위접속사 and가 적합하다.

35.
(A) After
(B) During
(C) So as
(D) Though

해설 부사절 접속사 문제이다. -------- you arrive on the 28th, please ring me at (202) 594-9967은 '28일 도착 후 (202) 594-9967번으로 연락해 달라'는 의미가 되어야 하므로 빈칸에는 after가 들어가야 한다.

36.
(A) in
(B) on
(C) at
(D) of

해설 전화번호, 이메일 주소 앞에는 전치사 at 을 쓴다.

불규칙 변화 동사표

현재	과거	과거분사	뜻
be	was / were	been	~이다, 있다
become	became	become	되다
begin	began	begun	시작하다
bend	bent	bent	구부리다
bet	bet	bet	내기하다
bite	bit	bitten	물다
bleed	bled	bled	피 흘리다
blow	blew	blown	불다
break	broke	broken	깨다
bring	brought	brought	가져오다
build	built	built	세우다
burst	burst	burst	터지다
buy	bought	bought	사다
catch	caught	caught	잡다
choose	chose	chosen	선택하다
come	came	come	오다
cost	cost	cost	비용이 들다
creep	crept	crept	기다
cut	cut	cut	자르다
deal	dealt	dealt	다루다
do	did	done	하다
draw	drew	drawn	그리다
drink	drank	drunk	마시다
drive	drove	driven	운전하다
eat	ate	eaten	먹다
fall	fell	fallen	떨어지다
feed	fed	fed	먹이다
feel	felt	felt	느끼다
fight	fought	fought	싸우다
find	found	found	발견하다
fit	fit	fit	꼭 맞다
fly	flew	flown	날다
forget	forgot	forgotten	잊다
forgive	forgave	forgiven	용서하다
freeze	froze	frozen	얼다

현재	과거	과거분사	뜻
get	got	gotten	얻다
give	gave	given	가지다
go	went	gone	가다
grow	grew	grown	성장하다
hang	hung	hung	자라다
have	had	had	가지다
hear	heard	heard	듣다
hide	hid	hidden	숨기다
hit	hit	hit	치다
hold	held	held	잡다
hurt	hurt	hurt	다치게 하다
keep	kept	kept	유지하다
know	knew	known	알다
lay	laid	laid	놓다
lead	led	led	이끌다
leave	left	left	떠나다
lend	lent	lent	빌려주다
let	let	let	시키다
lie	lay	lain	눕다
lose	lost	lost	잃다
make	made	made	만들다
mean	meant	meant	뜻하다
meet	met	met	만나다
pay	paid	paid	지불하다
put	put	put	놓다, 두다
quit	quit	quit	그만두다
read	read[red]	read[red]	읽다
ride	rode	ridden	올라타다
ring	rang	rung	(소리) 울리다
run	ran	run	달리다
say	said	said	말하다
see	saw	seen	보다
seek	sought	sought	찾다
sell	sold	sold	팔다
send	sent	sent	보내다

Memo

Memo

Memo

Memo

Memo

Memo

Memo

Memo

https://books.english.co.kr

https://books.english.co.kr